Our Own Book
A Victorian Guide to Life

Homespun Cuisine, Health, Romance, Etiquette, Raising Children and Farm Animals

Restored by Diane Janowski

New York History Review Press
Elmira, New York

From the **Victorian Pride** Series of Books

Our Own Book - A Victorian Guide to Life - Homespun Cuisine, Health, Romance, Etiquette, Raising Children and Farm Animals. From the Victorian Pride series of books.

Originally published by the (Elmira, New York) *Weekly Gazette & Free Press*, 1888. Reprinted by New York History Review Press, Elmira, New York. Diane Janowski, Publisher

For the latest on New York History Review or Victorian Pride, please visit
www.NewYorkHistoryReview.com
www.VictorianPride.com

This book was designed and laid out in Adobe InDesign using typeface Adobe Caslon Pro.

Caution: The information contained in this book is provided for your general historic information and entertainment only. New York History Review Press does not give medical advice or engage in the practice of medicine. Old home remedies are often not safe to use today and their use could put your health in serious risk. They are not offered here as sound medical advice. New York History Review Press *under no circumstances* recommends the particular treatments in this book.

ISBN: 978-0-6152-0679-0

First Edition

About this Book

This book is a reprint of *Our Own Book* first published in 1888 and distributed free of charge to subscribers of the Elmira, New York *Weekly Gazette & Free Press*. The copy used in the making of this new version is made of paper made of ground wood and unbleached fibers. It is in decrepid condition - extreme acid burn, brittle pages, and oxidation.

The New York History Review Press has a deep commitment to the digital preservation of rare historical works and their subsequent reintroduction to the current generation, thereby ensuring the works for generations to come. Without digital preservation, it would be impossible for anyone to see this book again. 21st century technology has allowed our conservators to "repair" this book for a new edition. All pages were brown and crispy from acid. Many pages were unreadable, loose, and torn. The binding barely holds together. Yet, it is still a charming book - an ode to the Victorian life - with many glimpses into a previous era.

This is not to imply that this version is perfect, it is merely better than the original in its present condition. Every effort was made to keep the integrity of the original book - including the charm of the added recipes and notes, and handwriting. It is evident that this was a very much loved book and the woman who owned it treasured it.

Cure for Diphtheria

Take two tablespoonfuls liquid of tar and two tablespoonfuls of turpentine, place in a dish in the room with the patients; set fire to it, and in a few minutes the room will be filled with a rich resinous smoke or vapor, which will be inhaled by the patients. Relief will follow in a very short time after inhaling the smoke. The microbesities will be loosened in the throat and xpectoration will soon follow, after which the patient will get a pleasant sleep or repose.

A CHOICE PICKLE CHAPTER.
CUCUMBERS.

I have put up pickles in several different ways but in no way do they keep as well and give such good satisfaction as they do in glass cans. Select small, plump cucumbers, wash them with a cloth in clear water, remove all the black points, and soak them in weak brine for 24 hours, take them out and drain in a colander and rinse off with clear water, then place in a kettle with enough vinegar to cover a little stronger than you want your pickles, for the salt will take some of its strength, half a cup of light brown sugar, tablespoon each of whole cloves and cinnamon and let them stand over slow fire till they come to boil, then can up the same as fruit and they are always ready when needed. Add a little whole pepper if desired.

TOMATO PICKLES.

Tomatoes are much better when peeled, using small or medium sized ones. Soak them in weak brine for twenty - four hours after peeling with a thin knife, drain well in a colander, then cook them until they can easily be pierced with a fork, in the following syrup: Take equal parts of light brown sugar and good cider vinegar and a tablespoon each of whole cloves and cinnamon—ground spices are sometimes used but they tend to darken the pickles. Tomatoes made this way are almost transparent and are much preferred to those sliced in the old fashioned way. Can them up while hot.

CHOCOLATE CAKE.

One cup of sugar; two eggs; one-half cup butter; one-half cup of sour milk; two cup of flour; one teaspoonful of saleratus. Ta one-third of a bar of chocolate; yelk of on egg; one-half cup of sweet milk, and one te spoonful of vanilla. Sweeten to taste, mix a together, and place in a basin of boiling wate Cook until it thickens, let it cool, then spre between the layers of cake. Loyally—
Minnie Tanquary, Sparland, Ill.

RECIPES WANTED.

HAPPY HOUSEHOLD: Please send me th best recipe for making blackberry and grap wine, and oblige—Jacob J. Amidon, Fores burg, Prince William County, Va.

Here are recipes for the blackberry win now will someone send direction for maki grape wine.

BLACKBERRY WINE.

To four quarts of berries put one quart boiling water. Let it stand 24 hours in stone ja then drain the liquid from the fru add one and one-half pounds of sugar. Bot it. It will be ready for use in three month

ANOTHER RECIPE.

Crush the berries well together wit wooden masher; cover with water, and well together; let them stand 24 hours; strain, and to one gallon of juice put six of common brown sugar; put into mouthed jars for several days, carefully ming of the scum that will rise to the put in several sheets of brown paper an them remain in it three days; skim and p into your cask. There let it remain und turbed six months; then strain and bot These directions if carefully carried out w insure excellent wine.

The Home Doctor.

A SURE cure for inflammatory rheumatism i made by taking one ounce pulverized saltpetre and putting it into a pint of sweet oil. Bathe th parts affected and a sound cure will speedily be made.

FOR soft corns dip a piece of linen cl h in turpentine and wrap it around the toe on which the corn is situated every night and morning, It will prove an immediate relief to the pain or soreness, and the corn will disappear after a few days.

NEURALGIA in the face has been cured by ab-

GROVER CLEVELAND.

JAMES G. BLAINE.

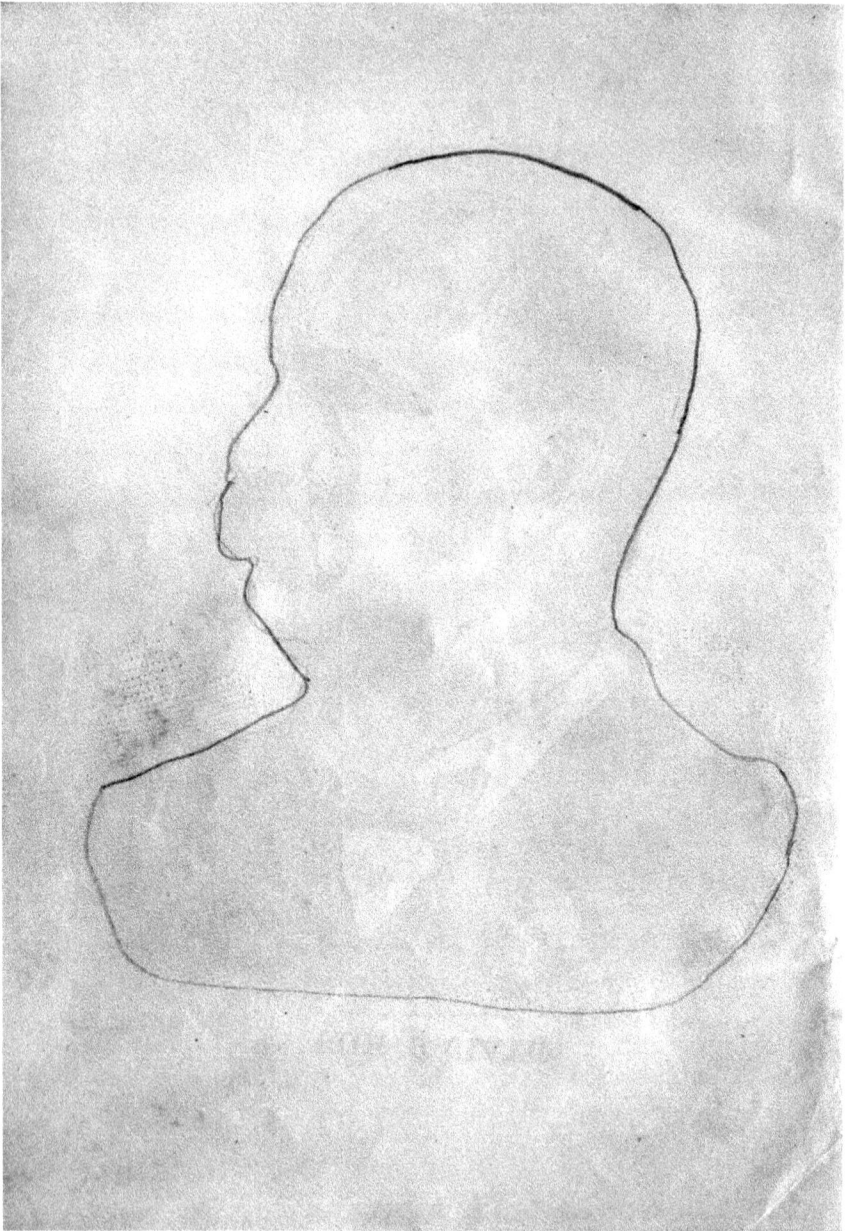

DAVID B. HILL.

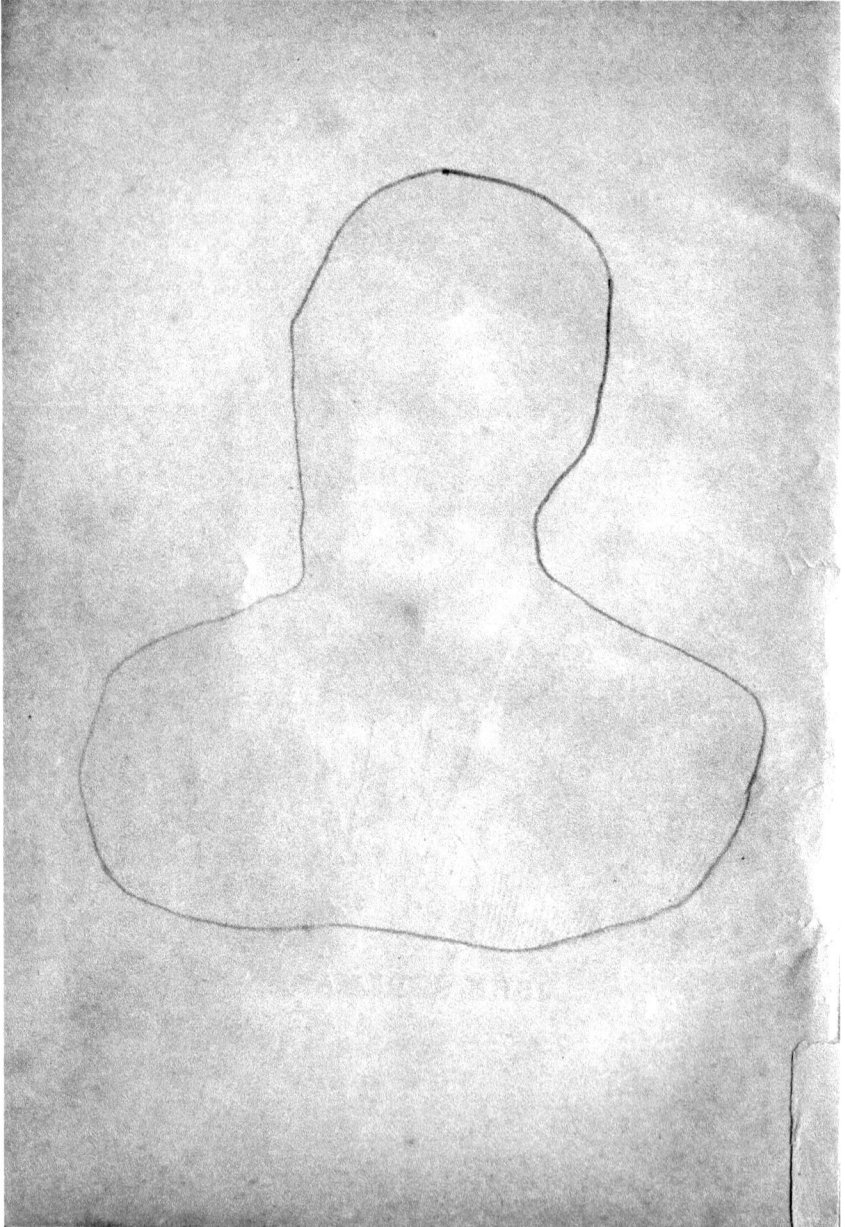

JOHN SHERMAN.

OUR OWN BOOK

----OF----

EVERY DAY WANTS,

CONTAINS PORTRAITS OF THE

Probable Presidential Candidates in 1888

THE HOME COOK BOOK :

A Manual for Farmers and their Wives, Merchants, Mechanics and their Children.

THE FAMILY PHYSICIAN & YOUNG PEOPLE'S GUIDE

SULLIVAN'S INDIAN CAMPAIGN IN 1779.

For subscribers of the
WEEKLY GAZETTE & FREE PRESS.

TABLE OF CONTENTS.

INDEX TO COOKERY DEPARTMENT.

INDEX.

PUDDINGS.

PASTRY.

CAKE.

INDEX.

INDEX.

COOKERY DEPARTMENT.

Tomato Soup.—One quart can of tomatoes, or twelve large ripe tomatoes, peeled and chopped ; boil an hour, then stir in half a teaspoonful of soda ; when the foaming ceases add two soft crackers rolled very fine, one quart of milk, one tablespoonful of butter, salt and pepper to taste. Cook fifteen minutes. If too thick add milk or boiling water.

Tomato Soup.—Put on a piece of beef, mutton or lamb to boil ; skim off all the fat before seasoning, then add two sliced onions, a little pepper and salt, two cloves and about a dozen tomatoes ; boil three hours, then add a little thickening of flour. If the tomatoes are very sour, add a tablespoonful of sugar.

Plain Beef Soup.—One gallon of cold water, one pound of beef and two tablespoonfulls of rice. Let this boil, then add an onion, or two or three leeks ; boil an hour. Peel and slice eight potatoes, wash them in warm water, add them to the soup with seasoning of salt and pepper ; stir frequently ; boil another hour, and then serve.

Pea Soup Without Meat.—Boil a pint of split peas in two quarts of water for four or five hours, or until quite tender, then add two turnips, two carrots, a stick of celery and some potatoes all cut in pieces. When tender pulp it through a sieve. Cut a large onion in slices and fry it in butter and flour, to thicken the soup. Season to taste.

If desired, a ham bone or a piece of beef can be stewed with the peas, to be taken out when the soup is pulped through the sieve. Serve with the soup, pieces of bread fried crisp in butter.

Vegetable Soup.—Peel and slice six large onions, six potatoes, six carrots and four turnips; fry them in half a pound of butter, and pour on them four quarts of boiling water. Toast a crust of bread as brown and hard as possible, but do not burn it, and put it in, with some celery, sweet herbs, white pepper and salt; stew it all gently for four hours, and then strain it through a coarse cloth. Have ready thinly sliced carrot, celery and a little turnip; add them to your liking, and stew them tender in the soup. If approved of a spoonful of tomato catsup may be added.

Stock—How to Make It.—Four pounds of beef, or a shin of beef, one gallon of cold water and two teaspoonfuls of salt; put it on the back of the stove and slowly come to a boil, and keep boiling until the water is boiled away one-half; strain and set to cool; when cold, take the grease off the top and it is ready for use. To make soup;—For a family of six, take one-quarter of the stock, to which add one quart of boiling water and any vegetables you desire, salt and pepper and boil three hours; Eat while hot. This stock will keep one week in cold weather.

Economical Veal Soup.—Boil a piece of veal, suitable for a fricassee, pie, or hash. When tender, take the meat up and slip out all the bones; put these back into the kettle and boil for two hours. Then strain the liquor and stand away until the next day. When wanted, take off the fat, put the soup into a clean pot, add pepper, salt, an onion, a half teacupful of rice, a tablespoonful of flour mixed in cold water, and slices of potatoes. Boil thirty minutes and serve hot.

Chicken Soup.—Boil a pair of chickens with great care, skimming constantly, and keeping them covered with water. When tender, take out the chicken and remove every bone from the meat ; put a large lump of butter into a frying-pan and dredge the chicken meat well with flour, lay in the hot pan : fry a nice brown, and keep it hot and dry. Take a pint of the chicken water, and stir in two large spoonfuls of curry powder, two of butter, and one of flour, one teaspoonful of salt and a little cayenne : stir until smooth, then mix it with the broth in the pot : when well mixed, simmer five minutes, then add the browned chicken. Serve with rice.

Soup for an Invalid.—Cut in small pieces 1 lb. of beef or mutton, or a part of both ; boil it gently in 2 quarts of water ; take off the scum, and when reduced to a pint, strain it. Season with a little salt, and take a teacupful at a time.

Oyster Soup.—To one hundred oysters take one quart of milk, half a pint of water, four spoonfuls of flour, half a cup of butter, and one teaspoonful of salt, with a very little cayenne pepper. Boil and skim the liquor off the oysters. Steam the flour and butter over the tea-kettle until soft enough to beat to a froth ; then stir it in the liquor while boiling ; after which add the other ingredients, and throw in the oysters, allowing them merely to scald.

Green Pea Soup.—Take two quarts of green peas, one small onion and a sprig of parsley cut fine ; add two quarts of hot water, and boil slowly for half an hour, then add a pint of small new potatoes which have been peeled and laid in cold water an hour; put in a teaspoonful of sugar and a little salt ; boil till the potatoes are done ; now add a teacupful of cream or a pint of milk, boil a minute or two, and serve with small slices of toasted bread or gems cut in halves.

Clam Soup.—Twenty-five clams, opened raw and chopped fine ; add three quarts of water; boil them one-half hour, then add a pint of milk, one onion chopped fine, thicken with butter and flour: beat three eggs in the tureen and pour your broth over them boiling hot.

Potato Soup.—One quart of milk, six potatoes boiled and peeled, one-quarter pound of butter, season with pepper and salt ; mash the potatoes very fine, and, while mashing, add the butter and salt and pepper; pour in gradually the milk, boiling ; stir it well and strain through a sieve : beat up an egg and put in the tureen ; after the soup is strained, heat it again, as it cools in straining. At the table, a little sherry is an improvement.

To Boil Fish.—Put the fish in the saucepan, and a little more than half cover it with boiling water. Cover the lid closely and boil gently until done. To determine when a fish is sufficiently boiled, draw it up upon the fish-plate, and if the thickest part of the fish can be easily divided from the bone with a knife, it should be at once taken from the water. A little saltpetre or a few spoonfuls of vinegar may be added to the water to render the boiled fish firm. Some cooks prefer to steep the fish in salt and water from five to ten minutes before putting it in the kettle to cook, instead of putting salt in the water in which it is boiled. By this means less scum rises.

To Bake a Large Fish Whole.—Cut off the head and split the fish down nearly to the tail ; prepare a nice dressing of bread, butter, pepper and salt, moistened with a little water. Fill the fish with this dressing, and bind it together with fine cotton cord or tape, so as to confine it ; the bindings may be three inches apart ; lay the fish on the grate on a bake-pan or a dripping-pan, and pour round it a little water and melted butter. Baste frequently. A good-sized fish will bake in an hour. Serve with the gravy of the fish, drawn butter or oyster sauce.

Fish Chowder.—Take a good haddock, cod or any other solid fish of three or four pounds, clean it well and cut in pieces of three inches square. Place in the bottom of your dinner-pot five or six slices of salt pork, fry brown, then add three onions sliced thin, and fry those brown. Remove the kettle from the fire, and place on the onions and pork a layer of fish ; sprinkle over a little pepper and salt, then a layer of pared and sliced potatoes, a layer of fish and potatoes, till the fish is used up. Cover with water and let it boil for half an hour. Pound six biscuits or crackers fine as meal and pour into the pot ; and, lastly, add a quart or a pint of milk ; let it scald well and serve.

To Pickle Fish.—Take any freshly caught fish, clean and scale them, wash and wipe dry. Cut them into slices a few inches thick, put them into a jar with some salt, some allspice and a little horseradish. When filled cover them with good strong vinegar. Cover it well with a good cover. Let it stand in your oven a few hours. Don't let the oven be too hot. This will keep six months. Put it immediately in the cellar, and in a few days they will be fit for use.

Cream Baked Trout.—Clean the trout, put in pepper and salt, and close them. Place the fish in the pan with just cream enough to cover the fins, and bake fifteen minutes.

Boiled Salmon.—A piece of six pounds should be rubbed with salt, tied carefully in cloth, and boil slowly for three-quarters of an hour. It should be eaten with egg or caper sauce. If any remains after dinner, it may be placed in a deep dish, a little salt sprinkled over, and a teacupful of boiling vinegar poured upon it. Cover it closely and it will make a nice breakfast dish.

Picked-up Codfish.—This is an old-fashioned dish and name, but none the less to be admired on that account, being with most persons, when properly prepared, a great favorite. Pick up the fish in small particles, separating the fibres as near as possible, the finer the better. Freshen by leaving it in water one hour. Pour off the water and fill up with fresh. Bring it to a scald, pour it off and put on the fish just enough milk to cover it. Add to a quart of the soaked fish a bit of butter the size of half an egg, a very little flour and a dust of pepper. Beat up two eggs, and after taking off the fish thicken it by stirring in the egg. Some let it boil after the egg is added, but if this is done the egg will be curdled. Another way is to boil eggs, chop and mix them in the gravy.

Fish Cakes.—The first and most important thing to be remembered is, have the ingredients cooked on the day you wish them to be eaten. Put your codfish to soak a day and a half, then boil until tender. Have your potatoes boiling, too. When the fish is done, chop it as fine as possible. Mash the potatoes until they are perfectly smooth ; add a little cream or milk and a little butter, but not enough to color them ; mix all thoroughly, proportion of one cupful of fish to three of potatoes, and roll into flat, small balls, about one-half inch thick. Be careful to make them a good shape. A little raw onion, chopped fine, is delicious mixed through them, just sufficient to flavor. Fry a good brown, in plenty of hot lard. Remember, the beauty is to have them fine and white inside.

Fish Cakes.—One pint bowl salt codfish, picked very fine, two pint bowls of old raw, peeled potatoes ; put together in cold water and boil till the potatoes are thoroughly cooked ; remove from fire and drain off all the water ; mash with potato masher ; add piece of butter the size of an egg, two well-beaten eggs and a little pepper ; mix well with a wooden spoon ; have a frying-pan with boiling lard or drippings, into which drop a spoonful of mixture and fry brown ; do not freshen the fish before boiling with potatoes, and do not mold cakes, but drop from spoon.

To Fry Halibut or Codfish.—Place in your fly-kettle half a dozen slices of fat pork ; fry to a brown, then remove them to a deep dish ; add to the fat three tablespoonfuls of fresh lard : when boiling hot put in your halibut, which should be cut in pieces about three inches square, and dipped in sifted meal ; sprinkle over it a little salt ; fry a good brown. After the fish is all fried (it may be necessary to add more lard if it is a large one), put it in the dish with the slices of pork, pour the boiling fat over it, and add one tablespoonful of boiling water ; cover with a plate tightly, and stand in the oven for twenty minutes.

Stewed Oysters.—Boil up the oysters in their own liquor, with a piece of butter the size of a walnut, and pepper and salt to taste. Have ready a pint or more of rich boiled milk, the quantity according to the number of oysters. Pour it hot into the soup tureen, and as the oysters come to a boil, skim them, let them boil up once, and then pour them into the milk.

Stewed Oysters.—Strain the oysters, and put the juice into a saucepan on the fire ; add a large spoonful of butter and the same of flour, well braided together ; add a cup of cream if you have it, if not, milk, a little salt and nutmeg or mace ; stir into the hot juice, and let it simmer for five minutes. Squeeze over the oysters the juice of a lemon, and just before they are required for table throw them into the boiling juice.

Oysters are very nice flavored with celery ; this is done by cutting the celery stalks into the juice instead of the spice. and take out before the oysters are added.

Scolloped Oysters.—Wash out of the liquor two quarts of oysters ; pound very fine eight soft crackers, or grate a stale loaf of bread : butter a deep dish, sprinkle in a layer of crumbs, then a layer of oysters, a little mace, pepper, and bits of butter : another layer of crumbs, another of oysters, then seasoning as before, and so on until the dish is filled : cover the dish over with bread crumbs, seasoning as before ; turn over it a cup of the oyster liquor. Set it in the oven for thirty or forty minutes to brown.

To Pickle Oysters.—Open as many oysters as will fill a gallon, together with the liquor—wash them well in their own liquor, carefully clearing away the particles of shell—then put them into an iron pot, and pour the liquor gently over them, adding two tablespoonfuls of salt, or a little more if they are fresh ; set them on the fire till they are ready to boil, and the fins much shriveled ; if the oysters are large, they may boil a minute or two ; then take them out and lay them on a table to cool ; take the liquor, putting some mace and whole pepper into it, and let it boil for some time, carefully skimming it as long as any scum remains ; then pour it into a pan. When perfectly cold, add a pint of white wine and half a pint of strong vinegar. Place the oysters gently in a jar ; pour the liquor on them so as to cover them.

Oyster Patties.—Make the usual puff-paste, say for a dozen patties ; bake an hour in a brisk oven ; set to cool ; wash and drain three dozen large, fresh oysters ; put them in a stewpan with only enough of their own liquor to keep them from burning. Season with cayenne and mace and a few of the green tops of celery, minced fine ; add a quarter of a pound of butter laid in bits among the oysters ; to enrich the gravy stir in the beaten yolks of two eggs or stir in some thick cream—most people like the latter the best. Let the oysters stand in the gravy about five minutes. When the patties are beginning to cool put three of the oysters in each. A thin lid of pastry, if you like, can be poured over the patties when put into the oven to bake.

Fried Oysters.—Select fine, large oysters, dry them out of their own liquor. Have ready a plate of eggs aud a plate of bread crumbs. Let them lay in the egg a few minutes.

and then roll them in the bread crumbs, allowing them to remain in these also, for a minute or two; this will make them adhere, and not come off as a skin, when in the pan. Fry in half butter and half lard, in order to give them a rich brown. Make it very hot before putting the oysters in.

Clam Fritters.—Take twelve large, or twenty-five small clams from their shells; if the clams are large divide them. Mix two gills of wheat flour with one gill of milk, half as much of the clam liquor and one egg well beaten. Make the batter smooth, and then stir in the clams. Drop the batter by tablespoonfuls in boiling lard; let them fry gently, turning them when done on one side.

Clam Chowder.—Twenty-five clams chopped fine, six potatoes chopped fine, two onions chopped fine, a piece of salt pork, also chopped, and butter about the size of an egg, salt and pepper to taste; the clam juice and one pint of milk, and the same of water; six crackers rolled, one nutmeg grated, teaspoonful celery seed. Boil these slowly for at least four hours, adding water if it becomes too thick; half an hour before serving add coffee-cupful of tomato catsup and two tablespoonfuls of Worcestershire sauce. When ready for table add tumbler of sherry; cut a lemon in slices and serve with it.

Clam Chowder.—Put in a kettle some small slices of fat salt pork, enough to line the bottom of it; on that a layer of potatoes, cut in small pieces; then a layer of chopped onions; then a layer of tomatoes, in slices, or canned tomatoes; on the latter a layer of clams, chopped; then a layer of crackers. Season each layer with pepper and salt. Repeat the process (omitting the pork) until the kettle is nearly full; cover with water; set on a slow fire, and when nearly done stir gently; finish cooking and serve hot. When done, if found too thin, boil a little longer; if too thick, add a little water and let it boil once. The more potatoes that are used the thicker it will be.

Beef.—To choose beef, the color should be a bright red, and in cold weather, or when cooled by ice should present a well mixed or marbled appearance. The fat should be a very light straw color. The suet must be of a brighter shade than the meat or muscle fat, dry and hard and break or crumble easily; also have but little fibre through it.

To Roast Beef.

To Roast Beef.—The nicest pieces for roasting are the sirloin and rib pieces; the "middle or second cut ribs" are considered the best, but the "first cut ribs" are the smallest and most suitable for a small family. Ask your butcher to remove the bone, roll the meat into a round shape, and tie securely with a stout string; then, before sending it to the table, you can remove the string and insert one or two steel skewers. Before placing the meat to roast dredge all over with flour, seasoned with salt; then place it upon a grating in your dripping-pan and put it in a very hot oven; baste frequently; if the meat is very fat you will need no water in your pan; if not, you had better pour a small cup of boiling water into the pan after it has been in the oven fifteen minutes. A piece weighing eight or nine pounds will cook in an hour; that is, if you like your meat rare. Remove the meat when done to a heated dish; skim the drippings, add a little boiling water (a little browned flour if you wish), and boil up once; then strain it and send to table in gravy-boat.

Beef Stewed with Onions.—Cut two pounds of tender beef into small pieces, and season with pepper and salt; slice one or two onions and add to it, with water enough in the stewpan to make a gravy. Let it stew slowly till the beef is thoroughly cooked, then add some pieces of butter rolled in flour, enough to make a rich gravy. Cold beef may be cooked in the same way, but the onions must then be cooked before adding them to the meat. Add more water if it dries too fast, but let it be boiling when poured in.

Boiled Corned Beef.—Wash it well, put it in a pot, and if very salt, cover well with cold water; if only slightly corned, use boiling water; skim often while boiling, and allow at least half an hour for every pound of meat. If it is to be eaten cold, do not remove as soon as done but allow it to remain in the liquor until nearly cold; then lay it in an earthern dish with a piece of board upon it, and press with a stone or a couple of flat irons The brisket is a good piece for a family dinner.

Beef Tongue (corned or smoked).—Soak the tongue twenty-four honrs before boiling. It will require from three to four hours, according to size. The skin should always be removed as soon as it is taken from the pot. An economical method is to lay the tongue, as soon as the skin is removed, in a jar, coiled up, with the tip outside the root, and a weight upon it. When it is cold, loosen the sides with a knife and turn it out. The slices being cut horizontally all round, the fat and lean will go together.

Stuffed Corned Beef.—Take a piece of well-corned rump or round, nine or ten pounds; make several deep cuts in it; fill with a stuffing of a handful of soaked bread, squeezed dry, a little fat or butter, a good pinch of cloves, allspice, pepper, a little finely-chopped onion, and a little marjoram or thyme; then tie it up tightly in a cloth and saturate it with vinegar; boil about three hours.

Dried Beef Frizzled in Cream.—Chip the beef as thin as paper with a very sharp knife. Melt in a frying-pan butter the size of an egg, stir the beef about in it two or three minutes, dust in a little flour, add half a teacupful of rich cream, boil, and serve in a covered dish.

Kidney Stew.—Take a large beef kidney, cut all the fat out, cut it up in slices; then let it lay in cold water, with a teaspoonful of salt added, fifteen minues; wipe dry, then put it in the pot with three half pints of cold water; let it boil two hours; half an hour before it is done, add one large onion, sliced; one teasponful of powdered sage, a very little grated nutmeg, and pepper and salt to season well; serve hot, with mashed potatoes.

Bouilli with Tomatoes.—Take a rump of beef, about ten pounds, and have the bone taken out by the butcher; put in water just enough to cover it, and let it boil slowly for three or four hours. Then season it to your taste with salt, pepper, mace and cloves, pounded fine. Dress tomatoes as a vegetable, strain them, pour them over the beef after it is dished, and let them mix with the gravy.

Savory Beef.—Take a shin of beef from the hind quarter, saw it into four pieces, put it in a pot, and boil it until the meat and gristle drop from the bones; chop the meat very fine, and put it in a dish, and season it with a little salt, pepper, cloves and sage, to suit your taste; pour in the liquor in which the meat was boiled, and place it away to harden; cut in slices and serve cold.

Stuffed Beefsteak.—Procure a steak cut from the rump of beef, and fill it with a dressing made of chopped bread, pork, sage, onions and sweet marjoram, and well seasoned; sew it up, put a slice or two of pork, or some of the dressing, on the top, and set it in a pan, into which pour a pint of water; cover down tight, and let it cook slowly in the oven three hours; then take off the lid, brown quickly, and serve hot.

Hash Balls of Corn Beef.—Prepare the hash by mincing with potatoes; make it into flat cakes; heat the griddle, and grease it with plenty of sweet butter; brown the balls first on one side, and then on the other, and serve hot.

Tripe.—Must be washed in warm water, and cut into squares of three inches; take one egg, three tablespoonfuls of flour, a little salt, and make a thick batter by adding milk;

fry out some slices of pork, dip the tripe into the batter, and fry a light brown.

Beef Balls.—Take a piece of beef boiled tender, chop it very finely with an onion, season with salt and pepper, add parsley, bread crumbs, lemon peel and grated nutmeg; moisten it with an egg, mix well together, and roll it into balls. Then dip them in flour and fry them in boiling lard or fresh dripping. Serve them with thickened brown gravy, or fried bread crumbs.

Boiled Bullock's Head.—This is a good dish for a large family. Place the head in salt water for six hours, to cleanse it; then wash and remove the palates, and place them again in salt and water; put the head in a saucepan, with sufficient water to cover; boil for five hours, adding two carrots, two turnips, and two onions, cut small; when done remove the head from the soup, and remove the bone from the meat; serve soup and meat in tureen; the palates when white, boiled until tender, then pressed until cold, make a delicious relish for lunch or supper. This is one of a few receipes for substantial dishes, suitable for persons of small means.

Meat Croquettes.—Any nice cold meat when finely minced will make good croquettes. Take about a quarter of a loaf of bread well soaked in water and squeezed dry, mix with the minced meat about a dessertspoonful of chopped parsley, three eggs, a pinch of ground mace, a dessertspoonful of ground ginger, pepper and salt; roll them into egg shaped balls; have ready two or three eggs well beaten in one plate and flour in another; firstly, roll in the flour, then in the egg; fry in boiling dripping; serve hot.

Beef a-la-Mode.—Take a piece of meat—cross-rib is best —put a slice of bacon or some lard in the bottom of the pot, then the meat, and fill up with water till the meat is covered; then take two onions, some peppercorns, cloves, bay leaves, one carrot, and a crust of brown bread, salt and some vinegar ; throw all this in over the beef ; keep the pot well covered ; fill up with more hot water, if it boils down, and let it boil three hours ; then burn a tablespoonful of flour, with some butter, a nice brown, thin with the gravy, and let it boil up once more with the meat ; then put the beef in a deep dish and strain the gravy over it ; add more vinegar to taste ; serve with fried potatoes and red cabbage.

Cold Roast Beef and Potato Pie.—Boil some potatoes until nearly soft, then mash them with a pestle and add some cream or butter, and salt to taste. Slice the cold beef and place it in a nappy, with a little chopped onions, salt and pepper, and ripe tomatoes sliced very thin. Add to it any gravy that was left, and a little flour; or it is best to dip each slice of meat into flour. Fill the dish two-thirds full, and cover the whole with a thick crust of mashed potatoes, making it rise to the centre above the edges of the dish. Score the crust with the point of a knife into squares of an equal size. Put the dish into the oven and bake it for half an hour—or until it is well browned.

Beef Tea.—Beef to be used for tea should be cut fine or chopped, and then soaked in cold water for two hours, if the time can be spared, and placed upon the fire in the same water. After thorough boiling it should be strained, all the fat carefully removed, and a little salt added. Allow a pint of water to every pound of meat.

Beef Liver.—Slice the liver and pour boiling water over it ; wipe dry and cut into very small pieces. Fry slices of fat, salt pork until brown ; take out the pork and fry the liver in the fat ; cook thoroughly. When done pour a little water over the liver and thicken a little with flour and water, mixed smooth, salt to taste.

Calf's Liver, Stewed.—Cut the liver into small slices, about three inches square. Into your saucepan place two onions, sliced fine, a tablespoonful of sage, one summer savory, a little pepper and salt; then add your liver and cover with water, and let it stew for two hours. Just before you serve it, dredge on a little flour, and add a tablespoonful of butter.

To Choose Veal.—Good veal should be finely grained, tender and juicy, the fat firm and of a whiteish color.

Roast Veal.—Make a dressing of bread crumbs, chopped thyme and parsley ; a little pepper and salt, one egg and a little butter. If too dry moisten with a little hot water. Take a loin of veal, make an incision in the flap and fill it with the stuffing ; secure it with small skewers and dredge the veal with a little flour, slightly salted. Bake in a moderate oven and baste often ; at first with a little salt and water, and afterwards with the drippings in the pan. When done, skim the gravy and thicken with a little brown flour. The breast and shoulder are nicely cooked in the same manner ; ask your butcher to make incisions for the stuffing. Serve roast veal with tomato sauce.

A Ragout of Cold Veal.—Cut the veal into slices ; put a large piece of butter into a frying-pan, and as soon as it is hot, dredge the meat well with flour, and fry a nice brown. Remove the meat, and put into the pan as much of your cold gravy as you think proper ; season with pepper and salt and a wineglassfull of tomato catsup ; then cut a few slices of cold ham, lay into the gravy, and add your slices of veal. It must be sent to the table hot.

Veal Minced.—Mince the veal as finely as possible, separating the skin, gristle and bones, with which a gravy should be made. Put a small quantity of the gravy into a stewpan, with a little lemon peal grated, and a spoonfull of milk or cream. Thicken it with a little butter and flour, mix gradually with the gravy ; season it with salt and a little lemon juice and cayenne pepper. Put in the minced veal and let it simmer a few minutes. Serve it upon sippets of toasted bread.

Knuckle of Veal.—Cut the veal in small thick slices, season with a little salt and pepper, flour lightly and fry it to a pale brown; then lay it in a saucepan and cover it with water. Skim well and season with thyme and parsley and a little mace. Simmer gently for two hours and a half, then thicken the gravy with a little flour and a piece of butter, and salt to taste. Add a little catsup if desired.

Veal Relish.—Three pounds of uncooked veal, quarter of a pound of pork; chop these fine; add two eggs, one cupful pounded crackers, one teaspoonful of salt, two of pepper; sage and summer savory to suit the taste; press hard in a pudding-dish, and bake one and a half hours; cut in thin slices when cold.

Veal Pie.—Very nice, made same as chicken pie.

Spiced Veal.—One pound of veal, chopped very fine; season with two well-beaten eggs, a teaspoonful of butter, teaspoonful of salt and sage each. Put it into a cake-pan, and bake about an hour. Slice when cold.

To Prepare Veal left over from Dinner.—Cut in small thin slices, peal and chop two medium sized onions, fry in a small piece of butter to a light brown, add a dessert spoonful of flour, then the gravy, if there was any left from dinner, add the meat to this gravy, and just heat through. Serve immediately.

Calf's Head.—Let the butcher split the head in halves. Take out the eyes and the snout bone; then lay it in cold water to soak, two hours before boiling; take out the brains and wash them well in several waters, then lay them in cold water. Put the head together, and lay it in a good-sized pot; cover it with cold water and throw in a tablespoonful of salt; let it boil slowly for two or three hours. When it has boiled a little more than an hour, take some of the liquor, about a quart, and put into a stewpan for the gravy ; add to this liquor some salt, pepper, a little parsley chopped fine, a teaspoonful of lemon pickle, and put over the fire to boil. Beat up an egg lightly, with two tablespoonfuls of flour, then remove carefully the skin from the brains, and beat them up with the egg and flour. When well beaten thicken the gravy with it, and stew about ten minutes.

Sweet Breads.—For every mode of dressing, they should be prepared by half boiling and then putting them in cold water ; this makes them whiter and firmer. Dip them in beaten egg and then into bread crumbs ; pepper and salt, and fry in lard. Nice served with peas or tomatoes.

Stewed Sweet Breads.—After they are parboiled and cold, lard them with fat pork ; put them in a stewpan, with some good veal gravy and juice of a small lemon ; stew them till very tender, and just before serving thicken with flour and butter ; serve with the gravy.

To Choose Mutton.—The fat to the best mutton is white, clear and hard, the scored skin on the fore-quarter nearly red ; the lean firm, succulent and juicy, and the leg bones nearly white.

To Choose Lamb.—Examine the fat on the back, and then that of the kidneys, both of which should be white, hard, and of the same color ; the vein in the neck should always be blue.

Leg of Mutton Stuffed.—Wash and wipe the mutton, grate a pint of bread crumbs, season with salt and pepper, a teaspoonful of sweet marjoram, two teaspoonfuls of sage and half a one of sweet basil (all dried and rubbed fine,) chop a medium-sized onion, and put it over the fire in a small saucepan with butter the size of a large egg, stew for five minutes, pour over the bread crumbs and stir in thoroughly ; with a sharp knife make a deep incision on the long side of the leg parallel with the bone, push the dressing in and make it go all through the length of the leg, skewer it at the opening where you stuffed it, season the leg with pepper and salt, dust it with flour and roast two hours in a hot oven, keeping a little water in the pan to baste it with, which should be done every fifteen or twenty minutes ; thicken the gravy with browned flour, put a few spoonfuls over the meat when you place it on the dish, and serve the remainder in a gravy-boat. To be eaten with currant jelly.

Shoulder of Mutton.—Take out the bone, and fill the space with a stuffing made of bread crumbs, salt pork, chopped fine, pepper, salt and sage, or sweet merjoram. A shoulder weighing eight pounds requires an hour and a half good fire.

Stewed Leg of Mutton.—Make a nice stuffing of finely chopped beef suet, bread crumbs, an onion chopped finely, pepper, salt, and a little ground clove. Make incisions in the leg, and stuff it well ; tie a little bundle of basil and parsley together, lay in the bottom of the dinner pot, and on it place the mutton ; just cover with water, and stew slowly. Two hours steady cooking will be all that is required : when tender, take out the mutton and add to the liquor a large spoonful of flour, made smooth with a little water, stir it well, and in five minutes take it off and strain it ; pour it back into the pot, and add a wineglassful of catsup, and lay the mutton in till it is served.

Leg of Lamb.—Boil it in water to cover it ; when half done add two cups of milk to the water, with a large spoonful of salt. It should be served with spinach and caper sauce. It will cook in an hour and a quarter, or half, according to size.

To Fry Lamb Steaks.—Dip each piece into well-beaten egg, cover with bread crumbs or corn meal, and fry in butter or new lard. Mashed potatoes and boiled rice are a necessary accompaniment. It is very nice to thicken the gravy with flour and butter, adding a little lemon juice, and pour it hot upon the steaks, and place the rice in spoonfuls around the dish to garnish it.

Irish Stew.—Put two pounds of mutton cutlets or chops, and four pounds good potatoes, peeled and sliced, in alternate layers in a large saucepan or stewpan, season to taste with pepper and salt, and a finely shred onion, if liked ; add a pint of cold water, and simmer gently for two hours. Serve very hot.

Cold Mutton Broiled.—Cut in thick slices cold boiled leg of mutton ; it should not be cooked too mnch or it will fall into pieces ; put on it salt and pepper, and then broil it. Let it be very hot, and add a thick sauce flavored with fresh tomatoes, or tomato sauce, and serve.

Lamb or Mutton Stew.—Part of a breast of mutton or lamb, cut in bits, as many potatoes, pepper and salt to taste ; two onions, a bunch of parsley, a bunch of sweet herbs. Stew all together, in sufficient water to cover them, for two hours, gently. Then put in a teacupful of tomato catsup, and boil up again. Serve hot.

Cottage Pie.—In the bottom of the pie-dish put a good layer of nicely minced mutton or beef, season to taste, add an onion chopped fine, cover with mashed potatoes, and bake in a sharp oven half an hour, or until the potatoes are well browned.

A Nice Breakfast Dish.—Boil and mash some nice, meally potatoes ; then, with one or two well beaten eggs make them into a paste ; work it well, dust it over with flour and roll out. Take some nice thin neck of mutton or lamb chops, carefully trim off the fat, pepper and salt them on both sides ; cut and paste into shape, cover over like a puff, pinch the edges, and fry a light brown ; they look better if a about an inch of the bone is left visible. Any kind of cold, underdone meat, minced fine and seasoned nicely, can be used instead of the chops: it is an excellent way of cooking cold meat.

To Choose Pork.—The skin should present a semi-transparent appearance, approaching white in color ; the fat firm and white, and the lean juicy and of a pale reddish color.

To Roast Pork.—A piece weighing eight or nine pounds will require nearly three hours to roast, although the time depends more on the thickness than the weight ; before placing it in the oven dredge with flour (it is best browned), season with sage, pepper and salt : after it has roasted half an hour, pour a little hot water in the dripping pan and baste the meat frequently till done. Serve apple sauce with all joints of roasted pork.

Corned Pork.—It should be soaked a few hours before boiling, then washed and scraped, and put into a fresh water. It must not be boiled fast, but put into cold water, and gradually warmed through ; skim frequently while boiling. A leg or shoulder weighing seven or eight pounds, should boil slowly for four hours. When taken up it must be skinned carefully, though some prefer the skin remaining on, as it looses much of the juice by skinning. It is very nice **cold.**

Pig's Head.—Clean it nicely and boil till very tender, chop it very fine, and season with salt, pepper, sage, and a little clove, while hot. Put in a deep dish, and cover with a plate that is smaller than the dish, that may rest on the meat. Press with a heavy weight for twenty-four hours.

Pork Chops.—Cut the chops about half an inch thick, and trim them neatly ; put a frying-pan on the fire, with a bit of butter ; as soon as it is hot, put in your chops, turning them often till brown all over ; they will be done in fifteen minutes ; a few minutes before they are done season with powdered sage, pepper and salt.

To Fricassee Pork.—Cut a small sparerib or chine of pork into pieces, cover with water and stew until tender ; remove the meat, and flavor the gravy with salt, pepper and thicken with a little flour. Serve in a deep dish, in the gravy, and garnish the dish with rice.

Sausages.—The proper seasoning is salt, pepper, sage, summer savory or thyme; they should be one-third fat, the remainder lean and finely chopped, and the seasonings well mixed, and proportioned so that one herb may not predominate over the others. If skins are used, they cannot be prepared with too much care ; but they are about as well made into cakes; spread the cakes on a clean white wood board, and keep them in a dry, cool place. To fry, put a bit of butter into a frying-pan ; as soon as it is melted put in the sausages, and fry them over a slow fire till they are nicely browned on both sides.

Sausages with Tomatoes.—Tomatoes and sausages are capital. Fry the sausages and arrange them in a dish in front of the fire. Cut the tomatoes into slices with some onions thinly sliced ; fry them, season them with pepper and salt, place them among the sausages and serve hot.

How to Cook Salt Pork.—Many people do not relish salt pork fried, but it is quite good to soak it in milk two or three hours, then roll it in Indian meal and fry to a light brown. This makes a good dish with mashed turnips, or raw onions cut in vinegar ; another way is to soak it over night in skim-milk and bake like fresh pork ; it is almost as good as fresh roast pork.

Pork Relish.—Fry some slices of salt pork till crisp, take them out, pour a little water to the fat and season it with pepper ; sprinkle in a little flour, then cut up the pork into small pieces, and put it into this thickened gravy.

Boiled Ham.—Soak in cold water over night ; in the morning wash thoroughly, and trim away any black or rusty edges; cover with cold water and put it on to boil; when it is nearly boiling hot, pour off the water and cover again with cold water; boil gently, and allow twenty minutes to every pound in cooking. Remove the skin when cold, stick cloves at intervals with a ring of pepper around them; garnish with parsley.

Steamed Ham.—Soak and clean, the same as for boiled ham; put into a steamer, cover, and keep the water underneath boiling briskly. Allow thirty minutes to a pound; when nearly done remove the skin and place the ham in a baking pan: pour over it a little vinegar and sprinkle with white sugar; bake in the oven a few minutes till a nice brown. This is a nice way to cook part of a ham; it wastes less than when boiled.

Ham Toast.—Mix with one tablespoonful of finely chopped or grated ham, the beaten-up yolk of an egg and a little cream and pepper; heat over the fire and then spread the mixture either on hot buttered toast, or on slices of bread fried quite crisp in butter; serve very hot.

Cold Ham and Meat Croquettes.—Take cold fowl or cold fresh meat of any kind, with a few slices of cold ham. fat and lean; chop together until very fine; add half as much stale bread, grated; salt, pepper, grated nutmeg, a teaspoonful of made mustard, one tablespoonful of catsup. a small lump of butter. Knead all well together; make into small, flat cakes (the yolk of an egg may be used to bind the ingredients, but it is not necessary). Brush with the yolk of a beaten egg, on both sides, cover thickly with grated bread crumbs, fry in a little lard or butter, a light brown. They are excellent.

Ham and Eggs.—Chop finely some cold boiled ham, fat and lean together, say a pound to four eggs; put a piece of butter in the pan, then the ham; let it get well warmed through, then beat the eggs light; stir them in briskly.

Directions for Roasting a Turkey.—Pluck the bird carefully and singe off the down with lighted paper; break the leg bone close to the foot and hang up the bird and draw out the strings from the thigh. Never cut the breast; make a slit down the back of the neck and take out the crop that way: then cut the neck-bone close, and after the bird is stuffed the skin can be turned over the back and the crop will look full and round. Cut around the vent, making the opening as small as possible, and draw carefully, taking care that the gall bag and the gut joining the gizzard are not broken. Open the gizzard and remove the contents and detatch the liver from the gall bladder. The liver, gizzard and heait, if used in the gravy, will need to be be boiled an hour and a half, and chopped as fine as possible. Wash the turkey and wipe thoroughly dry, inside and out; then fill the inside with stuffing, and either sew the skin of the neck over the back or fasten it with a small skewer. Sew up the opening at the vent; then run a long skewer into the pinion and thigh through the body, passing it through the opposite pinion and thigh. Put a skewer in the small part of the leg, close on the outside of the sidesman, and push it through. Pass a string over the points of the skewers and tie it securely at the back.

Dredge well with flour, and cover the breast with nicely buttered white paper, place on a grating in the dripping-pan and put in the oven to roast. Baste every fifteen minutes—a few times with butter and water, and afterwards with the gravy in the dripping-pan. Do not have too hot an oven. A turkey weighing ten pounds will require nearly three hours to bake. Stew the giblets in just water enough to cover them, and when the turkey is lifted from the pan add these (chopped very fine) with the water in which they were boiled, to the drippings; thicken with browned flour, boil up once and turn into the gravy-boat. If the drippings are too fat, skim well before putting in the giblets. Serve with cranberry sauce, currant or apple jelly.

Stuffing for a Turkey.—Take some bread crumbs and turn on just enough hot water to soften them ; put in a piece of butter, not melted, the size of a hen's egg, and a spoonful of pulverized sage, a teaspoonful of ground pepper, and a teaspoonful of salt ; then mix thoroughly and stuff your turkey.

Stuffing for a Turkey.—Mix thoroughly a quart of stale bread, very finely grated ; the grated rind of a lemon ; quarter of an ounce of minced parsley and thyme, one part thyme, two parts parsley ; and pepper and salt to season. Add to these one unbeaten egg and half a cup of butter : mix all well together and moisten with hot water or milk. Other herbs than parsley or thyme my be used if preferred, and a little onion, finely minced, added if desired. The proportions given here may be increased when more is required.

Roast Goose.—Geese and ducks, if old, are better parboiled before they are roasted. Put them in sufficient water to cover them, and simmer about two hours. Make a stuffing with four onions, one ounce of green sage, chopped fine, a large cupful of stale bread crumbs, and the same of mashed potatoes, one teaspoonful of butter, a little pepper and salt, and one unbeaten egg ; mix them well together, and stuff the body of the goose ; then place in the oven and bake about an hour and a half. Serve with apple sauce.

Roast Pigeons.—When cleaned and ready for roasting, fill the bird with a stuffing of bread crumbs, a spoonful of butter, a little salt and nutmeg, and three oysters to each bird (some prefer chopped apple). They must be well basted with melted butter, and require thirty minutes careful cooking. In the autumn they are best, and should be full grown.

Roast Duck.—Prepare your duck for roasting, and use the following stuffing : Chop fine and throw into cold water three good sized onions, one large spoonful of sage, two of bread crumbs, a piece of butter the size of a walnut, a little salt and pepper and the onions drained. Mix well together and stuff the duck.

An hour is enough for an ordinary sized duck. The gravy is made by straining the drippings; skim off the fat, then stir in a large spoonful of browned flour, a teaspoonful of mixed mustard, a wineglassful of claret. Simmer for ten minutes.

Boiled Turkey.—Prepare your turkey as for roasting; put it in a cloth and boil it slowly, if from eight to nine pounds, an hour and a half. Throw into the water a few cloves, a little black pepper, sweet marjoram and salt. It is to be served with oysters. Skim the turkey well while boiling, or it will not be white.

Chicken Pie. (*Economical.*)—Cut the chicken in pieces and parboil for three-quarters of an hour. Remove the chicken and add to the water in which it is boiled a little salt, pepper and a teacupful of milk thickened with a tablespoonful of flour. Line a deep dish with nice paste, put in the chicken and turn over it the gravy which you have prepared. Cover it with paste immediately: make a small hole in the centre; ornament with strips of paste, and bake for forty-five minutes.

Boiled Fowl or Chicken.—They should be cleaned and stuffed as for roasting. A young fowl requires an hour; if tough and old, three hours. A chicken will boil in three-quarters of an hour. They may be served with oyster, caper or egg sauce.

Prairie Chickens.—Skin the chickens, which makes them sweeter; cut them open on the back and through the breast. Fry them in butter, with salt and pepper to the taste. Cook them to a nice brown.

Hashed Fowl.—Cold fowls may be turned into a hot breakfast dish as follows: Chop the meat very fine; put half a pint of gravy into a stew-pan with a little piece of butter rolled in flour; season with nutmeg, pepper and salt; put in the turkey or chicken, and shake it over a clear fire till it is thoroughly hot. Serve with poached eggs laid on the hash, and garnish round the plate pieces of fried or toasted bread.

Pressed Chicken.—Cut the chicken into four parts, boil in as little water as possible; when done tender take out the meat, but keep the broth boiling; pick the meat from the bones, chop it, and add butter, pepper and salt. Take all fat from your broth, then pour over the chopped chicken. Then press it and serve cold.

Chicken Fricassee. Prepare a couple of nice chickens; joint them, dividing the wings, side, breast and backbone, and let them lie in salt and water half an hour; remove them then to a stewpan, with a half pound of good, sweet salt pork cut up in pieces; barely cover with water, and *simmer* on the top of the stove or range for three hours; when sufficiently tender take out the chicken, mix a table-spoonful of flour smoothly with cold milk, and add a little fine dried or chopped parsley, sage and thyme, or summer savory, and stir gradually into the liquor; keep stirring till it boils; season with pepper and salt to taste; and then put back the chicken and let it boil up for a few moments in the gravy; garnish with the green tops of celery.

Stewed Chicken.—Divide a chicken into pieces by the joints, and put into a stewpan, with salt, pepper, some parsley and thyme; pour in a quart of water, with a piece of butter: and when it has stewed an hour and a half, take the chicken out of the pan. If there is no gravy, put in another piece of butter, add some water and flour, and let it boil a few minutes. When done, it should not be quite as thick as drawn butter. For the dumplings: Take one quart of sifted flour, one teaspoonful of salt, two of cream of tartar and one of soda; mix with milk and form into biscuit; place them upon a tin in a steamer over the kettle where the chicken is boiling. They will steam in twenty minutes. You can rub a little butter in the flour, if you wish them very nice.

Chicken Pot Pie.—Divide the chicken into pieces at the joints; boil until part done, or about twenty minutes, then take it out. Fry two or three slices of fat salt pork, and put in the bottom: then place the chicken on it with three pints of water, two ounces of butter, a teaspoonful of pepper, and cover over the top with a light crust, made the same as for biscuit. Cook one hour.

To Cook Poultry.—All kinds of poultry and meat can be cooked quicker by adding to the water in which they are boiled a little vinegar or a piece of lemon. By the use of a little acid there will be a considerable saving of fuel, as well as shortening of time. Its action is beneficial on old tough meats, rendering them quite tender and easy of digestion. Tainted meats and fowls will lose their bad taste and odor if cooked in this way, and if not used too freely no taste of it will be acquired.

To Roast Wild Fowl.—The flavor is best preserved without stuffing. Put pepper, salt, and a piece of butter into each. Wild fowl require much less dressing than tame. A rich brown gravy should be sent in the dish; and when the breast is cut into slices, before taking off the bone, a squeeze of lemon, with pepper and salt, is a great improvement to the flavor. To take off the fishy taste which wild fowl sometimes have, put an onion, salt, and hot water into the dripping-pan, and baste them for the first ten minutes with this; then take away the pan and baste constantly with butter.

How to Cook Vegetables.—Potatoes and many other vegetables are much nicer steamed than boiled. It is a common idea that it requires no skill to cook vegetables; but many a dinner is spoiled by neglect in this department. Cook them until done, season well, use plenty of butter and serve them hot if you wish them to be good.

In order to boil vegetables of a good green color, put them on in boiling water and boil very fast; do not cover them, and take them out as soon as done, or the color will change. To boil them green in hard water use a little carbonate of soda, put into the water before the vegetables are put in.

Boiled Potatoes.—Pare the potatoes very thin and let them lie in cold water an hour or longer. Some potatoes are best put on in cold water (old potatoes especially), and others are nicest if dropped iuto boiling water. Put some salt in the water, a tablespoonful for each dozen potatoes, and cook till done, not a moment longer. Pour off all the water and let them stand five minutes in the saucepan (the lid partly off) on the back of the stove. Serve in a covered dish.

Old Potatoes.—Old potatoes are best to boil until soft, then peel and mash fine, with a little salt, butter, and a very little milk, beat well together with a spoon ; then put into a dish, smooth over with a knife, sprinkle a little flour over it : put in the oven to brown.

Fried Potatoes.—Peal good-sized potatoes, slice them as evenly as possible and drop them into very cold water : have a kettle of very hot lard, as for cakes, put a few at a time into a towel and shake, to dry the moisture out of them, and then drop them into the boiling lard. Stir them occasionally, and when of a light brown take them out with a skimmer, and they will be crisp and not greasy. Sprinkle salt over them while hot.

Fried Potatoes.—Pare a dozen medium-sized potatoes, cut them up small, and let them remain in cold water for half an hour; take them out and put them in a frying-pan, with half a cup of butter and a little salt ; cover, and every little while shake and turn them ; when they are tender, and of a light, rich brown, they are done.

Lyonaise Potatoes.—Put a pint of milk in a frying-pan ; add a piece of butter the size of a butternut, some salt and pepper ; let it boil ; take a heaping teaspoonful of corn-starch, mix with a little cold milk ; add, stiring till it thickens; have six or seven good sized peeled potatoes (boiled or baked the day before,) cut them in small pieces, put all together; cook fifteen minutes, stiring to prevent burning. They make delicious breakfast dish, cheap and wholesome.

Stewed Potatoes.—Pare the potatoes, cut them in slices, (let them lie in cold water, if you have time,) and put them in a saucepan with boiling water. When nearly done, pour off the water, pour on milk to cover the potatoes season with pepper, salt and a little butter, and thicken with a little flour. Simmer a few minutes till potatoes are tender then send to the table hot.

Potatoe Cakes.—Mash the potatoes, season with salt, add a very small piece of butter and one egg ; make into flat cakes, flour and fry in lard or good drippings, until a nice brown.

Fried Sweet Potatoes.—Parboil them, skin and cut lengthwise into slices quarter of an inch thick. Fry in sweet dripping. Cold boiled potatoes are nice cooked the same way.

Boiled Asparagus.—Reject the woody portions and scrape clean the white part that remains: throw into cold water as you scrape them. Tie them in bundles of about twenty each, and cut the stalks even. put them on in boil-ing water, with a handful of salt, and cook until they are tender at the stalk. Toast some bread, dip into the water in which the asparagus was boiled ; lay the asparagus upon the toast, the white ends outwards each way; serve with melted or drawn butter.

Asparagus Stewed.—Cut the points as far as they are perfectly tender, in pieces not more than half an inch in length; wash them very clean and throw them into plenty of boiling water, salted. When they are tender, take out the asparagus and lay aside for a few minutes. Have some pieces of toasted bread, dip them into the water in which the asparagus was boiled, butter them and lay them in dish, and place the asparagus on top. Pour a little milk into the saucepan, thicken with a little flour and add a piece of butter; salt to taste. Pour the mixture over the asparagus and serve very hot.

Celery.—Cut off the roots and wash and scrape the stalks. Cut off the green leaves and reject the toughest stalks. Retain the leaves that grow near the heart. Lay in cold water till ready to serve. The habitual daily use of this vegetable is much more beneficial to man than most people are aware of. Everybody engaged in labor weakening to the nerves should use celery daily in the season, and onions in its stead when not in season.

Young Beets, Boiled.—Wash them very clean, but neither scrape nor cut them. Put them in boiling water, and according to their size, boil them from one to two hours; take off the skin when done, and put over them pepper, salt and a little butter. Beets are very nice baked, but require a much longer time to cook.

Lima Beans.—Shell them into cold water; let them lie half an hour, or longer; put them into a saucepan with plenty of boiling water, a little salt, and cook till tender. Drain and butter well, and pepper to taste.

String Beans.—Break off both ends and string carefully; if necessary, pare poth edges with a knife. Cut the beans in pieces an inch long and put in cold water a few minutes. Drain and put them into boiling water with a piece of bacon or salt pork. Boil quickly for half an hour, or till tender. Drain in a colander and dish with plenty of butter.

Green Corn.—This should be cooked on the same day it is gathered; it loses its sweetness in a few hours, and must be artificially supplied. Strip off the husks, pick out all the silk, and put it in boiling water; if not entirely fresh, add a tablespoonful of sugar to the water, but *no salt*; boil twenty minutes, fast, and serve; or you may cut it from the cob, put in plenty of butter and a little salt, and serve in a covered vegetable dish.

Succotash.—Cut off the corn from the cobs, and put the cobs in just water enough to cover them, and boil one hour; then remove the cobs, and put in the corn and a quart of Lima beans, and boil thirty minutes. When boiled, add some cream or milk, salt, and butter.

Buttered Parsnips.—Scrape and wash the parsnips and slice them lengthwise; boil in just water enough to cover them till thoroughly done; drain off the water, put in a piece of butter, a little salt and pepper; beat up an egg with half a cup of milk, and turn over them.

Fried Parsnips.—Boil until tender, scrape off the skin and cut in lengthwise slices. Dredge with flour and fry in hot dripping, turning when one side is browned.

Cauliflower.—Take off all the green leaves, cut the flower close at the bottom from the stalk; if large, divide into four quarters. Put into cold water, let it lie not over an hour, then put into boiling milk and water, or water only —milk makes it white—skim while boiling. When the stalks are tender, take it up, which must be done before it loses its crispness. Lay it on a cloth or colander to drain, and serve with melted butter.

Boiled Cabbage.—Take off the outer leaves, cut the head in quarters, and boil in a large quantity of water, until done. Drain and press out the water, chop fine and season. Boil three-quarters of an hour, or till tender. The water can be drained off when they are half done, and fresh water added if desired.

Green Peas.—They should be fresh and newly shelled. Put them into salted boiling water, and cook them with the lid of the saucepan off. If young and fresh they will cook in twenty minutes. Drain and dish with plenty of butter. A sprig of mint and a very little white sugar added to the water in which they are boiled improves taste and color.

Boiled Onions.—Skin them and soak them in cold water an hour or longer, then put into a saucepan and cover with boiling water, well salted; when nearly done, pour off the water, add a little milk, and simmer till tender. Season with butter, pepper and salt.

Winter Squash.—Cut it in pieces, take out the seeds and pare as thin as possible; steam and boil until soft and tender. Drain and press well, then mash with butter, pepper, salt and a very little sugar. Summer squash may be cooked the same way; if extremely tender they need not be pared.

Spinach.—Wash and clean the spinach thoroughly from grit, then boil it in salt and water; press the water entirely out of it, and chop it fine. A quarter of an hour before serving put it into a saucepan with a piece of butter, mixed with a tablespoonful of flour and half a tumblerful of boiling water or milk, some salt and pepper, and let it simmer fifteen minutes. Serve with hard-boiled eggs, cut in rings, on the top.

Turnips.—Pare the turnips, cut them in two or more pieces and boil briskly in water with salt in it. When they are done, drain and mash them with pepper and salt and a piece of butter. If preferred, they may be sent to the table without mashing, and have melted butter poured over them.

Stewed Tomatoes.—Pour boiling water over the tomatoes, and remove the skins; cut them in pieces and stew them without water, seasoning them with butter and salt, and a little pepper if desired.

Tomato Toast.—Prepare the tomatoes as for sauce, and while they are cooking toast some slices of bread very brown, but not burned; butter them on both sides and pour the tomato sauce over them.

Tomatoes Fried.—(*Very nice.*) Do not pare them, but cut in slices as an apple; dip in cracker, pounded and sifted, and fry in a little good butter.

Eggs a-la-Mode.—Remove the skin from a dozen tomatoes, medium size, cut them up in a saucepan, add a little butter, pepper and salt; when sufficiently boiled, beat up five or six eggs, and just before you serve turn them into the saucepan with the tomato, and stir one way for two minutes, allowing them time to be well done.

To Boil Eggs.—Three minutes will boil them very soft; five minutes will cook hard, all but the yolk, and eight minutes will cook them hard all through.

Scrambled Eggs.—Beat up four eggs, with salt and pepper to taste. Put an ounce of butter into a saucepan; directly it is melted put in the eggs, and keep constantly stirring with a spoon until they are nearly set. A little finely minced parsley added is a great improvement.

Omelet.—Take four eggs and beat as light as possible. For every egg add a tablespoonful of milk. Put a piece of butter in the omelet pan, and when hot pour in the mixture. With a fork scrape the egg very lightly toward the center of the pan as it cooks, and when done fold it together with a pancake turner.

Poached Eggs.—The eggs should be fresh. Have the boiling water in a shallow pan, break the eggs separately in a saucer, and slip gently into the boiling water; when all are in the water, place the pan over the fire, until the white of each is perfectly set; remove with a slicer, and lay on buttered toast or broiled ham.

Baked Eggs.—Have a little beef fat in your tin, let it be hot, then break in your eggs as for frying; salt them and set in hot oven a few minutes and they are done. Eat with buttered toast.

Pickled Peaches.—Nine pounds peaches, three pounds sugar, three quarts good cider vinegar. Peel the peaches, put two cloves in each peach, then put them with the sugar and vinegar in a porcelain-lined kettle; cook from five to ten minutes. Add a little whole allspice.

Sweet Tomato Pickles.—Eight pounds peeled tomatoes, four of powdered sugar, cinnamon, cloves and allspice, each one ounce. Boil one hour, and then add a quart of boiling vinegar.

Cold Slaw.—A white, hard head of cabbage, cut in halves and laid in cold water, then shave it very fine. Boil from a half to a pint of vinegar, stir into it the well-beaten yolk of an egg, and then turn over the cabbage, but not till a short time before using.

Pickled Cucumbers.—To a gallon of water add a quart of salt, put in the cucumbers and let them stay over night. In the morning wash them out of the brine, and put them carefully into a stone jar. Boil a gallon of vinegar, put in, while cold, quarter of a pound of cloves and a tablespoonful of alum; when it boils hard, skim it well and turn over the cucumbers. In a week they will be fit for use.

Green Pickles for Daily Use.—A gallon of vinegar, three-quarters pound of salt, quarter pound of ginger, an ounce of mace, quarter ounce of cayenne pepper, and an ounce of mustard seed, simmered in vinegar, and when cold put in a jar. You may throw in fruits and vegetables when you choose.

Tomato Catsup.—One gallon skinned tomatoes, three heaping tablespoonfuls of salt, same of black pepper, two of allspice, three of ground mustard, half a dozen pods of red pepper. Stew all slowly together in a quart of vinegar for three hours ; strain the liquor, simmer down to half a gallon. Bottle hot and cork tight.

Tomato Catsup.—Cut the tomatoes in two, and boil for half an hour ; then press through a hair sieve, and add spices in proportion given below ; after which, boil for about three hours over a slow fire. Remove from the fire, turn it out, and let it stand till next day, when you must add half a pint of vinegar for each peck of tomatoes. For every like amount of the vegetable add, while boiling, one-eighth of an ounce of red and one-quarter of an ounce of black pepper, half an ounce each of mace, allspice and cloves, and two ounces of mustard—all finely powdered. Salt to suit, and put in a little ginger and essence of celery, if you so desire. Bottle, seal the corks, and keep in a dark, cool place.

Pepper Catsup.—Fifty pods of large red peppers, with the seeds. Add a pint of vinegar, and boil until the pulp will mash through a sieve. Add to the pulp a second pint of vinegar, two spoonfuls of sugar, cloves, mace, spice, onions and salt. Put all in a kettle and boil to a proper consistency.

Pickled Red Cabbage.—Cut the red cabbage in thin slices, spread it on a sieve and sprinkle with salt. Let it drain for twenty-four hours, dry it, pack it in pickle jars, fill them with cold vinegar, put in spice to taste, and tie the jars up firmly. Open the jars in a few days, and if the cabbage has shrunk, fill up with vinegar.

Pickled Green Tomatoes.—Let the tomatoes stand in salt and water for twelve hours. Then stick four or five cloves in each one and pour boiling vinegar over them. Place them in a jar and set them in a cool place.

Spiced Currants.—Five pounds of currants, two pounds sugar, one pint vinegar, one tablespoonful each of salt, pepper, cinnamon and cloves ; mash well together and boil twenty minutes. Spiced gooseberries are very nice.

Tomato Soy.—To one peck of green tomatoes, sliced thin, add one pint of salt ; stand twenty-four hours, strain, and put on the fire with twelve raw onions, an ounce of black pepper, an ounce of allspice, quarter of a pound of ground mustard, half a pound of white mustard seed, and a little cayenne pepper. Cover with vinegar, and boil till as thick as a jam, stirring occasionally with a wooden spoon, to prevent burning.

Mock Capers.—Take green nasturtium seeds when they are full grown, but not yellow ; dry for a day in the sun ; then put them in jars and cover with boiling vinegar, spiced, and when cool, cork closely. Fit for use in six weeks. They are nice in drawn butter for fish or boiled meat.

Red Cabbage (Pickled).—One red cabbage chopped fine, one quart of vinegar ; if very strong, reduce it by taking one-half water, one heaping tablespoonful ground mace, one heaping tablespoonful ground cinnamon, one heaping tablespoonful ground cloves, one heaping tablespoonful ground allspice ; make a bag for these spices and put them in the vinegar ; two tablespoonfuls of salt, one tablespoonful of pepper, a small piece of alum and some whole cloves. Boil all together about five minutes.

French Pickles (*Delicious*). — One colander of sliced green tomatoes, one quart of sliced onions, one colander of cucumbers, pared and sliced, two good handfuls of salt. Let all stand twenty-four honrs, then drain through a sieve ; one-half ounce of celery seed, one-half ounce of allspice, one tea-cupful of white mustard seed, one-half teacupful of black pepper, one tablespoonful of turmeric, one pound of brown sugar, two tablespoonfuls of mustard, one gallon of vinegar.

Pickled Pears.—Ten pounds of pears, three pounds of light brown sugar, one quart of vinegar, one ounce of cinnamon, one ounce of cloves (ground), one-quarter pound of citron ; put all in together and boil until the pears are tender ; skim the pears out and let the syrup boil a half hour longer.

French Mustard.—Take a quarter of a pound of best yellow mustard, pour over it half a pint each of water and vinegar. Add a pinch of salt and a piece of calamus root the size of a pea. Put it on the fire, and while it boils add a tablespoonful of flour ; let it boil twenty minutes, stirring it constantly. Just before taking it off stir in a teaspoonful of sugar or honey. When cool, put it into bottles and cork tightly.

Chow Chow.—A peck of tomatoes, two quarts of green peppers, half a peck of onions, two cabbages cut as for slaw, and two quarts of mustard seed. Have a large firkin, put in a layer of sliced tomatoes, then one of onions, next one of peppers, lastly cabbage ; sprinkle over some of the mustard seed, repeat the layers again, and so on until you have used up the above quantity. Boil a gallon of vinegar, with a bit of alum, two ounces of cloves and two of allspice tied in a little bag, and boiled with the vinegar; skim it well and turn into the firkin. Let it stand twenty-four hours, then pour the whole into a large kettle, and let it boil five minutes ; turn into the firkin, and stand it away for future use.

Chicken Salad.—Boil a chicken ; do not chop very fine ; cut up one bunch of celery, the size of a cent ; to make the dressing, wash smooth the yolk of a hard-boiled egg, one full teaspoonful of salt, one or two tablespoonfuls of made mustard; stir in slowly four tablespoonfuls of sweet oil, then two tablespoonfuls of vinegar; pour over the chicken and celery.

Lobster Salad.—To make the dressing: boil two eggs for twelve minutes, and put them in a basin of cold water for a few minutes, till the yolks become thoroughly cold and hard. Rub the yolks through a sieve with a wooden spoon, and mix them with a tablespoonful of water; then add two tablespoonfuls of olive oil; when these are well mixed, add by degrees a teaspoonful of salt, and the same of made mustard; when these are smoothly united add very gradually three tablespoonfuls of vinegar.

Take out the finest parts of a lobster and mince them small. Just before it is to be served, mince two heads of white-heart lettuce; mix it with the lobster and the dressing. Cut up the white of the eggs and garnish the salad with it.

Potato Salad.—Six cold-boiled potatoes, one medium-sized onion, sliced thin into a tureen; first a layer of potato, then of onion, alternately, until the dish is full; sprinkle with pepper and salt occasionally while filling the dish; do the same on top; put on four tablespoonfuls of sweet cream; melt one-half cup of butter or lard from fried pork, with half a pint of vinegar; when boiling hot pour over the salad and it is ready to serve.

Salad Dessert.—Boil and mash fine a white potato, add the yolks of two cold hard-boiled eggs. While the potato is warm, beat all smoothly together, add melted butter or oil-prepared mustard, salt and vinegar to taste. The potato increases the quantity of dressing, and cannot be distinguished from eggs.

Lettuce Dressing.—Five eggs beaten together, a level teaspoonful of salt, same of pepper, tablespoonful each of butter, cream and mixed mustard, and half a teacupful of weak vinegar. Put all into a dish and place it in a vessel of boiling water, stirring all the time until it thickens. When cold, add four tablespoonfuls of salad oil.

Bread.—One quart of lukewarm water, tablespoonful of salt, teaspoonful of sugar, half a cup of yeast. Dissolve a tablespoonful of butter or lard and add to the above. Stir in flour to form a stiff dough. Knead well, cover and set in a warm place to rise. Next morning knead again, divide it into three loaves, place in pans near stove to rise; will be ready to bake in about an hour.

If made in the morning and set over a kettle of warm water near the stove the bread may be baked by noon.

Three things must be exactly right in order to have good bread—the quality of the yeast ; the lightness or fermentation of the dough, and the heat of the oven. It requires observation, reflection, and a quick, nice judgment to decide when all are right ; no precise rules can be given.

Delicious Bread.—Melt a cake of German or condensed yeast in a cup of blood-warm water ; sift six quarts of flour in pan ; add three full handfuls Indian meal, two handfuls salt, and stir all together ; make a hole in middle ; have ready pitcher of lukewarm water ; pour some in ; add yeast ; and make pretty thick sponge ; let it rise till light mix in the morning ; it will be light if in a warm place in three hours ; flour your board ; mix your flour in your pan in the sponge, not so much but that it will be soft ; take out, mold, and knead a few minutes ; put in greased pans, and set in warm place to rise ; when it is cracked on top it is ready for oven ; one can see the cracks by holding up the pan and looking across it.

Brown Bread.—Two cups of Indian meal even full, three cups of flour or Graham meal heaped, a pint and a half of sour milk, a cup of molasses, teaspoonful and a half of soda, one of salt, steamed four hours. Brown lightly in the oven afterwards.

Brown Bread.—One quart of Indian meal and one quart of rye, mixed well together ; half a cup of molasses, one tablespoonful of salt, tablespoonful of cream of tartar, two-thirds of a tablespoonful of soda, dissolved in a pint of cold water. When dissolved wet the mixture with it, and if it does not thoroughly wet it add a little more. It should be nearly as stiff as bread. Bake moderately from four to five hours. Some people add raisins, which makes it very nice.

Milk Bread.—One pint of boiling water, one pint of new milk, one teaspoonful soda, the same of salt, flour enough to form a batter ; let it rise, and add sufficient flour to form a dough, and bake immediately.

Soda Biscuits.—Into one quart of flour, rub a tablespoonful of lard and one of butter, with two teaspoonfuls of cream of tartar. Dissolve a teaspoonful of soda, and one and a half of salt in half a pint of water, and if this will not wet the flour sufficiently add a little more cold water ; roll it out, handling as little as possible, and cut with a tin into rounds. Bake in a quick oven ; quarter of an hour should bake them. Everything depends on a quick oven. Many use milk instead of water, but if made and baked properly, water is nice enough to render them fit for any epicure.

Sour Milk Biscuits.—To be made as the above, with the exception sour milk is used in the place of cream of tartar, and the soda is dissolved in the milk. Teaspoonful of soda to a pint of sour milk.

Drop Biscuits.—One pint sour milk, teaspoonful of soda dissolved in the milk, tablespoonful of butter, tablespoonful of white sugar, a little salt, and flour enough to make it stiff enough to drop.

Tea Biscuits.—One quart of sifted flour, a little salt, three teaspoonfuls baking powder, a small handful of sugar ; mix lightly through the flour ; rub a large teaspoonful of lard through the dry mixture; mix with water (it is better than milk), the colder the better; roll out soft to thickness of about one-third of an inch; cut with a large size cutter, and bake in a really hot oven.

Rolls.—Two quarts of sifted flour, a lump of lard about the size of an egg—one a little larger of butter; stir into the flour the same as in making pastry. When well stirred add blood-warm water, or milk and water, to mix; add a little salt, half teacupful of yeast, and a tablespoonful of sugar. Mix in the evening as for bread, and let it rise. In the morning knead, roll out, cut with a tih, shape them, and let them rise ten or fifteen minutes after putting them in the pan, then bake; fifteen minutes will suffice if the oven is sufficiently heated. Good bread may be made in the same way, with a proportionally smaller quantity of lard and butter. Can be made in the morning and baked for tea.

Economical Fritters.—Rusked bread, or that which is old and sour, can be made into very nice fritters. The bread should be cut in small pieces, and soaked in *cold* water till very soft. Drain off the water and mash the bread fine.

To three pints of bread thus prepared, add two eggs, four tablespoonfuls of flour, a little salt, one teaspoonful of soda in a cup of milk, which must be stirred into the bread, and a little more milk added, until thin enough to fry.

Blackberry Fritters—Are made by mixing a thick batter of flour and sour milk, or cream as for pancakes, only quite stiff. If cream is used allow one more egg than for sour milk, then stir thick with berries. Have ready a kettle of hot lard, dip a tablespoon into the lard, then take a spoonful of batter and drop it into the boiling lard; the grease will prevent the batter from sticking to the spoon, and will let it drop off in nice oval shapes. Eat with syrup.

French Twists.—To one quart of warm milk, add one coffeecupful of potato yeast, a little salt, flour enough to make a stiff batter. Let it rise; when very light work in two spoonfuls of butter, one egg, and flour until stiff enough to roll. Cut in strips, braid it, let it rise again. When light bake on buttered tins half an hour.

Sally Lunn.—Take one and a half quarts of flour, two tablespoonfuls of melted butter, one pint of warm milk, three beaten eggs, one teaspoonful of salt, and half a cup of yeast; mix well, put in a buttered pan, cover and set to rise; when light, bake in a moderate oven.

Dyspepsia Bread.—One pint bowl of Graham flour, dissolve one-half teaspoonful of soda in two-thirds of a cup of home-made yeast, and add to the mixture one teacupful of molasses; pour in sufficient warm water to make it somewhat thinner than flour bread.

French Rolls.—One pint of milk, one small cup of yeast, flour enough to make a stiff batter; raise over night. In the morning add one egg, one tablespoonful of butter and flour to make it stiff enough to knead. Let it rise, then knead it again (to make it fine and white), roll out, cut with a round tin, brush with milk and fold over; put them in a pan and cover very close. Set them in a warm place until they are very light; bake quickly, and you will have delicious rolls.

Grandmother's Johnny Cake (1776).—One quart Indian meal, teaspoonful of salt, scalded well with boiling water. Bake half an inch thick. When done cut in squares for the table. Very nice split through the middle and dipped in melted butter.

Huckleberry Tea Cake.—Two cups of sour milk, half a cup of white sugar, one egg, teaspoonful of soda, teaspoonful of salt, flour enough to make it a stiff dough. Beat it well and fill with berries. To be eaten hot with butter. If made with sweet milk, use baking powder instead of soda.

Berry Corn Cake.—Two cups Indian meal, one cup of flour, three tablespoonfuls sugar, two eggs, teaspoonful of salt, teaspoonful of soda, dissolved in a pint of sour milk. or, if the milk is sweet, use two teaspoonfuls of cream of tartar. To be filled with berries and baked till a nice brown.

Rice Fritters.—Take one cup of cold-boiled rice, one pint of flour, one teaspoonful of salt, two eggs beaten lightly, and milk enough to make this a thick batter; beat all together well and bake on a griddle.

Corn Bread.—Take one quart of sweet milk, corn meal enough to thicken, three eggs, half a cup of butter, two tablespoonfuls of brown sugar, one teaspoonful of soda, and two of cream of tartar; bake in a moderate oven.

Muffins.—Beat one egg lightly, add a quart of warm milk, cut up into a spoonful of lard and a spoonful of butter, with a little salt, let it be of the consistency of a rather thick batter; set it to rise and bake in rings.

Waffles.—Beat carefully into one quart of flour one quart of sweet milk, one cup of melted butter, half a teaspoonful of salt, and a scant half cup of good home-made yeast. When raised, add two eggs well beaten, and let the batter rise half an hour longer. Bake as soon as light in hot, greased waffle-irons.

Rice Waffles.—A pint bowl of cold-boiled rice, thin it with cold milk, beaten well, one egg, a small piece of butter, and flour to make a batter stiff enough to bake.

Use pork to grease your waffle-iron.

Waffles. *Simple receipt.*—One pint of sour cream, one pint of flour, three eggs, half a spoonful of soda. Thin with a little sweet milk.

Corn Muffins.—Two cups of Indian meal, two cups of flour, two eggs, piece of butter size of an egg, melted, two teaspoonfuls of cream of tartar, one teaspoonful of soda and one pint of milk.

Buckwheat Cakes.—Take one cupful of flour, two of buckwheat flour, and one of yeast; one tablespoonful of sugar, and salt according to taste. Mix with enough water to form a stiff batter, and set to rise over night. In the morning add water in sufficient quantity to make the batter run when poured on the griddle. They are nice with a little Indian meal instead of flour.

Soda Griddle Cakes.—Stir together in one pint of milk, one teaspoonful of soda, one teaspoonful of salt, two teaspoonfuls of cream of tartar, sufficient flour to make a thick batter, and fry them on the griddle.

Corn Fritters.—To a dozen ears of corn, grated, add two eggs and a teaspoonful of salt. (If the corn is old add a little milk.) Fry in hot butter and lard, half of each.

Flannel Cakes.—Put two ounces of butter into a pint of hot milk, let it melt; add then a pint of cold milk, four beaten eggs, a teaspoonful of salt, two tablespoonfuls of yeast and sufficient flour to make a stiff batter. Set in a warm place three hours to rise, then fry on the griddle.

Rusks.—Three pints of flour, one pint of sugar, a quarter of a pound of butter rubbed in the flour, one tablespoonful of yeast, one pint of warm milk. Set a sponge and put all in. Mix soft. This is good for doughnuts.

Raised Breakfast Cakes.—Scald one quart of milk; into this, while hot, put a piece of butter the size of an egg; when lukewarm add one beaten egg and a teacupful of yeast, then stir in flour enough to make a stiff batter; cover and rise over night; in the morning stir, put in muffin pans and rise again; when light bake quickly. They can be made at noon and will be ready to bake at tea time.

Green Corn Cakes.—Mix a pint of grated green corn with a teacupful of flour, half a teacupful of milk, half a teacupful of melted butter, one egg, a teaspoonful of salt and a little pepper. Drop on a buttered pan by the spoonful, and bake or fry for ten or fifteen minutes

Green Corn Cakes.—Six ears of green corn, grated ; one cup of milk, one egg, one teaspoonful of salt, one-half teaspoonful of pepper, and flour to make batter as for griddle cakes.

Brown Bread.—Take one pint of Indian meal, one-half a pint of rye meal, one-half a cup of molasses and a little salt ; mix with cold water to the consistency of griddle cakes ; then pour it into an iron pan and cover with another pan. Bake three hours. Covering the bread prevents it having a hard crust.

Squash Muffins.—To one pint of sifted squash add two tablespoonfuls each of sugar, sweet milk and melted butter, a teaspoonful of salt and a cup of yeast ; then stir in flour till it is stiff enough to knead ; when it is risen very light, knead, roll out and put them in a pan till light enough to bake.

Squash Muffins.—Take one cup of squash, one cup of sour milk, two tablespoonfuls of sugar, one tablespoonful of melted butter, a little salt and one teaspoonful of soda ; add flour till they are stiff enough to roll out. Bake and serve hot.

Graham Muffins.—Three cups of Graham flour, three tablespoonfuls of molasses, one tablespoonful of butter, two cups of milk, one teaspoonful of salt, one teaspoonful of soda, two teaspoonfuls of cream of tartar. This is also nice made in a loaf, and covered while baking.

Rye Drop Cakes.—Three cups of sour milk, half a cup of molasses, a heaping teaspoonful of soda and a little salt ;

add meal enough to make a very thick batter, and drop into hot iron gem pans.

Milk Toast.—Take stale slices of bread, toast, and dip in boiling milk salted to taste; then lay them in a covered dish; boil some milk, a little more than enough to cover the bread, add a good-sized piece of butter, some salt, and pour over it all. It is very nice thickened with a little flour.

Pop-Overs.—One cup of milk, two eggs, one teaspoonful of melted butter, a little salt, and flour enough to make batter as thick as for griddle cakes.

Graham Muffins.—One pint of sour milk; one teaspoonful of soda, a little salt, one tablespoonful of molasses, two cups Graham flour, one cup wheat flour. With baking powder use sweet milk and small piece of butter.

Strawberry Shortcake.—First, take the berries, sugar them well, press a little, if you like, and set them aside; then take one quart of sifted flour, one teaspoonful salt, quarter of a pound of butter, rub them well into the flour; wet with water as for pie-crust; handle lightly, and roll without kneading; bake in a biscuit pan. When done, split the cake, butter it and lay berries between. Peaches cut up, sugared and laid between, are very nice also.

New York Strawberry Shortcake.—Mix dough as for soda biscuit; that is to say, one quart of sifted flour, piece of butter the size of an egg, two teaspoonfuls of cream of tartar, one of soda, a pinch of salt, and sweet milk to form a soft dough. Put the cream of tartar in the flour, and soda in *dry* also, and, when thoroughly mixed, roll out half an inch thick and bake in a shallow pan fifteen or twenty minutes; have ready two quarts of fresh, fine strawberries; split the cake, place half the strawberries between and cover thickly with white sugar and cream; put the other half on the top and cover in the same way; send to the table immediately. Use baking powder, if preferred.

Blackberries make a very nice shortcake by preparing a crust as for soda biscuit, only twice as rich. Roll an inch and a half thick, and after baking, split, butter on both sides, then put in all the berries that can be laid on.

Breakfast Dishes.—Hominy, oatmeal, cracked wheat, etc., are best cooked in a covered dish, set in a kettle of boiling water; or, if you have time, steamed. Sea moss, farina, and all other articles mixed with milk, if cooked in this manner, are not liable to be scorched.

To Boil Hominy.—Take three cups of water to one cup of hominy, boil slowly for an hour; the longer it boils, the better it is; then add a teacupful of sweet milk, and boil fifteen minutes more; stir it frequently while boiling. It is very nice if soaked over night.

Hominy Fritters.—Two teacupfuls of cold-boiled hominy, add to it one scant teacupful of sweet milk and a little salt, stir till smooth, then add four tablespoonfuls of flour and one egg; beat the yolk and white separately, adding the white last. Have ready a pan with hot butter and lard (half of each), drop the batter in by spoonfuls and fry a light brown.

Hominy Croquettes.—To a cupful of cold-boiled hominy, add a teaspoonful melted butter, and stir it well, adding by degrees a cupful of milk, till all is made into a soft light paste; add a teaspoonful white sugar, and one well-beaten egg. Roll it into oval balls with floured hands; dip in beaten egg, then rolled cracker crumbs, and fry in hot lard.

Fried Bread.—Beat four eggs very light, add three tablespoonfuls of good brown sugar, a little grated nutmeg, a tablespoonful of orange or rose water, and a quart of milk. Cut into nice slices, an inch thick, a stale loaf of bread; remove the crust from the sides, and cut each slice into halves. Butter your frying-pan, and when hot lay in your bread (dipped in the custard) and brown on both sides. Lay them on a hot dish, and sprinkle over them a little loaf sugar.

Puddings—General Directions—If you intend to boil or steam a pudding, always have the water boiling before you put in the pudding. Do not let it stop boiling for an instant while the pudding is cooking.

Puddings are boiled in cloths, or in molds tied in cloths; they should be tied tightly, and the molds be buttered before the puddings are put in them. A pudding-cloth should be made of thick, twilled muslin, and always, before using it, wash it out in clean water and flour it well before pouring in the pudding, allowing room for the pudding to swell.

Puddings are much lighter and nicer steamed than boiled. Have the steamer hot before putting in the pudding. The simplest and cheapest steamer is easily had by having a steamer made to fit the large iron kettle that every kitchen has. The steamer, of tin, made to fit the kettle, the sides fitting down, say one inch, a snug, perfect fit ; one inch from this rim is a bottom with holes cut in it, half an inch in diameter and one inch apart. The steamer, like a basin with straight or perpendicular sides, nine inches deep, a tin cover to fit perfectly tight, the cover made to run up higher in the middle two or three inches. The steamer can be made for $1.50.

All puddings in which berries are used require more flour than those without; and it must be remembered, fruit (dusted with a little flour) should always be added the last thing.

All puddings of the custard kind require a very gentle oven. Those made of batter should be put into one sufficiently brisk to raise them quickly, without scorching them. Such as contain suet and fruit must have a well-heated, but not a fierce oven.

Tapioca Cream Pudding.—One cup tapioca soaked over night in cold water. Boil one quart of milk and stir in the tapioca; boil ten minutes, stirring all the time. Dissolve one tablespoonful of corn starch in half a cup of milk, add the beaten yolks of four eggs, and stir into the tapioca ; add a little salt, sweeten to taste and boil up once. Flavor to taste. Beat the whites of four eggs and two tablespoonfuls of sugar; flavor, spread over the pudding, and brown lightly in the oven.

Half-Hour Pudding (*Very nice*).—Boil one and a half pints of milk; pour half of it over as many stale pieces of bread as it will soften ; let it stand ten minutes and add one unbeaten egg, one tablespoonful of sugar, a little butter, salt and nutmeg, one teaspoonful of cream tartar and one half a teaspoonful of soda ; beat all well together and add the rest of the milk, then stir in half a cup of currants dusted with a little flour. Pour into a buttered bowl and steam half an hour. Serve with a sauce. Very nice without the currants.

Apple Tapioca Pudding.—Soak one cup of tapioca in enough boiling water to cover it ; when it is quite soft stir in three beaten eggs, two tablespoonfuls of sugar, and add one quart of milk, also a little salt. Have your pudding dish filled with apples, pared and cored ; stir the mixture well and pour over the apples ; bake and eat with cream and sugar.

Nursery Tapioca Pudding.—Take two ounces of tapioca aud boil it in half a pint of water until it begins to melt, then add half a pint of milk by degrees, or boil until the tapioca becomes very thick ; add a well-beaten egg, sugar, and flavoring to taste, and bake gently for three-quarters of an hour. The preparation of tapioca is superior to any other, is nourishing, and suitable for delicate children.

Sago Pudding.—Put seven-eighths of a cup of sago to a quart of cold milk, add half a teaspoonful of salt, and turn into a tin saucepan ; place a large pan with boiling water on the stove, and place the saucepan in it; let it remain until the sago is thick, then remove it from the saucepan to your pudding-dish, and while hot add half a cup of butter ; when cool add four eggs, well beaten, a cup of white sugar and the grated peel and juice of a lemon. Bake until a nice brown. It is very nice with a gill of rose-water or half a glass of wine added to it.

Will's Sago Pudding.—One quart of boiling water turned upon a cup of sago. Have your pudding dish filled with apples pared and quartered, stir the sago well, and turn over the apple ; bake, and eat with sauce or cream and sugar. You can cook tapioca the same way.

Farina Pudding.—Boil one quart of milk, sprinkle in gradually two even tablespoonfuls of farina and stir well until it thickens, then let it boil slowly about five minutes. Take three beaten eggs, half a cup of sugar, two tablespoonfuls of melted butter, a little salt, and stir into the farina and milk. Flavor with lemon. Bake half an hour in quick oven and eat warm.

Steamed Apple Dumplings.—One pound of suet, one pound of flour ; heaping teaspoonful of salt ; chop the suet in a little of the flour to prevent its caking; chop very fine, as fine as meal ; then add flour and mix thoroughly ; then add cold water enough to make a paste ; roll as thin as pie crust ; pare a dozen large apples, quarter and core them, keeping each apple by itself, place the quarters together again and cover each apple with a square of the paste ; then butter, slightly, the bottom of a steamer, and lay in your dumplings. They will cook in an hour. Serve with hard sauce.

Baked Apple Dumpling.—Make a crust as for soda biscuit, peel and core your apples, cut the dough in square pieces, and put one apple for each dumpling; put them in a dripping-pan, and place in the oven for five minutes, then make a syrup with water and sugar (one cupful of sugar to a pint of water), and pour into the dripping-pan; baste with the syrup while they are cooking; when done eat with sweet cream.

Nellie's Corn Pudding.—Grate twelve ears sweet corn, stir into one quart of milk, add four beaten eggs, two cups of sugar and a tablespoonful of salt. Pour the mixture into a dish and put small pieces of butter on top; bake three-quarters of an hour in a quick oven and eat hot with butter.

Arrowroot Pudding.—Mix four spoonfuls of arrowroot with a teacupful of new milk, then boil nearly a quart of milk and stir in the arrowroot. When almost cold add two well-beaten eggs, two spoonfuls of melted butter, sugar to taste and a little nutmeg. Bake about twenty minutes.

Queen Pudding.—One quart of milk, one and three-fourths cupfuls of bread crumbs, yolks of four beaten eggs, and sugar to taste; bake until done, taking care not to have it watery. Whip the whites of four eggs, and a tablespoonful of sugar, and flavor with lemon. Spread over the pudding a layer of sweetmeats or jelly. Put the whites of the eggs on and brown lightly. Serve cold with cream.

Maizena Pudding.—Four tablespoonfuls of maizena, stirred into two eggs, and milk enough to make it smooth. Set a quart of milk to boil, and just before it boils stir in the above, constantly stirring the same way till it thickens; remove from the fire and flavor. To be cold, and eaten with milk or cream, and sugar. It is very nice to omit the eggs and take six tablespoonfuls of maizena to a quart of milk (stirring the same way), and eaten warm with a sauce.

Baked Custard.—Pour a quart of hot milk over four or five well-beaten eggs. Add a teaspoonful of butter. Season with vanilla, rose-water or nutmeg, and sweeten to taste. Bake in cups or pudding-dish.

Bird's Nest Pudding.—Pare and core as many apples as will stand in a dish, and fill the holes with sugar. Make a custard of a quart of milk, eight eggs, and a quarter of a pound of sugar. Pour it over the apples, grate a nutmeg over the top, and bake one hour.

Minnie's Rice Pudding.—To twelve cups of milk, one cup of rice well washed. Sweeten to taste; flavor with vanilla or nutmeg; add a little salt and about a teaspoonful of butter. Bake in a slow oven for three or four hours, stir-ing it frequently until the last hour; then let it brown nicely. Excellent, if baked right.

Apple Corn-Starch Pudding.—Set a quart of milk over night, take off the cream in the morning, and heat your milk in a spider to a boiling point. Wet two dessertspoon-fuls of corn-starch in a little cold milk and stir into it, and continue stirring it till it thickens. Set it off from the fire. Beat together two eggs and half a cupful of white sugar; then pour your corn-starch into this, stirring it together care-fully, and add a teaspoonful of salt. Pare and slice thin six large, pleasant apples; lay them into your pudding-dish, pour the custard over them, and bake an hour, or until the pud-ding is tender. For sauce, add sugar, nutmeg, and a little extract to the cream. This is a very economical and deli-cious pudding.

Corn-Starch Pudding.—Boil one quart of milk, then beat the yolks of four eggs with four tablespoonfuls of corn-starch and a little milk; stir into the boiling milk, let it boil up once; flavor to taste, and turn into a pudding-dish; then beat the whites of the eggs to a froth, add four spoonfuls of white, powdered sugar, flavor a little and cover the pudding with the mixture : set in the oven and brown lightly.

Rice Pudding.—One quart of milk, half cupful of white sugar, one teaspoonful of rose or vanilla extract, one teaspoonful of butter, half a cup of rice; merely wash the rice, and after adding it to the sweetened pudding, put in the oven, occasionally stirring for the first ten minutes. It will be of the consistency of ice cream, and very delicate. Bake until browned on top.

Farina Pudding.—Heat one quart of milk to the boiling point. Stir in dry five tablespoonfuls of farina, and continue to stir it until quite thick. Add one cupful of sugar and half a teaspoonful of salt. Flavor with lemon or vanilla, and eat with sweetened milk or cream, with a little nutmeg or other flavoring added.

Peach Tapioca Pudding.—Soak half a pint of tapioca in cold water for two or three hours, then set on the stove until it boils; sweeten with white sugar ; peel and slice ripe peaches to nearly fill a baking-dish; sprinkle over them white sugar, then pour over the tapioca, and bake slowly for one hour. To be eaten with cream and sugar.

Potato Suet Pudding.—Take a pound of mealy potatoes, boiled and mashed smooth ; add four ounces of chopped beef suet, three eggs, a little milk, sugar to taste, and a good dessertspoonful of cinnamon or allspice. Put it into a dish, cover tight, and steam for an hour. Serve with sweet sauce.

Steamed Indian Pudding.—A quart of sour milk, half a cup of molasses, a cup of raisins, a cup of chopped suet, a teaspoonful of saleratus, and meal enough to make it stiff. Cover tight, and steam three hours.

Boiled Indian Pudding.—Two eggs, a piece of butter the size of an egg, one pint of milk, one-half teaspoonful of soda, dissolved in boiling water. Thicken with about three teacupfuls of Indian meal. Steam about two hours. This makes only a small pudding.

Boiled Indian Pudding.—Take one quart of Indian meal and two teaspoonfuls of salt, scald with boiling water enough to swell the meal, then add half a pound of suet, chopped fine, raisins or apples, as you choose, and boil for four hours.
This is very nice to eat with roast pork.

Baked Indian Pudding.—Boil a quart of milk; stir into it gradually three gills of yellow Indian meal and half a pint of molasses; scald thoroughly, and add two tablespoonfuls of powdered ginger and a teaspoonful of salt; butter a brown earthern pan; put into ito it half a pound of beef suet chopped fine; turn in a quart of cold milk; then add the pudding and stir up well; bake five hours. Serve either plain or with hard sauce.

Baked Indian Pudding.—Take a large cup of meal and a teacupful of molasses and beat them well together; then add to them a quart of boiling milk, some salt, and a tablespoonful each of cinnamon and butter; let it stand awhile in the dish you are going to bake it in until it thickens, and when you put it into the oven pour over it from half to a pint of milk, but do not stir it in, as this makes the jelly. Bake three or four hours.

Baked Indian Pudding.—One quart of milk, three handfuls of Indian meal stirred in while the milk is hot; let it cool, and add one egg; molasses to sweeten; butter, half the size of an egg; cinnamon and salt to your taste; bake three-quarters of an hour.

Apple Indian Pudding.—One quart of milk, boiled, one pint of Indian meal, two cups of molasses, a dozen sweet apples cut in thin slices; bake it with a steady fire three hours.

Apple Fritters.—Peel some apples and cut them in slices; put a little sugar over them and some lemon juice. Let the pieces soak a couple of hours; then dip each piece in flour, and have ready a frying pan with two inches deep of fat. When hot, put the slices of apple in one at a time, turn over with a slice as they are doing, and serve with powdered loaf sugar.

Apple Fritters.—Beat three eggs very light, then stir in one teaspoonful of salt, one tablespoonful of sugar, the grated rind of half a lemon and the juice, one pint of milk, two cups of chopped apple, and two cups of flour; stir it well together, and fry in lard, or can be baked on a griddle as pancakes. Sift sugar over them and send to the table.

Plain Bread Pudding.—Take stale pieces of bread, pour boiling water over them, and cover down tight. When they are soft mash to a pulp. Mix in one tablespoonful of cornstarch, one egg, a cup of milk, a little salt, sugar to taste, and a few currants, or a cup of chopped apples. Bake in a dish with a few pieces of butter on the top, and a little nutmeg grated over.

Thanksgiving Pudding.—Pound twenty crackers fine, add five cups of milk, and let it swell. Beat well fourteen eggs, a pint bowl of sugar, teacupful of molasses, two small nutmegs, two teaspoonfuls of ground cloves, three of ground cinnamon, two of salt, and half a teaspoonful of soda, and add to the cracker lastly a pint bowl heaped of raisins, and citron if you like. This quantity will make two puddings.

Lizzie's Cracker Pudding.—Pour one quart of boiling milk over six soft crackers, let it stand till the crackers are very soft; then add four beaten eggs, half a pound of raisins, and salt, sugar and spices to taste. Steam three or four hours. Use brown sugar.

Boiled Cracker Pudding.—Split four soft crackers, pour a pint of boiling milk over them, and add immediately a cup of suet well chopped ; when cool, add five eggs, well beaten, a little mace, and as many raisins as you like. Boil or steam three hours, and eat with sauce.

Cocoanut Pudding.—One quart of milk, half a cocoanut, grated, four eggs, a little salt and sugar to taste ; bake in a quick oven about thirty minutes. Serve with sauce.

Minute Pudding.—Mix five tablespoonfuls of flour with half a pint of cold, sweet milk, a very little salt, one-fourth of a nutmeg ; stir it into a pint and a half of boiling sweet milk ; boil one minute, stirring constantly ; set it off from the fire until it gets lukewarm ; add three beaten eggs ; stir until it boils, and eat with cream and sugar.

Plain Batter Pudding.—One quart of milk, four eggs, six spoonfuls of flour, a little salt ; bake twenty minutes.

Currant Pudding.—One cup finely cut suet, one of dried currants, one-third cup of molasses, two-thirds cup of milk or water, one teaspoonful allspice, cloves and cinnamon mixed, three cups of flour ; mix well and steam three hours.

Troy Pudding.—One cup each of chopped suet, stoned raisins, molasses and milk, and one egg, three cups of sifted flour, a little salt, and a pinch of soda ; boil or steam three hours ; serve with sweet sauce.

Apple Batter Pudding.—Core and peel eight apples, put in a dish, fill the places from which the cores have been taken with brown sugar, cover and bake. Beat the yolks of four eggs light, add two teacupfuls of flour, with three even teaspoonfuls of baking powder sifted with it, one pint of milk, and a teaspoonful of salt, then the whites, well beaten ; pour over the apples and bake. Use sauce with it. Very nice.

Apple Batter Pudding.—One pint of milk, three eggs, two cups of flour, two cups of apples, cut small. Bake one hour, and eat with sauce.

Orleans Pudding.—Two cups of flour, one-half cup butter, one cup molasses, one cup raisins, one and one-half cups milk, one teaspoonful saleratus dissolved in milk ; boil two hours in tin boiler. Serve with sauce.

Plain Plum Pudding.—Three teacupfuls of flour, one of milk, one of molasses, one of chopped suet, one of raisins, and a little salt ; three teaspoonfuls of baking powder, one of cinnamon, one of nutmeg, and one of cloves. Boil or steam three or four hours. Excellent.

English Plum Pudding.—One pound raisins, one pound currants, one pound suet, one pound flour, half pound citron, one nutmeg, one tablespoonful allspice, six eggs, one pound brown sugar, one wineglassful brandy ; boil six hours.

Bread Pudding.—Butter a tart-dish, sprinkle the bottom with finely minced candied peel and a very little shred suet, then a thin layer of light bread, and so on until the dish is full. For a pint dish make a liquid custard of one egg and half a pint of milk; sweeten pour over the pudding, and bake very slowly or two hours.

Berry Pudding.—One pint of milk, two beaten eggs, spoonful of salt, one-fourth of a teaspoonful of soda, one-half a teaspoonful of cream of tartar and flour to make a thick batter. Dissolve the soda in a little water and sift cream of tartar through the flour. One pint huckleberries, raspberries, currants or blackberries, dredged with flour, stirred in the last thing. Steam one hour.

Berry Pudding. (*No Eggs.*)—One pint of molasses, heaping teaspoonful of soda, a teaspoonful of salt, and flour enough to make a very stiff batter, so that the spoon will stand up in it ; add as many berries as you can possibly stir in ; steam three hours. Eat with butter or a sauce.

Fruit Puddings (Batter.)—One quart of flour, two table-spoonfuls of baking powder, and a little salt. Add two ta-blespoonfuls of melted butter, and mix to the consistency of drop biscuit. Butter a mold or deep dish, and lay in it a layer of the batter, then a layer of fruit, alternating them until the dish is nearly filled ; cover it tight and steam an hour and a half. Eat with a sweet sauce.

Fruit Puddings (To Roll.)—Roll out half an inch thick a paste made of suet chopped fine, flour, water, and a little salt. Spread over it preserves of any small kind. Dust a little flour over it, roll up, wet and pinch the ends tight, and tie in a cloth which has been wet in cold water and floured. Steam one or two hours, according to size.

Apple Roley-Poley.—It is very nice made like the above fruit pudding ; use butter instead of suet, and slice the apples thin.

Cranberry Pudding.—Sift well together one quart of flour, one teaspoonful of soda, and two teaspoonfuls of cream of tartar. Mix into a soft dough with sweet milk, roll thin in an oblong shape, and spread over it one quart of cranber-ries sprinkled well with sugar. Dust with a little flour, and roll over and over, then tie in a pudding cloth and steam for an hour. Any tart fruit is nice made in same way.

Family Pie Paste.—One coffeecupful of flour will make the paste for a medium-sized pie. Use three-fourths of a cup of shortening to each cup of flour ; you may use all but-ter or part lard if preferred. Take one-third of the shorten-ing, a little salt, and rub well into the flour with the hand, then stir in as little water as possible and form with a spoon into a very stiff paste ; put it on a pie board, roll lightly, and spread with one-third of the remaining shortening, sprinkle on a little flour, fold and roll out enough for the under crust. Take the rest of the paste, spread on half the remain-ing butter, fold and roll as before, repeat the process, roll

thin and use it for the upper crusts. Always make a few
slits in the centre of the upper crust to allow the steam to
escape. Never put in the filling until you are ready to bake
them. A nice pie will be brown, tender and flaky.

Common Paste.—Rub half a pound of shortening (lard
or butter) into a quart of flour, add a little salt and cold water enough to make a dough; flour your molding board and
roll out the dough. Be sure and not mold it, but handle as
little as possible.

Sliced Apple Pie.—Take ripe, tart apples, pare, core and
cut them into very thin slices, fill the under crust; then
strew over the apples as much sugar as you think they required, a little nutmeg or cinnamon to taste, and a teaspoonful of butter. Cover with the upper paste, make a few small
incisions in the middle of the upper crust and bake in a
mild oven.

Apple Pan Pie.—Take a deep, earthern pudding-pot, fill
it with slices of apple, then pour on as much molasses as
the apple requires to sweeten it; sprinkle over a little cinnamon, put over a paste, with a small slit in the middle and
place in the oven. After the first paste is baked it may be
taken off and another put on in its place. This should be
taken off, and the apple remain long enough to be a deep
red. When cooked enough, take from the oven, and immediately break the paste in small pieces, and stir into the
sauce while hot. To be eaten cold. It is a favorite dish
with many people, and very nice.

Dried Apple Pies.—Soak the apples; then put them in
a brown earthern pot; cover them with water, cover the pot
and bake four or five hours, sweeten with sugar or molasses
the last half hour, and mash well with a spoon; when the
apples are thoroughly cooked flavor with lemon juice and
add a little butter. You can bake between two crusts, or
put bands of the paste across the top.

Apple Meringue.—Pare, slice, stew and sweeten ripe, juicy apples ; mash smooth, and season with nutmeg or lemon peel ; fill a pie plate with an under-crust, and bake till done. Then whip the whites of three eggs for each pie to a stiff froth, with a little sugar, one tablespoonful to an egg ; beat till it stands alone, then spread over the pie three-fourths of an inch thick ; return to the oven three or four minutes to brown.

Dried Plum Pies.—Soak the plums, and stew them gently ; season them with spice and sugar to taste ; put a puff paste on to the plate; then put a layer of the plums, stewed ; roll out a piece of the paste thin, cover them, add another layer of plums, and cover for the last time. You may have as many stories to your pie as you choose.

Custard Pie.—Make a custard of a quart of milk, six eggs, well beaten, a cup of white sugar, not heaped, and a teaspoonful of vanilla. Line your plates with paste, pour in the custard and bake immediately. If you wish pudding, line your pudding-dish with paste and bake thick.

Corn-Starch Custard Pie.—Very nice pies are made with two eggs, and two large tablespoonfuls of corn-starch to a quart of milk ; sweeten and spice to taste ; the corn-starch should be mixed smooth with milk and eggs beaten up in it, then thin out with more milk ; sweeten, season, pour into pans lined with paste, and grate a little nutmeg over the top.

Apple Custard Pies. *Very Nice.*—Grate or steam twelve apples ; to this add a teaspoonful of salt, sugar, nutmeg, three eggs well beaten, a pint of milk and a tablespoonful of melted butter, the grated rinds of two lemons and the juice of one ; pour the mixture into lined plates, and arrange strips of paste in a net work over the top. Sift powdered sugar over them when done.

Rhubarb Pie.—Skin the stalks, cut in small pieces ; line the plate and cover well with the raw fruit ; strew lavishly with sugar, and sprinkle over this a little flour. Cover and bake about three-quarters of an hour. This, like all fruit pies, is eaten cold.

Auntie's Cream Pies.—Make the paste for three pies, roll out and cover your plates, then roll out and cover a second time, and bake. When baked, and while warm, separate the edges with a knife, and lift the upper from the lower paste ; fill in the cream, and put on the upper paste.

The cream—put on a pint of milk to boil. Break two eggs into a dish, and add one cup of sugar and half a cup of flour ; after beating well, stir into the milk just as it commences to boil ; keep on stirring one way till it thickens ; use any flavor you may prefer.

Apple Pie.—Stew a dozen tart apples ; when soft, add a tablespoonful of butter, one cup of sugar, half a glass of rosewater and a little nutmeg. Bake the paste as for cream pie, and fill with apple instead of cream.

Fried Apple Pies.—Stew a quart of dried apples and one lemon together ; sweeten to the taste with sugar ; add a little salt, but no spice. For crust, take a tablespoonful of lard, one quart of flour, one tablespoonful of yeast, and water to form a stiff batter, and let it stand over night, or till light. Then, when wanted for use, add a very little soda, and knead up not very stiff ; roll out your crust, cut in rounds with a saucer ; lay in a spoonful of your apple on one-half ; fold the other over ; secure the edges carefully, and fry in hot lard.

Cherry Pie.—Line the dish and fill with ripe cherries, regulating the quantity of sugar you use by their sweetness ; sift over this a small teaspoonful of flour, add a very little butter, then cover and bake.

Washington Pie.—One cup of sugar, one egg, one-third of a cup of butter, half a cup of sweet milk, half a teaspoonful of soda, one teaspoonful of cream of tartar, one and a third cups of flour; flavor with lemon. Bake on two round tins; when done spread one cake with nice apple sauce, then put the other cake on top, and sift powdered sugar over it.

Lemon Cream Pies.—The juice and grated rind of one lemon, one cup of white sugar, the yolk of two eggs, three tablespoonfuls of sifted flour, milk to fill the plate. This makes a large pie, and should be made with an under-crust, but not any top crust. Bake until nearly done, then take from the oven, and pour over it a frosting made of the beaten whites of two eggs, and two tablespoonfuls of powdered sugar, then set back in the oven and brown lightly.

Lemon Pie.—Two lemons; squeeze out the juice, and chop the lemons fine (take out the seeds); three cups of water, three cups of sugar, one egg, two-thirds of a cup of flour; beat the egg well with half a cup of water and the flour; then stir lemons, juice and all, together; this will fill three pies. This is easily made.

Lemon Pie.—One cup of hot water, one tablespoonful of corn-starch, one cup of white sugar, one tablespoonful of butter, juice and grated rind of one lemon. Cook for a few minutes; add one egg; bake with a top and bottom crust. This is for one pie.

Lemon Pie.—Grate the yellow rind of two lemons, beat together the rind, juice, ten tablespoonfuls of loaf sugar, and the yolks of four eggs until very light, then add two tablespoonfuls of water. Line a large plate, and fill with the mixture; bake until the paste is done; beat the whites stiff, and stir into them two tablespoonfuls of sugar; spread it over the top, and bake a light brown.

Whortleberry Pie.—Wash and pick over the berries, place them an inch thick on the under-crust, cover them thickly with sugar; sprinkle with a pinch of salt, or add a small piece of butter, put on the upper crust and bake about half an hour. Blackberry and raspberry pies are made in the same way. They require no spice; but whortleberries are greatly improved by having a few currants or juice of a lemon sprinkled among them. Sift powdered sugar over all fruit pies before serving.

Peach Pie.—Make a nice short crust and cover your pie dishes; have ready pared and quartered ripe peaches, put a layer of them in the dish, sprinkle thickly with good brown sugar, roll out another crust, double it over and cut a row of slits through the centre; wet the edges of the lower crust, press lightly on the edges, trim it around close to the dish with a knife, dipped in flour, and bake in a quick oven half or three quarters of an hour. All fruit or summer pies should be eaten the same day they are baked.

Potato Pie.—Boil either Irish or sweet potatoes until well done; mash and sift them through a coarse wire sieve; to a pint of pulp, add three pints of sweet milk, a tablspoon-ful of melted butter, two eggs, a teacupful of sugar, half a teaspoonful of salt, nutmeg or lemon to flavor. Bake it with an under-crust of rich paste.

Sweet Apple Pie.—Pies made of sweet apples used in precisely the same way as pumpkins, omitting the ginger and adding a little lemon, if liked, for seasoning, are better to the taste of some than pumpkin pie itself. Pare, cut and stew the apples. If cooked in a covered dish in the oven, they are better. Strain through a colander; add a little milk; cream is better. If there be no eggs to spare, stir in a handful of flour, or about a spoonful to a pie. Sweeten to taste.

Squash Pie.—Steam or boil some squash, then sift it. Take two cups of sifted squash, one and a half cups of milk, three tablespoonfuls of sugar, two eggs, and flavor with ginger and cinnamon, or a little nutmeg. This will make one good-sized pie. Pumpkin pie can be made in the same way.

Squash Pie.—One quart of sifted squash, one and a half cups of sugar; add a little ginger and salt, and thin with milk. It must be considerably thicker than if eggs were used.

Mince Pie.—Boil four pounds of lean meat, chop very fine, and add twice the quantity of apples, also chopped, and half a pound of raw suet chopped very fine, then add three pounds of raisins seeded and chopped; two pounds of currants, one heaping teaspoonful each of cinnamon and nutmeg, the same of cloves and half the quantity of mace. Sweeten to taste with brown sugar, and add three quarts of cider and one pint of brandy.

Mince Pie.—Two pounds of beef, boiled and chopped; half a pound of suet, chopped fine; six large apples, pared and chopped; two pounds of currants, half a pint of wine, glass of rose-water; sugar and spice to your taste.

Mince Pie.—A shin of beef boiled down till very tender, one pound of nice, clear, beef suet chopped very fine, a tablespoonful of salt, six pounds of greening apples peeled, cored and chopped, three pounds of raisins stoned, three of currants carefully cleaned, one pound of brown sugar, a cup of maple syrup, half a pound of citron, shredded, half a pound of candied lemon peel, a quart of the best cider. This mixture makes rich pies, particularly fine in flavor. Instead of cider, some persons put in a quart of Maderia wine and a little brandy.

Hints for Making Cake.—The flour should always be very dry and well sifted.

White sugar is purer and sweeter for cakes and pastries than brown sugar.

If the butter is very hard soften, but do not melt it.

The butter and sugar should be worked to a cream.

Eggs should be broken separately in a cup, then if one is bad it will not spoil the others; they should be cold to beat well; always use a shallow dish in whipping the whites, and never stop after you commence beating them until they are light; unless they are very nice and fresh do not try to whip them until you can turn the dish over without their slipping.

When soda is used, dissolve it before adding to the general mixture.

Fruit should be thoroughly dry; as, if added to the other ingredients damp, cakes will be liable to be heavy. Dust your fruit with a little of the flour to be used for the cake, and stir into the other ingredients just before putting in the rest of the flour. The ingredients should be well beaten before mixing in the flour, except in a few plain cakes that are beaten all together.

All cakes bake nicer if the pans used are lined with buttered paper.

To know when a cake is sufficiently baked, insert a knitting needle, or clean broom corn, draw it out, and if it does not look the least sticky the baking is finished.

Nut Cake.—Two cups sugar, one cup butter, three cups flour, one cup cold water, four eggs, one tablespoonful soda, and two of cream of tartar; mix well, and last of all add two cups of kernels of hickory nuts or walnuts.

Pound Cake.—Beat six eggs to a froth, then add a pound of sugar and half a pound of butter, beat all well together; dissolve half a teaspoonful of soda in half a cup of milk. Take a pound of sifted flour and rub a teaspoonful of cream of tartar through it with your hands ; add the eggs, sugar and butter : stir all thoroughly together, flavor to your taste, and bake in a quick oven.

Chocolate Cream Cake.—One-half a pound sweet vanilla chocolate, grated ; one coffeecupful powdered sugar, yolks of two eggs, and one gill boiling milk. Stir all together until it makes a cream. To be spread between some nice cake.

Huckleberry Cake.—One cup of sugar, one egg, piece of butter size of an egg, half a cup of milk, one teaspoonful of soda, two of cream of tartar, a teaspoonful of any preferred essence, and two and a half cups of flour. Put cream of tartar in the flour, soda in the milk, and beat thoroughly. Add last a pint of huckleberries and bake in a quick oven. This is good eaten hot or cold.

Currant Cake.—Five cups of flour, three of sugar, one and a half of butter, six eggs, one cup of milk, with a scant teaspoonful of soda, one grated nutmeg and three-quarters of a pound of currants.

Plain Raisin Cake.—One cup of sour milk, one cup of sugar, one-half cup of butter, two cups of flour, one egg, one level teaspoonful of soda, half a cup of raisins, chopped and spiced to taste.

Cold Water Pound Cake.—Half a cup of butter, two cups of sugar, three eggs, one cup of cold water, three cups of flour, one teaspoonful cream of tartar, one-half teaspoonful soda.

Jelly Cake.—Two cups of sugar, one-half cup of butter, one cup of sweet milk, three cups of flour, three eggs beaten separately, one teaspoonful of soda and two of cream of tartar. Flavor with the rind of a fresh lemon. Bake in jelly tins. This will make two cakes of three layers each. It is also nice if baked in a loaf and frosted.

Pound Cake.—One pound of butter, worked back to a cream; then add slowly, beating the while, one pound of powdered sugar, ten eggs beaten to a froth, added gradually, half a glass of brandy, one glass of wine, and one pound of flour; after which beat well for half an hour, and bake with an even heat

Cream Cake.—One cup sugar, butter the size of an egg, one-half cup of milk, two eggs (beat them well), one heaping cup of flour, in which one teaspoonful of baking powder has been thoroughly sifted; bake in jelly tins. For the cream, boil one-half pint milk. Take a tablespoonful of flour, or corn-starch, beaten with a little milk; when the milk comes to a boil, stir this in slowly, and cook a minute; then add one-half cup of sugar, and stir in one well beaten egg. Flavor to taste. A very small piece of butter added is an improvement.

Jelly Roll.—Three eggs, one cup of sugar, one teaspoonful of cream of tartar, one-half teaspoonful of soda, one cup of flour; pour it thin into a baking-pan; bake slowly; spread jelly over it and roll it up. Wrap it in a cloth.

One Egg Cake.—One and one-third cups of flour, one-third cup of sweet milk, one cup of sugar, one tablespoonful of melted butter, one egg, and two teaspoonfuls baking powder.

Nut Cake.—One and one-half cups sugar, one-half cup of butter, three-fourths cup sweet milk, two cups flour, whites of four eggs, one-half teaspoonful soda, one teaspoonful cream of tartar, one large cup of walnuts or hickory nuts.

Pork Cake.—Half a pound of salt pork chopped fine, two cups of molasses, half pound raisins chopped well, two eggs, two teaspoonfuls each of clove, allspice and mace, half a tablespoonful of saleratus or soda and flour enough to make a stiff batter. The oven must not be too hot.

Good Girl's Cake.—One cup butter, one and a half cups sugar, three eggs, one cup chopped raisins, one teaspoonful of soda dissolved in two tablespoonfuls of milk; spice to taste, and add flour enough to roll as cookies.

Susie's Cake.—One cup of butter, two of sugar, three of flour (heaping), and four eggs. Sift one tablespoonful of cream of tartar and half a teaspoonful of soda into the flour.

Cream Cake.—Two cups of flour, one cup of cream, one cup of sugar, two eggs and half a teaspoonful of soda.

Gold Cake.—Two cups of flour, one-half a cup of milk, one-half a cup of butter, one cup of sugar, yolks of three eggs, one teaspoonful of soda and two teaspoonfuls of cream of tartar.

Silver Cake.—May be made the same as gold cake, only use a little more butter.

No Egg Cake (*Nice*)**.**—Two and a half cups of flour, half a cup each of butter and milk, one and a half cups of brown sugar, and one teaspoonful of soda. Flavor with nutmeg.

Corn-Starch Cake.—Two cups sugar, one cup butter, two cups flour, one cup corn-starch, one cup milk, four eggs, one teaspoonful soda, and two of cream of tartar: sift the flour, corn-starch and cream of tartar altogether. Flavor with almond only.

Snow Flake Cake.—Three eggs, one cup and a half sugar, half cup butter, half cup milk, half teaspoonful soda, one teaspoonful cream of tartar, two cups flour, whites of two eggs, half a cup of sugar, beaten together. Bake in jelly-cake tins, frost each layer and sprinkle with grated cocoanut. This is excellent.

Sugar Gingerbread.—One egg, one cup sugar, one-half cup shortening, four tablespoonfuls of milk, one teaspoonful cream of tartar, one-half teaspoonful of soda, one teaspoonful of ginger; add flour and mix hard.

Molasses Gingerbread.—Two cups of molasses, one cup sugar, one cup of shortening, one cup boiling water, two teaspoonfuls of soda; add ginger to taste, and flour enough to mold hard.

Plain Molasses Cake.—One cup molasses, one-half cup of butter, two eggs, two heaping cups of flour, one teaspoonful soda, and spice to taste.

Auntie's Ginger Snaps.—One cup of molasses, half a cup of butter, one teaspoonful of soda and one tablespoonful of ginger; flour to form a stiff dough; roll as thin as possible.

Minnie's Molasses Cake.—One cup brown sugar, one cup molasses, one cup milk, half a cup of butter, one egg, one teaspoonful of soda, and two and a half cups of flour. Flavor with lemon or nutmeg.

Molasses Cake.—A cup and a half of molasses, three-quarters of a cup of butter, one egg thrown in without beating. When these are well mixed, fill a cup with boiling water, throw half in at once, and mix with the other a heaping teaspoonful of soda (no cream of tartar), flour enough to just make it run off the spoon; either ginger or cinnamon to taste; bake in not too hot an oven.

Soft Gingerbread (Without Eggs.)—One tablespoonful butter, one tablespoonful ginger, one-half cup brown sugar two cups molasses, two cups water or sour milk, one and a half teaspoonful soda; do not stir very long; bake in a moderate oven.

Tea Cake.—One cup of sugar, two and one-half cups of flour, one tablespoonful of butter, one cup of milk, one egg, one teaspoonful of soda, and two teaspoonfuls of cream of tartar; dissolve soda and butter in a little warm water, and beat all together for fifteen minutes. Bake in small cakes or a loaf. To be eaten hot with butter.

Madge Cakes.—Three eggs, half a pound of sugar, one cup of butter, a pint and a half of flour, rolled thin in sugar.

Doughnuts (*Nice*).—Four eggs, eight tablespoonfuls sugar, butter big as an egg, a little salt, one nutmeg, half a cup of milk, half a teaspoonful of soda, and flour enough to roll out.

One Egg Crullers.—One cup of sugar, one cup of buttermilk or sour milk, three tablespoonfuls melted butter, one egg, one teaspoonful of saleratus; flavor with nutmeg; a little salt; mix as soft as possible, and cut any desired shape. Have your fat hot. If a piece of raw potato be peeled and thrown in the fat, it will keep the crullers from burning.

Crullers.—Two coffee-cupfuls of sugar, one coffee-cupful of milk, four eggs, six tablespoonfuls of lard, two teaspoonfuls of cream of tartar, one teaspoonful of soda, flour to make stiff enough to roll; fry in boiling lard; spice to suit the taste.

No Egg Cookies.—Two cups of sugar, three-fourths cup of butter, one cup sour milk, one teaspoonful of soda, and flour enough to roll. If made with sweet milk, use baking powder, or soda, and cream of tartar.

Minute Cake.—Two cups white sugar, one scant cup of butter, one cup of sweet milk, three heaping cups of flour, three eggs, two teaspoonfuls cream of tartar, one teaspoonful of soda. Put sugar, butter, eggs (not previously beaten) soda and cream of tartar all together, beat to a froth; add the milk, beating well; flavor with lemon extract; add the flour gradually; pour into a cake tin lined with buttered paper; sprinkle a little powdered sugar over the cake before baking. It is well to cover it when first put in the oven, in order not to harden the top too soon. This is very nice and quickly made.

Railroad Cake.—One cup sugar, one tablespoonful of butter beaten to a cream, three eggs beaten to a froth, one cup of flour, three tablespoonfuls sweet milk, one teaspoonful cream of tartar, half teaspoonful soda, half teaspoonful salt.

Sponge Cake.—Three eggs, beaten one minute; one and one-half cups white sugar, beaten five minutes; one cup of flour, beaten one minute; one-half cup cold water and another cup of flour, with two teaspoonfuls of baking powder, beaten one minute; bake in a slow oven.

Sponge Cake.—Beat six eggs together thoroughly; when well beaten, stir in two cups of granulated sugar, two cups of flour, and half a teaspoonful of soda dissolved in a tablespoonful of milk; beat all well together, then add the grated peel and juice of a good-sized lemon or two small ones; bake immediately in a quick oven.

School Cake.—One egg, a piece of butter the size of an egg, one cup of sugar, one cup of milk, one pint of flour, two teaspoonfuls of cream of tartar, one of soda. Divide the milk, and dissolve the cream of tartar in one and the soda in the other, and pour one into the other to effervesce, then add to the other ingredients.

New Year's Marble Cake (*White Part*).—Whites of four eggs, one cup white sugar, half cup butter, half cup sweet milk, two teaspoonfuls of baking powder, one teaspoonful of vanilla or lemon, and two and a half cups of sifted flour.

Dark Part.—Yolks of four eggs, one cup brown sugar, half cup molasses, half cup butter, half cup sour milk, one teaspoonful cloves, one teaspoonful cinnamon, one teaspoonful mace, one nutmeg, one teaspoonful soda, and one and a half cups sifted flour. Put it in the cake dish alternately, first one part and then the other.

Fruit Cake (No Eggs).—Five cups of flour, two of sugar, one of molasses, one of butter, half cup of lard, teaspoonful salt, teaspoonful of soda dissolved in a cup of sour milk, two teaspoonfuls of ground cloves, two of allspice, one of mace, one pound chopped raisins, two ounces of citron sliced thin.

Lemon Cake.—One cup butter, three cups sugar, four cups flour, one cup milk, five eggs, one teaspoonful soda, juice and rind of one lemon.

New York Cup Cake.—Three cups of sugar, two of butter, six of flour, one of sour milk (or sweet), with a little cream, five eggs, nutmeg, and a little fruit of any kind, one teaspoonful of soda, two of cream of tartar; two loaves.

Raised Cake.—Three cups of new milk, one cup of yeast, two cups of sugar; work it into a stiff batter with flour; let it rise over night; in the morning put in one and a half cups of butter, one more cup of sugar, one teaspoonful of soda, dissolved in milk; put in spices, and raisins as long as you can stir it with a spoon, then put in pans to rise till light enough to bake.

Bread Batter Cake.—Three cups of bread batter, risen very light, two cups of sugar, one of butter, and two eggs; stir well and set to rise; when light, bake in a quick oven.

Coffee Cake.—Five cups of flour, one cup of made coffee, one cup sugar, half cup molasses, one cup of butter, teaspoonful soda, two teaspoonfuls of cinnamon, one of clove, raisins or currants.

Buns.—Two cups of milk, one of sugar, one of yeast, and flour enough to thicken; rise over night; in the morning add a piece of butter the size of an egg, another cup of sugar, one cup of Sultana raisins, or other raisins, chopped; roll out to bake, cut in rounds and rise again before baking.

Harrison Cake.—Four cups of flour, two cups of sugar, four eggs, one cup of butter, one of molasses, one of milk, half a teaspoonful of soda, half a teaspoonful of ground clove.

Every-Day Cake.—One cup molasses, one cup of sugar, one cup of butter, two eggs, two-thirds of a cup of milk, with one teaspoonful of soda dissolved in it. Two teaspoonfuls cream of tartar, and flour enough to make it as other loaf cake, one teaspoonful of salt, one of clove, one of cinnamon, one nutmeg.

Plain Cake.—Three cups of flour, one and a half cups of sugar, half a cup of butter, half a cup of milk, one teaspoonful of soda, three eggs, one nutmeg, and a tablespoonful of rose-water.

Brooklyn Cake.—One cup lard and butter mixed, one of molasses, one of sugar, three eggs, half a cup of sour milk, teaspoonful of soda; spice to your taste, and flour enough to make it as stiff as loaf cake.

Cup Cake.—Four cups of flour, four eggs, three cups of sugar, one of butter, cup of milk, teaspoonful of soda.

Jumbles.—Sift four cups of flour; cream two cups of nice, brown sugar, and a small teacupful of butter; beat two eggs very light, grate a little nutmeg, add one-half a teaspoonful of soda in half a cup of sweet milk; add flour enough to roll into cakes; handle as little as possible; bake in a long, tin pan, in a quick oven.

Caraway Cookies.—Two cups of sugar, one half cup of butter, one cup of sweet milk, one teaspoonful of baking powder, caraway seeds, flour enough to roll. These are deliciously light and tender.

Party Puffs.—Make a rich paste, roll out thin, and cut with a biscuit cutter. Lay them on a shallow tin pan, which has been buttered, and roll out a puff paste, which cut of the same size. In the centre of each of the pieces of puff paste cut a hole with a small wine glass, leaving a rim, which place on the top of your first pieces of paste, and bake all together a light brown. Before putting in the oven, brush them over with sweetened white of egg; it greatly improves the appearance. Fill with jelly or sweetmeats of any kind.

Wedding Cake.—One pound of butter, one pound of sugar, nine eggs, one pound of flour, three pounds of clean currants, two pounds of stoned raisins, one-half teacup of wine or brandy, from one-half to three-quarters of a pound of citron, one grated nutmeg, some mace and cinnamon. Rub the butter and sugar together; when light, add first the yolks and then the whites of the eggs—the yolks and whites of the eggs to be beaten separately—then put in nearly all your flour, keeping out just enough to dust your raisins; cut your citron in slips, and put in as you put the cake in the pan; after mixing your fruit in the cake, grease a four-quart pan carefully, line it with buttered paper; put your cake in and bake, in not too quick an oven, for it burns easily. After it is baked take it out of the pan, paper and all, and let it cool. The next day, to keep it fresh and moist, put it back in the pan, or in a tin cake box and keep it tightly covered.

Icing.—For a good-sized cake take the whites of two eggs, and about half a pound of powdered sugar. Beat the whites, slowly adding the sugar. This is better than beating the whites first and then adding sugar. A little lemon juice makes it whiter and better. When the cake is almost cold cover it with the icing evenly, using a knife dipped in water.

Chocolate Icing.—A cup of milk, a quarter of a pound of good chocolate, one cup of powdered sugar, one teaspoonful of vanilla. Scald the milk and chocolate, then add the sugar, and pour it on the well beaten white of an egg. This will ice a good-sized cake or pudding.

To Blanch Almonds.—Put them in boiling water.

Preserved Apples. (*Nice.*)—Core and pare a dozen good-sized apples, and cut into eighths; make a syrup of a pound of sugar to half a pint of water; let it boil, and then put in as much apple as can be boiled without breaking; remove them carefully when tender; after all are done, add a little more sugar, boil a few minutes, flavor with lemon and pour over the apples.

Preserved Pine-Apple.—A pound of sugar to a pound of pine-apple; put the slices in water, and boil a quarter of an hour; then remove them, and add the sugar to the water; put in the apple and boil fifteen minutes. Boil the syrup till thick.

Charlotte Russe.—Soak one ounce of gelatine in two tumblerfuls of milk fifteen minutes; then boil till the gelatine is all dissolved. Beat the yolks of six eggs and half a pound of powdered sugar, and stir them into the boiling milk long enough for them to thicken like a custard; then stir in the whites, beaten to a stiff froth. Season with bitter almond or vanilla. Whip a pint of cream to a stiff froth and stir into the custard. Line a mold with sponge cake or lady's fingers and fill with the mixture. Set it on ice.

Apple Jelly.—Take some ripe apples, fine-flavored and juicy, pare and cut them in quarters; put them in water as you cut them, or they will turn black. When all are cut, put them in a preserving kettle and pour over them a little water; let them cook until they are quite soft; then strain through a flannel bag; boil the juice with an equal weight of sugar until it will jelly (you can test it by placing a little on a plate), and pour it, while hot, into the jelly molds or jars. Golden pippin apples make the finest jelly. If wanted for immediate use only, you can use less sugar.

Quince Jelly.—Make the same as apple jelly.

Currant Jelly.—Mash the currants well to expel the juice; strain through a cloth, and to every pint of juice allow a pound of sugar. Put the sugar in the preserving-pan and add a very little water; heat gradually and boil it ten minutes, stirring constantly; skim the sugar and add the currant juice; let the sugar and currant juice cook ten minutes after they begin to boil. Skim well and pour at once into the glasses or jars.

Grape Jelly.—Take grapes before they are fully ripe and boil them gently with a very little water; then strain and proceed as with currant jelly. Wild grapes will not make as firm a jelly as cultivated ones.

Apple Jam.—Core and pare a good quantity of apples, chop them well, allow equal quantity of weight, apples and sugar, make a syrup of your sugar by adding a little water, boilng and skimming well, then throw in some grated lemon peel and a little white ginger with the apples; boil until the fruit looks clear.

Green Gage Jam.—Rub ripe, green gages through a sieve, put all the pulp into a pan with an equal weight of loaf sugar pounded and sifted. Boil the whole until sufficiently thick, and put into pots.

Raspberry Jam.—Pick them carefully, take equal quantities of berries and sugar, stir it continually; put the fruit first into a saucepan, and when the watery parts are evaporated add the sugar; simmer slowly for fifteen or twenty minutes.

Gooseberry Jam.—Select ripe, red gooseberries, as many as you require, and after removing the stalks place the berries in a preserving-pan. As they warm stir and bruise them to bring out the juice. Let them boil for ten minutes, and add sugar in the proportion of three-quarters of a pound to every pound of fruit, and place it on the fire again; let it boil slowly, and continue boiling for two hours longer stirring it all the while to prevent burning. When it thickens, and is jelly-like on a plate when cold, it is done enough. Put into pots, and allow it to remain a day or two before it is covered.

Gelatine Jelly.—To make two quarts, take a two-ounce package of the gelatine and soak for one hour in a pint of cold water; add to this one and one-half pounds of sugar, the juice of four lemons, some orange peel, stick cinnamon or other flavoring; when the gelatine is thoroughly soaked, pour on three pints of boiling water and strain immediately through a jelly bag or coarse toweling; next pour into molds and set aside to cool; in warm weather use a little more gelatine.

Grape Jam.—Boil the grapes in a little water long enough to make them tender, then add a pound of sugar to a pound of grapes, and boil half an hour.

Rhubarb Marmalade.—Take six oranges, peel them, and take away the white rind and pips, then slice the pulp into a stew pan along with the peel, cut very small; add thereto one quart of rhubarb, cut finely, and from one pound to one pound and a half of sugar. Boil the whole down in the usual way, as for other preserves.

Baked Cup Custards.—Take one quart of milk, four eggs, beaten very light, five tablespoonfuls of sugar and a little nutmeg; mix well and pour into custard cups; set them in a pan of hot water, grate a little nutmeg on each, and bake carefully. Eat cold.

Orange Custard.—The juice of six oranges, strained and sweetened with loaf sugar; stir over a slow fire till the sugar is dissolved, taking off the scum; when nearly cold, add the yolks of six eggs well beaten and a pint of cream or milk. Stir over the fire till it thickens, and serve in glasses; double the quantity, if required.

Gelatine Blanc Mange.—One quart of milk, one ounce gelatine, sugar to sweeten to taste; put it on the fire and keep stirring until it is all melted, then pour it into a bowl and stir it until it is cold; season with vanilla; pour it into a mold and put it into a cool place to stiffen. Soak the gelatine in the milk twenty minutes before you put it on to boil.

Moss Blanc Mange.—Take an ounce of moss, wash thoroughly, and put into two quarts of new milk; let it simmer slowly till it thickens; strain through a sieve, flavor and put it into molds.

Rice Custard.—One quart milk, three eggs, half a cup of rice, one lemon, teaspoonful of salt, and thirteen teaspoonfuls of powdered sugar. Boil the milk, rice and salt together until the rice is soft. Separate the yolks of eggs from the whites, and beat the yolks with three teaspoonfuls af sugar, and the grated peel of the lemon; beat the whites with ten teaspoonfuls of sugar and the juice of the lemon. When the rice is soft take it from the fire, and stir to it the beaten yolks till it thickens, turn into your pudding dish, put whites over the top; place in oven to color the top. To be eaten cold.

Lizzie's Trifle.—Soak a dozen sponge drops in sweet wine; after they are well soaked, drain off any of the wine that may remain; make a custard of a pint of cream, the yolks of four eggs and white of one, flavored and sweetened to your taste; when cool, pour over the cakes, then beat the whites with sugar and lemon, and put on the custard as high as you can.

Floating Island.—Take a large glass of currant jelly, the whites of three eggs, a little lemon juice and peel grated; whip it up with a rod, and put into the middle of a dish of cream.

Floating Island.—Take six eggs, separate them; beat the yolks and stir into a quart of milk; sweeten to taste; flavor with lemon or nutmeg. Put this mixture in a dish, and half immerse it in a saucepan of boiling water. Keep stirring it until the custard gets thick, which will be in about thirty minutes. Whip the whites of the eggs to a strong froth. When the custard is done, put into a deep dish and heap the frothed egg upon it. Serve cold.

Quinces for the Tea Table.—Bake ripe quinces thoroughly. When cold, strip off the skins, place them in a glass dish and sprinkle with white sugar, and serve them with cream. They make a fine-looking dish for the tea-table, and a more luscious and inexpensive one than the same fruit made into sweetmeats.

Preserved Strawberries.—Pick off all the stems, and to every quart of fruit add a quart of sugar; mix well with the sugar and put them over a slow fire till the syrup commences to form, then put them over a hot fire and let them boil quickly for fifteen minutes, skimming it well. Put them boiling hot into stone jars, seal up tightly.

Strawberry Syrup.—Make a syrup in the proportion of three pounds of sugar to half a pint of water. Boil and skim until clear. Have ready the strained juice of the strawberries. It is best to let drip through a bag without pressure, so as to be clear. Allow two and a half pints of strawberry juice to the half pint of water. After you add this, let it boil hard for not more than five minutes. Take it from the fire before it loses its fine color, and pour hot into self-sealing glass jars—the kind that only need the top to be screwed on. This syrup preserves even the odor of the fresh strawberry when opened months afterward, and flavors ice cream delightfully.

Preserved Lemon Peel.—Make a thick syrup of white sugar, chop the lemon peel fine, and boil it in the syrup ten minutes; put in glass tumblers and paste paper over. A teaspoonful of this makes a loaf of cake or a dish of sauce nice.

How to Crystallize Fruit.—Pick out the finest of any kind of fruit, leave on their stalks, beat the whites of three eggs to a stiff froth, lay the fruit in the beaten egg with the stalks upward, drain them and beat the part that drips off again, select them out one by one and dip them into a cup of finely powdered sugar; cover a pan with a sheet of fine paper, place the fruit inside of it, and put it in an oven that is cooling; when the icing on the fruit becomes firm, pile them on a dish and set them in a cool place.

Preserved Tomatoes.—A pound of sugar to a pound of tomatoes. Take six pounds of each, the peel and juice of four lemons, and quarter of a pound of ginger tied up in a bag; put on the side of the range, and boil slowly for three hours.

Cider Apple Sauce.—Take a porcelain-lined kettle, fill it with rich, sweet cider; boil more than half away, then empty into a stone pot. Have ready sweet apples pared and quartersd; fill the kettle with them, pour on part of the cider, cover and let them stew until the apples are done;

add the rest of the cider and a little sugar, and stir until quite thick. It is better to boil it several hours, as the longer it is boiled the longer it can be kept; while boiling add spice to taste.

Sauce for Roast Beef.—Grate horse-radish on a grater into a basin, add two tablespoonfuls of cream, with a little mustard and salt, mix well together, add four tablespoonfuls of the best vinegar, and mix the whole thoroughly. The vinegar and cream are both to be cold.

Oyster Sauce for Turkeys, etc.—Strain fifty oysters, put the juice into a saucepan, add one pint of new milk, let it simmer, and skim off any froth which may rise; then rub a large spoonful of flour and two of butter together; stir this into the liquor; add a little salt and pepper. Let it simmer five minutes, but do not add your oysters till just as they are to be sent to the table, as if they are too much cooked they are hard.

Oyster Sauce.—Beat a quarter of a pound of butter and three even tablespoonfuls of flour into a cream, then turn on a pint of boiling water, stirring briskly; let it boil once, then add a pint of solid oysters and boil two minutes. If desired, can flavor with chopped celery or parsley.

Cranberry Sauce.—A quart of cranberries, a large pint of sugar, and a pint of water. Boil slowly, and when the berries are soft, beat well and strain through a colander.

White Sauce.—In three tablespoonfuls of nice melted butter mix thoroughly one tablespoonful of sifted flour, add three-fourths of a pint of milk, boil once, and then stir quickly. For color, add a little yolk of egg, and for flavor, lemon juice.

Egg Sauce.—Take quarter of a pound of butter and braid it well into three even spoonfuls of flour; then turn on a scant pint of boiling water, chop well three boiled eggs, and stir into the butter as it goes to the table.

Caper Sauce.—Is to be made as egg sauce, and two tablespoonfuls of capers stirred in instead of eggs.

Drawn Butter.—Take one pint of sweet milk, a piece of butter the size of an egg, two or three tablespoonfuls of flour or corn-starch ; rub the butter and flour together; when the milk is boiling, stir in the butter and flour ; have ready two hard-boiled eggs ; take off the shells and chop or slice them ; stir them in as you take the butter from the fire ; pepper and salt to taste ; send to table immediately.

Mint Sauce.—Choose fresh and young mint, strip the leaves from the stems, wash and drain, chop them finely, and add two tablespoonfuls of pounded sugar to three heaping tablespoonfuls of mint. Mix thoroughly, and pour in gradually six tablespoonfuls of good vinegar. The proportions can be varied according to taste.

Mint Vinegar.—Put into a wide-mouthed bottle fresh, clean mint leaves, enough to fill it loosely ; then fill up the bottle with good vinegar, and after it has been stopped close for two or three weeks, it is to be poured off clean into another bottle, and kept well corked for use. Serve with lamb when mint cannot be obtained.

Apple Sauce for Roast Pork.—Pare, core and cut up a quart of apples, add half a cup of water, boil them till tender, then add sugar, and any flavor desired, to taste. Nice with a very little butter added.

Tomato Sauce.—Remove the skin and seeds from about a dozen tomatoes, slice them and put them in the stewpan, with pepper and salt to taste, and three pounded crackers. Stew slowly one hour.

To Brown Flour.—Spread upon an iron pan and set upon the stove, or in a very hot oven, and stir continually after it begins to color. Brown evenly all through. Keep in a glass jar in a dry place.

Good Common Sauce.—One coffee-cupful of brown sugar, two tablespoonfuls of butter and a tablespoonful of flour ; beat well together, then add a cupful of boiling water and simmer for a few minutes. Flavor with nutmeg or lemon, or a little cider.

Hard Sauce.—Take one cup of butter, two of sugar. and beat well together. Flavor as desired. Set in a cool place.

Brandy Sauce.—Beat one-quarter of a pound of butter to a cream, add gradually one pound of white sugar, one wineglassful of brandy, and half a small nutmeg. Beat until light and white, and then pile up into a pyramid.

Liquid Sauce.—Two cups white sugar, a piece of butter the size of an egg, one egg well beaten, one teaspoonful corn-starch or flour, beat all well, now add a teacupful of boiling water, put in saucepan on fire till it thickens like cream ; do not let it boil.

Wine Sauce.—One cup of powdered sugar, and one half cup of butter beaten to a cream, the yolk of one egg beaten and added, then the white of the egg beaten and also added ; melt over the tea-kettle and add half a glass of wine.

Sauce for Apple Pudding.—Take equal parts of sugar and molasses, boil together about twenty minutes, and add half a teaspoonful of butter and a little vinegar or lemon juice.

Milk Sauce.—Rub one tablespoonful of butter into a large cup of sugar, add two beaten eggs and work all to a froth. Wet one-half a teaspoonful of corn-starch and stir into the mixture ; then stir in five tablespoonfuls of boiling milk, beating well all the time. Set the dish in a pan of boiling water and simmer for five minutes. Flavor to taste.

COOKERY FOR INVALIDS.

Barley Water.—Pearl barley, two ounces ; boiling water, two quarts ; boil to one half and strain. A little lemon juice and sugar may be added, if desirable. To be taken freely in inflammatory diseases.

Barley Coffee.—Roast one pint of common barley in the same way in which coffee is roasted. Add two large spoonfuls of this to a quart of boiling water ; boil five minutes. Add a little sugar.

Rice Water.—Rice, two ounces ; water, two quarts ; boil an hour and a half, and add sugar and nutmeg. Rice, when boiled for a considerable time, becomes a kind of jelly, and, mixed with milk, is an excellent diet for children. It has in some measure a constipating property, which may be increased by boiling the milk.

Lemon Water.—Put two slices of lemon, thinly pared, into a bowl, a little bit of the peel and a little sugar. Pour in a pint of boiling water and cover it close two hours.

Lemonade.—This is invaluable in fevers, and also in rheumatic affections. Rub two medium-sized lemons soft, cut them through the center, and squeeze out the juice, take out the seeds. Put two tablespoonfuls of white sugar to each lemon, and add a pint of cold or boiling water, according as you desire the lemonade, hot or cold.

Apple Water.—Roast two tart apples until they are soft; put them in a pitcher, pour upon them a pint of cold water, and let it stand in a cool place an hour, It is used in fevers and eruptive diseases, and does not require sweetening.

A Refreshing Drink in Fevers.—Put a little sage, two sprigs of balm, and a little sorrel into a stone jar, having first washed and dried them. Peel thin a small lemon, slice it, and put a small piece of the peel in; then pour in three pints of boiling water. Sweeten, and cover it close.

Another.—Boil an ounce and a half of tamarinds, three ounces of cranberries, and two ounces of stoned raisins, in three pints of water, till the water is reduced to two pints. Strain and add a bit of lemon peel, which must be removed in an hour, as it gives a bitter taste if left too long.

A Very Pleasant Drink.—Put a teacupful of cranberries into a cup of water, and mash them. In the meantime, boil two quarts of water with one large spoonful of corn or oatmeal and a bit of lemon peel; then add the cranberries. As much fine sugar as shall leave a smart flavor of the fruit, and a wineglassful of sherry. Boil the whole gently fifteen minutes, and strain.

Sage Tea.—Dried leaves of sage, half an ounce; boiling water, one quart. Infuse for half an hour, and strain. Add sugar and lemon juice as required by the patient. Balm and other teas are made in the same manner. The above form agreeable and useful drinks in fevers, and their diaphoretic powers may be increased by adding a little sweet spirits of nitre.

Crust Coffee.—Toast slowly one or two slices of brown or white bread, pour boiling water over it, and drink hot or cold, according to preference.

Infusion of Malt.—To one pint of ground malt add three pints of scalding water; that is, water not quite brought to the boiling point; infuse two hours and strain. Add sugar or lemon juice, as desired. An excellent preparation in inflammatory fevers.

Water Gruel.—Oat or corn meal, two tablespoonfuls; water, one quart. Boil for ten or fifteen minutes, and strain, adding salt, and sugar if desired.

Rice Gruel.—Ground rice, one heaping tablespoonful; ground cinnamon, one teaspoonful; water, one quart. Boil gently for twenty minutes, adding the cinnamon near the conclusion. Strain and sweeten. Wine may be added in some cases.

Panada.—White bread, one ounce; ground cinnamon, one teaspoonful; water, one pint. Boil them until well mixed, and add a little sugar and nutmeg. Wine or butter may also be added, if desirable.

Panada.—Break up three arrowroot crackers into small pieces; pour upon them boiling water and cover close for a minute, then add a teaspoonful of white sugar and a little milk. It is an excellent breakfast or supper for an invalid or a child. Instead of the milk, the juice of a lemon may be squeezed in and another teaspoonful of sugar added.

Sago Gruel.—Sago, two tablespoonfuls: water, one pint. Boil gently until it thickens, stirring frequently. Wine, sugar and nutmeg may be added, according to circumstances.

Arrowroot Gruel. — Arrowroot, one tablespoonful; sweet milk, half a pint; boiling water, half a pint. To be sweetened with loaf sugar. Excellent aliment for children when the bowels are irritable.

Tapioca Jelly.—Tapioca, two tablespoonfuls; water, one pint. Boil gently for an hour, or until it assumes a jelly-like appearance. Add sugar, wine and nutmeg, with lemon juice to suit the taste of the patient and the nature of the case.

Jelly of Irish Moss.—Irish moss, half an ounce; fresh milk, a pint and a half. Boil down to a pint. Remove any sediment by straining, and add the proper quantity of sugar and lemon juice, or peach-water, to give it an agreeable flavor.

Isinglass Jelly.—Isinglass, one roll. Boil in one pint of water until it is dissolved. Strain, and add one pint of sweet milk. Put it again over the fire, and let it just boil up. Sweeten it with loaf sugar, and grate nutmeg upon it. When properly made, it resembles custard. This is excellent for persons recovering from sickness, and is well adapted to the bowel complaints of children.

Calf's Foot Jelly.—Take two calf's feet, and add to them one gallon of water; boil down to one quart; strain, and when cold, skim off the fat; add to this the white of six or eight eggs well beaten, a pint of wine, half a pound of loaf sugar, and the juice of four lemons, and let them be well mixed. Boil the whole for a few minutes, stirring constantly, and then strain through a flannel. This forms a very nutritious article of diet for the sick, and for those recovering from disease. The wine may be omitted or added, according to choice.

Chicken Water.—Take half a chicken, divested of all fat, and break the bones; add to this two quarts of water, and boil for half an hour. Season with salt.

Milk Porridge.—Wheat flour, corn meal or oatmeal, two tablespoonfuls; milk, one pint; water, one pint; mix the flour or meal with cold water, to form a thin paste; put the milk and water over the fire, and when they come to the boiling point, add the paste, carefully stirring. Boil at least half an hour.

French Milk Porridge.—Stir some oatmeal and water together; let the mixture stand to clear, and pour off the water. Then put more water to the meal, stir it well and let it stand till the next day. Strain through a fine sieve and boil the water, adding milk while so doing. The proportion of water must be small. With toast this is a good preparation for weak persons.

Boiled Flour.—Tie up as tight as possible, in a linen cloth, one pound of flour, and, after frequently dipping it in cold water, dredge the outside with flour till a crust is formed round it, which will prevent the water soaking into it while boiling. Place it in water and boil until it becomes a hard, dry mass. Two or three spoonfuls of this may be grated, and prepared in the same manner as arrowroot gruel, for which it is an excellent substitute.

Essence of Beef.—Lean beef, chopped fine. Put a sufficient quantity in a bottle to fill up its body, cork it *loosely,* and place it in a pot of cold water, attaching the neck, by means of a string, to the handle of the vessel. Boil this for an hour and a half or two hours, then pour off the liquor and skim it. To this preparation may be added spices, salt, wine, brandy, etc., according to the taste of the patient and nature of the disease.

Restorative.—Take two calf's feet, one quart of water, and one quart of new milk; place all in a close-covered jar, and bake three hours and a half. When cold, remove the fat. Any desired flavor may be given, by adding lemon peel, cinnamon, or mace, while baking. Add sugar afterwards.

Vegetable Soup.—Take one turnip, one potato, and one onion, let them be sliced and boiled in one quart of water for an hour. Add as much salt as is agreeable, and pour the whole upon a piece of dry toast. This forms an agreeable substitute for animal food, and may be given when the latter is inadmissible.

Oyster Soup.—Make a little broth of lean veal, or mutton, simmer with it a little celery. Strain it; put it again on the fire, and when it boils throw in the oysters with their liquor, and a trifle of pepper and salt. Serve as soon as it comes to a boil on little squares of toast.

Sippets.—On an extremely hot plate, put two or three slices of bread, and pour over them some of the juices of boiled beef, mutton or veal, if there be no butter in the dish. Sprinkle over them a little salt.

Vinegar Whey.—Milk, one pint; vinegar, one table-spoonful. Boil for a few minutes, and separate the curd.

Alum Whey.—Alum, one teaspoonful; milk, one pint. Boil together, and strain to separate the curd.

Orange Whey.—Milk, one pint; the juice of an orange with a portion of the peel. Boil the milk; then put the orange to it and let it stand till coagulation takes place. Strain.

Whey with Tamarinds.—Milk, boiling, one pint; tamarinds, two ounces. Boil them together till coagulation takes place.

Wine Whey.—Milk, two-thirds of a pint; water, one-third of a pint; Madeira, or other wine, one gill; sugar, one dessertspoonful. Place the milk and water together in a deep pan, and when it begins to boil pour in the wine and the sugar, stirring assiduously while it boils, for twelve or fifteen minutes. Lastly, strain through a sieve. This is excellent in all forms of fever, given in small quantities. It may be drank either cold or tepid, a wineglassful at a time.

Roast Apples.—These can nearly always be eaten with safety, when they are eaten with relish. Choose good-sized, fair apples of a tart and juicy, but not sour kind. Rub them off clean, and put them in rather a slow oven, which may increase in warmth, so that they shall be thoroughly done in an hour. When so soft that the savory pulp breaks through the browned skin in every direction, take them out, sift white sugar over them, and carry one at a time on a saucer to the patient.

Stewed Prunes.—These are extremely good in measles, scarlet fever, and the like, both as food and medicine. Get the box prunes, as they are generally of a much better quality than the open sort. Soak them for one hour in cold water, then put them in a porcelain-lined saucepan, with a little more water if necessary, and a little coffee crushed sugar. Cover, and let them stew slowly an hour, or until they are swollen large and quite soft. They are excellent as an accompaniment to breakfast for a sick person.

Milk Toast.—This is a favorite dish with nearly all sick people when they are getting well. Cut stale baker's bread in thin slices, toast a nice brown, and lay them in a deep dish. Meanwhile, boil some milk, salt to taste, and pour it over the toast, cover and serve quick. For an invalid, no butter should be put in the milk.

Thickened Milk.—With a little milk, mix smooth a tablespoonful of flour and a pinch of salt. Pour upon it a quart of boiling milk, and when it is thoroughly mixed put all back into the saucepan, and boil up once, being careful not to burn, and stirring all the time, to keep it perfectly smooth and free from lumps. Serve with slices of dry toast. It is excellent in diarrhœa, and becomes a specific by scorching the flour before mixing with the milk.

Soft Boiled Eggs.—Fresh eggs for invalids who like them cooked soft, should be put in a pan of boiling water, and set on a part of the stove where they will not boil for several minutes. At the end of that time they will be like jelly, perfectly soft but nicely done, and quite digestible by even weak stomachs.

Milk and Eggs.—Beat up a fresh egg, with a grain of salt, pour upon it a pint of boiling milk, stirring all the time. Serve hot, with or without toast.

Invalid Cup Pudding.—One tablespoonful of flour, one egg; mix with cold milk, and a pinch of salt to a batter.

Boil or steam fifteen minutes in a buttered cup. Eat with sauce, fruit or plain sugar.

Tapioca Cup Pudding.—This is very light, and delicate for invalids. An even tablespoonful of tapioca, soaked for two hours in nearly a cup of new milk. Stir into this the the yolk of a fresh egg, a little sugar, a grain of salt, and bake in a cup for fifteen minutes. A little jelly may be eaten with it, if allowed, or a few fresh strawberries.

Invalid Apple Pie.—Slice up one or more nice tart apples in a saucer, sweeten with white sugar, and cover with a moderately thick slice of bread buttered slightly on the under side. When the bread is browned, the apples, if of a tender kind, and thinly sliced, will be done.

Broiled Tenderloin.—This is highly enjoyed when the patient is becoming convalescent. Cut out the round piece from the inside of a sirloin steak, broil it quick over a bright fire, turn it, with its gravy, upon a piece of freshly made toast, sprinkle with salt and pepper, but no butter, place between two hot plates, and serve directly. A tender mutton chop, or half the breast of a chicken may be served the same way, only the chicken will require longer and somewhat slower cooking

MISCELLANEOUS.

Boston Baked Beans.—Soak three pints small, dried beans over night; in the morning pour off the water, and add fresh water, in which is dissolved a quarter of a teaspoonful of baking soda; parboil them till soft, being careful not to let them break; when done enough, pour into a colander, and rinse with clear water, drain and put them in the bean-crock with a pound and a quarter of fat and lean salt pork in the centre; cover with water, in which is dissolved a little salt, and molasses if desired. Bake all day, occasionally looking at them to see if more water is required; when half done, put a spoon in the middle and see if they are salt enough;

cover a few hours before they are done to prevent the top from becoming too brown. Brown bread is a necessary accompaniment.

Blackberries with Cream,—Take one and a half pounds of carefully cleaned and perfectly ripe berries; one-half a pound of sugar, one-half a teacupful of molasses, and half a teacupful of flour; cook the berries till done, then add the flour; cook five minutes, turn into a mold, and eat cold, with cream.

Green Pears or Apples.—The above fruit, which is continually falling during the summer, may be parboiled; then, after draining, add about as much sugar as it will take to sweeten them (about half a pound of sugar to a pound of fruit); put back and cook slowly half an hour. If they seem too dry, add a little water. Flavor with preserving ginger, vanilla bean, or lemon, sliced. Cooked in this way they are nice for tea.

Potato Fritters.—Grate six cold-boiled potatoes; add one pint of cream or milk, and flour enough to make stiff as other fritters; the yolks of three eggs; then the beaten whites; a little salt, and fry in hot lard. They are delicious.

Cider Cake.—Five cups of flour, three of sugar, one of butter, five eggs, two teaspoonfuls of soda dissolved in two cups of cider. Work the butter to cream; beat eggs and sugar together; pour the cider on the flour; spice to taste. When the oven is ready, mix all together and bake.

German Toast.—Cut thick slices of bread—baker's is the best—dip them each side in milk enough to soften, then dip in beaten egg; put in a pan greased with just sufficient butter to fry; fry till brown as an omelet, then serve, well sprinkled with white sugar. Two eggs would be sufficient to dip nearly a dozen slices of bread. Like pancakes, the hotter the toast the better.

Doughnuts.—Half a pint of sweet milk, half a cup of butter (scant), one cup of yeast, salt ; flavor with nutmeg or cinnamon. Mix them at night. In the' morning, roll out and let them raise until very light, and drop in hot fat. They are very nice, after they are fried, to roll them in pulverized sugar.

Hop Yeast.—Two tablespoonfuls of hops to a quart of water ; let them steep well ; make a thickening of six potatoes mashed fine, and three tablespoonfuls of flour worked into the potatoes ; strain the hop water upon it, stir it well, and when cool enough add yeast to work it. Bottle and keep in a cool place.

Potato Yeast.—Two good-sized potatoes, grated raw ; pour on half a pint of boiling water, half cup of white sugar, teaspoonful salt ; when cool, put in half a cup of good yeast; let it rise ; when light, put in a bottle and cork tight. Half a cup makes two loaves of bread ; reserve a half cupful every time for raising.

Mush, or Hasty Pudding.—Set on a quart of water to boil ; in the meantime stir half a pint of sifted Indian meal into water enough to make it smooth ; add salt to taste. When the water boils, stir in a tablespoonful and boil, then another and let it boil, and so on till you have the thickening in ; then add enough sifted raw meal gradually, stirring all the time till thick enough, and it is done. This is a very nice receipt.

Fried Mush.—Made as above the day before it is wanted, and cut in slices, and fried with fat enough to prevent its sticking to the griddle.

Pears for Tea.—Very ripe, soft pears should be pared and cut in slices and covered with sugar and cream.

Peaches for Tea.—They should be prepared as above, and are very nice.

Strawberries for Tea.—They should have nearly their weight in sugar, and a sweet, rich cream to serve with them. There is no greater luxury.

Apple Cream.—Peel and core five large apples ; boil them in a little water, till soft enough to press through a sieve ; sweeten, and beat with them the whites of five eggs. Serve it with cream poured round it.

To Clarify Sugar.—To two pounds of granulated sugar put a pint of water, and dissolve it. When dissolved place to boil, and before hot stir in well the whites of two eggs ; watch it carefully, skimming well. When clear, cool and bottle it. This will keep a long time if kept in a cool place.

Blackberry Brandy.—Two quarts of the juice of black-berries, one pound of loaf sugar, one-half ounce of nutmeg, one-half ounce of cinnamon, one-half ounce of cloves, one-quarter ounce of pimento (the spices are pulverized) ; boil to-gether about half an hour, and when cold add a pint of the best brandy.

Cherry Rum.—A peck of black wild cherries, soaked in cold water for twenty-four hours. Put them in a demijohn, add two pounds brown sugar, two quarts blackberries, and a gallon of best New England rum. The older it is the bet-ter, if kept well corked ; it is excellent for summer com-plaints.

Lemon Extract.—To prepare the best lemon extract for flavoring purposes, procure a quart bottle, have it perfectly neat and clean, pare the yellow rind off the lemon carefully, taking off as little of the white skin as possible, cut it in fine bits, put in the bottle and fill up with the best alcohol—only the best will cut the oil, which is the flavoring desired, and exists in the outside rind only. A dozen lemons will make a quart of the extract. The cheapest way is to have your bottle ready, and whenever a lemon is used, save the outside rind and drop it in the alcohol. In that way you have a much better extract than any that can be bought, and the cost is comparatively small.

Ice-Cream. (*Without the ordinary facilities.*)—Take three pints of milk, four eggs, well beaten, three-fourths pound sugar, and one tablespoonful corn-starch; mix in a three-quart tin pail; boil in a kettle of water till quite thick; add one pint of sweet cream, and flavor to taste. Freeze in a common water pail, or any vessel of suitable size, with equal parts of ice chopped fine, and coarse salt. Rotate the pail and stir frequently.

Strawberry Ice-Cream. (*Excellent.*)—Pass a pint of picked strawberries through a sieve with a wooden spoon, add four ounces of powdered sugar and a pint of cream and freeze.

Water Ices. (*Generally.*)—If made from jams, you must rub them through a sieve, adding thick boiled syrup and lemon juice, and some jelly, and coloring it for pink, and the white of an egg whipped up before you add it to the best of a pint of spring water; if of jam, you must have a good pint of mixture in all to make a quart mold; if from fruits with syrup you will not require water.

Mild Mustard.—For immediate use mustard may be mixed with milk, to which a spoonful of very thin cream may be added.

Recipe for Corning Beef.—For one hundred pounds of beef, take seven pounds of salt, two pounds sugar, two ounces saltpetre, two ounces pepper, two ounces soda; dissolve in two and a half gallons water; boil, skim, and pour on hot.

Pickle for Butter.—Allow half a pound of salt, an ounce of saltpetre, and half a pound of sugar to three quarts of water. Dissolve them together; scald and skim the pickle; let it be entirely cold, and then pour it over the butter.

Cocoa-Nut Drops.—Take equal parts of powdered co-coas and loaf sugar, add the whites of eggs beaten to a stiff froth, half a dozen to the pound; mix the whole together, and drop on buttered tins. Bake in a moderate oven.

Molasses Candy.—One pint of white coffee sugar, one pint of molasses, one tablespoonful of vinegar, one table-spoonful of butter; cook slowly a long time until it "strings" from the spoon when dipped up; pour upon a greased tin pan; then pull it until it becomes white.

Pop Corn Balls.—To six quarts of pop corn, boil one pint of molasses about fifteen minutes; then put the corn in-to a large pan, pour the boiling molasses over it, stirring briskly until thoroughly mixed. Then, with clean hands, make into balls of the desired size.

How to Make Peppermint Drops.—There are various ways of making them; a simple one is the following: Take a quantity of sugar and put it in a dish, with water enough to hardly dissolve all the sugar; put on a quick fire and boil; then put in a few drops of peppermint (only a few drops); drop on a tin plate to suit yourself; stir the solution until ready to make the drops.

Chocolate Cream Drops.—Take one pound of the best crushed sugar, half a teaspoonful of cream of tartar, one and one-half gills of water; put them in a porcelain-lined kettle, and place over a brisk fire and boil. Dip out a large spoon-ful of the boiling sugar, and cool the same in a saucer of water; dip in it the thumb and first finger; if, on separating them, the syrup is thick enough to be drawn out from the thumb and finger in a long thread without breaking, it is cooked enough. Set aside to cool for fifteen minutes; To cream it then rub the syrup against the sides of the kettle with a wooden spoon or paddle, when it will turn into cream; you can then form into shape ; first flavor as you wish. To cover with chocolate, take one-half pound of the best chocolate, place into an ordinary tin saucepan, and set into a kettle of boiling water ; when melted, drop into it the balls of cream, and roll until covered with the chocolate ; then remove with a fork, allow the surplus chocolate to drip, place on a greased plate, or thick paper, to dry.

Chocolate Caramels.—Two cups of molasses, one cup of grated chocolate, one cup of milk, two teaspoonfuls of vanilla extract, one tablespoonful of butter. Boil about twenty-five minutes, then set to cool in a buttered pan. Mark in squares.

Chocolate Caramels.—Take two cups of sugar, one cup of molasses, and one cup of milk ; put them in a buttered saucepan and boil fifteen minutes ; then add one teaspoonful each of butter and flour, beaten to a cream ; let all boil together five minutes, and add the chocolate, grated, and boil till thick. Turn into a buttered pan, and before it is cold, mark in squares with a knife.

Rays of the Sun.—The rays of the sun may be kept from penetrating a window by applying to it an ounce of powdered gum tragacanth in the whites of six eggs, well beaten.

Furniture.—Beeswax and strong lye will clean and polish furniture.

To Remove White Stains from Furniture.—Have ready three pieces of woolen cloth, with one well dipped in lamp oil (or, if that is not convenient, linseed oil), rub the spot briskly, wet the second with alcohol and apply to oily surface, rubbing quickly, as too much alcohol will destroy the varnish, and finally polish with the third cloth, moistened with oil or furniture polish.

Another way is to use equal parts of vinegar, sweet oil

and spirits of turpentine ; shake all well together in a bottle ; apply with a flannel cloth and rub dry with old silk or linen.

To Clean Paint.—Mix common whiting to the consistency of common paste, in warm water. Rub the surface to be cleaned quite briskly with a piece of flannel dipped in the whiting, and wash off with pure cold water. Grease spots, etc., will be removed without injury to the paint.

Papered Walls.—Rub the walls with a cloth sprinkled with Indian meal. Or gently sweep off the dust and rub with a soft muslin cloth.

To Make Paper Adhere to Whitewashed Walls.—Paper may be made to adhere to whitewashed walls by washing the walls with vinegar. When dry, apply the paper in the usual way.

To Remove Mildew or Stains from Linen.—Take your cloth when dry, wet thoroughly with soft soap and salt mixed. Chalk or starch scraped to a powder may be used instead of salt. Lay out to bleach. If one operation does not answer, two will, and the linen will be clear and clean as ever.

Iron Stains.—These may be removed with juice of lemon, or of sorrel leaves; but if these fail, moisten the stain spots with water and rub on a little powdered oxalic acid. Wash the acid off thoroughly soon after it is put on, or it will eat the cloth. Also, wash it from your hands, and keep it away from children, for it is poisonous in the mouth. Inkstains may be taken out in this way. Acids had better be used only on white goods.

To Keep Linen White.—Washing and bleaching well, and rinsing in very blue water, and putting away rough dry will keep linen perfectly white.

Grease Spots.—An ounce of pulverized boraz, put into a quart of boiling water and bottled for use, will be found invaluable for removing grease spots from woolen goods.

To Clean Black Cashmere.—Wash in hot suds, with a little borax in the water; rinse in bluing water—very blue—and iron while damp. It will look equal to new.

To Restore Velvet.—When velvet has been crushed, hold the wrong side over a basin of quite boiling water, and the bile will gradually rise. Do not lose patience, for it takes a considerable time, but the result is marvelous.

How to Wash Black Calicoes.—Put the calicoes in a boiler, with enough cold water to cover them well, and let them come to a boil. Then take out into clean water, and soap, and rub any part of the white (if there is any) which still looks soiled, after which rinse, wring as dry as possible, and dry quickly.

To Set the Color of Calico.—Salt thrown into the water will set the color of black calico.

How to Stiffen a Crape Veil.—Always keep it folded and pressed under a heavy book, and when it looks gray, take alcohol enough to wet it thoroughly, then shake it dry, fold it nicely and press.

To Restore Black Crape.—Black crape can be perfectly restored by holding it over the steam of a boiling kettle.

To Renovate Black Silk.—Sponge it with clear, strong, cold tea, shake it out, and hang it up to dry, or iron it while damp. Another way is, rip out the seams, rub it with a piece of crape, then put it in cold water twenty-four hours, iron it with a hot iron on the wrong side; be careful not to wring the silk.

116

THE FAMILY MANUAL.

We shall not attempt a description of the nature or symptoms of disease, but proceed upon the supposition that the character of the disease is understood by the patient. After naming the disease, we shall prescribe a few simple but well-tried remedies. In all cases of danger or doubt, send at once for a good physician.

ASTHMA.

1. Syrup of squills, in small doses, is the most simple remedy.

2. Or the tincture of ipecac, or lobelia, may be given at intervals, till it produces nausea without vomiting.

3. Skunk cabbage root, taken in the form of a syrup, or dried and smoked through a pipe, will give relief.

4. Burn a piece of brown paper, as big as your two hands, that has been wet in strong saltpetre water, in your room on going to bed—it will give great relief.

POOR APPETITE.

1. Take a tonic bitter made as follows;—Six parts bayberry root, one part wormwood, one part tansy; boil out the strength and sweeten to your taste. Dose, half wineglass three or four times a day.

2. Or steep 1 oz. quassia, 2 oz. thoroughwort, in pint and and a half of water; when cool, strain, and add half pint good port wine. Dose, half wineglass three times a day.

BLEEDING AT THE NOSE.

1. Soak the feet in warm water; put lint up the nose, wet with hot drops, and keep the temples wet with cold water.

2. Or, pour cold water upon the back of the neck, and put a ball of rag up the nostril, dipped in equal parts of white of egg, sugar, and burnt alum.

BLEEDING AT THE LUNGS.

1. Eat freely of raw table-salt.

2. Or, take a teaspoonful, three or four times a day equal parts of powdered loaf sugar and rosin.

3. Or, boil an ounce of dried yellow dock root in a pint of milk. Take a cupful two or three times a day.

BOILS.

1. Apply a poultice of warm bread and milk.

2. Or, a poultice of rye meal, with the addition of a teaspoonful paregoric.

BRUISES.

1. Apply a warm poultice of bruised wormwood and rum, or vinegar.

2. Or, bathe frequently with hot drops.

CANCER.

1. Take yolk of an egg, with as much fine salt as it will absorb ; stir it to a salve, and apply a plaster of it, spread upon silk, twice a day.

2. Or, bathe the cancer three or four times a day with a solution of brandy and salt.

CATARRH.

1. Take freely the catarrh snuff.

2. Or, for the cough, take tincture of lobelia in small doses.

3. Or, use the composition powders and elixir, with a warm bath.

CONSUMPTION.

1. But little can be done by medicine. Bring the blood to the surface by frequent washing and rubbing, or the warm bath.

2. Take a small quantity of the expressed juice of hoarhound (the herb), and mix it with half a pint of new milk; drink it warm every morning;—if persevered in, it will perform wonders.

3. Or, a strictly sober life, regular, active exercise, and a cheerful and contented mind, are the most certain means to effect a cure.

COLDS AND COUGH.

1. Drink freely of life-everlasting tea—it is excellent.

2. Or, take 5 oz. honey, 4 oz. molasses, and 7 oz. vinegar; mix, and simmer over the fire fifteen minutes; then add two drachms of wine of ipecac. Dose, tablespoonful every four hours.

3. Or, pour a half cup of molasses over a hot boiled turnip, let it stand fifteen minutes, turn off the syrup and squeeze the turnip. To be taken warm on going to bed.

WHOOPING COUGH.

1. Take a teaspoonful of castor oil, to a tablespoonful of molasses. Dose, give a teaspoonful whenever the cough is troublesome.

2. Or, take frequently slight emetics of wine of ipecac, or tincture of lobelia. Keep the bowels open.

CROUP.

1. Cut onions into thin slices; between and over them put brown sugar, and let it dissolve. A tablespoonful of the syrup will produce instant relief.

2. Or, take goose grease, rubbing the throat with it at the same time, till it produces vomiting.

CRAMP IN THE STOMACH.

1. Take freely of composition powder, or hot drops.
2. If the pain is severe, give sixty drops of paregoric.
3. Or, teaspoonful of essence of peppermint.
4. Or, half glass raw brandy, with ten drops of laudanum.

COLIC.

Use the same remedies as in case of cramp.

CHOLERA MORBUS.

1. Apply flannel cloths, wrung out in hot water or spirits, over the whole surface of the stomach. Give freely the composition powder and hot drops, so as to produce a copious sweat.

2. If the pain is very severe, use any of the remedies prescribed for the cramp.

COSTIVENESS

1. Use wheat and rye, or rye and indian bread.
2. Or, golden seal infused in wine, and taken as a bitter.
3. Or, take a little rhubarb every day.

CORNS.

1. Dissolve two cents' worth of caustic potash in one ounce of water, and wet the corn every night.

2. Or, take equal parts of roasted onions and soft soap : beat well, and apply the mixture hot on going to bed.

CANKER.

1. Take a tea made of low blackberry leaves or raspberry
2. Or, burnt alum held in the mouth is very good.

CHILBLAINS.

1. Common copal varnish is an efficacious remedy.

2. Or, use pig's foot oil, which will effect an immediate cure.

DROPSY.

1. Take two handfuls of inner bark of elder, steep it in two quarts of white wine for twenty-four hours. Dose, a gill every morning, fasting.

2. Or, take cream of tartar, dissolved in water, every day.

3. Or, take juniper ashes, with molasses and gin. This will carry off the water, and effect a cure.

4. Or, take quarter pound dried milkweed, cut small; pour to it a quart boiling water, and simmer to a pint; when cool, add pint Holland gin; cork tight, and let it stand twelve hours. Dose, half wineglass every three hours.

DYSENTERY.

1. Take one or two doses of rhubarb, and regulate the bowels by a suitable diet.

2. Or, take a dose of castor oil, apply a mustard poultice to the bowels and bathe the stomach and bowels frequently with hot drops.

DIARRHŒA.

1. Parch half a pint of rice perfectly brown; then boil it as usual, and eat it slowly,—it will check it in a few hours.

2. Or, take tablespoonful of West India rum, tablespoonful of sugar molasses, and same of sweet oil, well simmered together. An excellent remedy.

DYSPEPSIA.

1. Beef bones, burnt and reduced to powder. Take a teaspoonful three times a day, mixed with molasses. This is highly recommended.

2. Or, fill a decanter half full of wild cherries, then fill it up with best old Jamaica spirits. Take half wineglass twice a day. Use no sugar. This has cured many.

EAR-ACHE.

1. Apply to the ear cotton wool, wet with sweet oil and paregoric.

2. Or, put into the ear the heart of a roasted onion.

3. In case of an abscess, use poultices of bread and milk, or of roasted onions. Renew them till the abscess breaks.

ERYSIPELAS.

1. Apply plats of raw cotton.

2 Or, take half an ounce of cream of tartar to a quart of cold water. Dose, half wineglassful every two hours, day after day. Keep the bowels open with Epsom salts.

FAINTING.

First loosen the patient's clothes, and let him have fresh air; sprinkle the face with cold water; apply a smelling bottle to the nose, and rub the body with hot drops.

FELON, OR WHITLOW.

. Soak the finger in a strong warm lye of ashes, for half an hour at a time, frequently.

2. Or, make use of poultices, in connection with weak lye.

FLATULENCY.

1. Take a tea made of the seeds of *anise, caraway* and *coriander*.

2. Or, take the essence of peppermint, with a few drops of paregoric.

GOUT.

1. Use the composition and pennyroyal freely.

2. Keep the leg and foot lightly bandaged, covered with soft wool, wet in sweet oil.

GRAVEL.

1. Drink lime-water frequently. Dose, one gill. Very good.

2. Or, drink warm gum Arabic tea, or strong coffee without sugar. Keep the bowels open.

3. Or, take a handful smartweed, make a tea of it, and add

one gill Holland gin. Take it all in twelve hours. One of the best of remedies.

HEAD-ACHE.

1. Drink freely of strong thoroughwort tea—very efficient.

2. Or, open the bowels by a dose or two of physic.

3. Or, if the stomach be foul, take an emetic.

HICCOUGHS.

1. Take a long draught of cold water, or a few swallows of vinegar.

2. Or, take thirty or forty drops of paregoric, and apply hops and wormwood, simmered in vinegar, to the stomach.

HEARTBURN.

1. Take a teaspoonful of carbonate of soda, dissolved in a half tumbler of sweetened water.

2. Or, take a dose of composition powders.

INDIGESTION.

Eat bread made of unbolted wheat; make daily use of the cold bath and flesh-brush: and exercise freely in the fresh air.

ITCH.

1. Make use of sulphur—it is an old but effectual remedy.

2. Or, take half pound of fresh butter, and teacupful of vinegar; simmer till it evaporates; add one nutmeg, grated, a tablespoonful of ground allspice; let it cool to the thickness of cream, and add one teaspoonful of sulphur. Anoint three days in succession, and it will effect an entire cure. It will need no change of garments.

JAUNDICE.

1. Take an emetic to cleanse the stomach, then use a bitter to regulate the bile and restore the digestive powers.

2. A long journey often effects a permanent cure.

INFLAMMATION OF THE KIDNEYS.

1. Rub small of the back with sweet oil, and drink freely of balm tea.

2. Or, apply cloths wrung out in hot vinegar ; bring down the inflammation by leeches.

LIVER COMPLAINT.

1. Make free use of composition powder, and wear a plaster on the side constantly.

2. Or, take a strong infusion of Virginia snake-root three times a day.

LOCKJAW.

1. When the lockjaw is apprehended from any scratch or wound, bathe the part freely with lye, or pearlash and water.

2. Or, bind a rind of pork on the wound.

3. Or, use a batter made of strong soft soap, mixed with pulverized chalk.

NIGHT SWEATS.

1. Drink freely of cold sage—said to be a certain remedy.

2. Or, take elixir of vitriol in a little sweetened water. Dose, from twenty to thirty drops.

PALPITATION OF THE HEART.

1. Take from ten to fifteen drops, three times a day, of the tincture of stramonium.

2. Or, take the tincture of gum guaiacum. Dose, a teaspoonful twice a day, in a little milk.

PALSY.

1. Keep the bowels open, and encourage perspiration by the use of hot medicine.

2. Or, apply mustard poultices to the feet, and rub the part affected briskly with a flannel dipped in hot drops.

PILES.

1. Make constant use of a syringe, with warm water and molasses; it will certainly effect a cure if persevered in.

2. For an ointment, make use of lard, sulphur and cream of tartar, simmered together.

PLEURISY.

1. Take a teaspoonful of pleurisy-root in powder, or a gill of the decoction, or infusion, several times a day; this is nearly a specific.

2. A full course of Thomsonian medicine, and bathing the side with hot drops, will effect a speedy cure.

SALT-RHEUM.

1. Use a wash made of one pound of plantain leaves, boiled in two quarts of beef brine and one quart of urine—boil one hour.

2. Cleanse the blood by a syrup made of elder bark, yellow dock root, sassafras and sarsaparilla.

RHEUMATISM.

1. To a handful of blue flag root add a pint of good spirits; let it stand a week. Dose, a spoonful three times a day, and increase by degrees to three tablespoonfuls a day. An Indian remedy.

2. Or, apply a poultice of hot potatoes—renew as often as it becomes cool or hard. Said to be a very excellent remedy.

RINGWORM.

1. Strong tobacco juice, used as a wash, is an infallible remedy.

2. The common mushroom catsup, rubbed upon the affected part, was never known to fail of effecting a cure.

SCROFULA.

1. A mixture of part brandy and one part salt, applied externally, is good; take also two tablespoonfuls of same morning and evening.

2. Or, bathe the swellings with a strong decoction of hemlock.

3. Or, bathe daily in sea-water, and take small drinks of the same.

SPRAINS.

1. Apply a poultice of wheat bran, or rye bran and vinegar.

2. Or, bind on bruised wormwood, wet with hot drops.

SCALDS AND BURNS.

1. Bathe the burn often with strong green tea.

2. Or, apply cotton wool to the part, wet with sweet oil.

3. Lard and soot make a very good ointment for burns. Keep the bowels open.

SCURVY.

Eat freely of vegetables and fresh meat, and gargle the throat often with cayenne pepper and vinegar.

SICKNESS AT STOMACH.

Drink peppermint tea, or hot drops.

SORE THROAT OR MOUTH.

1. Gargle the throat with a solution of one teaspoonful of cayenne, two teaspoonfuls fine salt, and a cup of water.

2. Or, take draught of pepper-sauce.

3. Or, chew white pond-lily root.

STRANGURY.

This may generally be relieved by using a teaspoonful of powdered gum Arabic in half a tumblerful of any mild drink.

TOOTH-ACHE.

1. Alum reduced to powder, two drachms; nitrous spirits of ether, seven drachms; mix, and apply a little to the tooth. This is a certain cure.

2. Or, put into the tooth a pill made of camphor and opium.

TUMORS.

Apply a poultice made of slippery elm and Indian meal, equal parts; mix with weak lye, and a little salt added.

ULCERS.

Apply a poultice made of cracker, wet with new rum. This is the most effectual of any poultice whatever, for *old ulcers* and putrid sores.

WOUNDS AND CUTS.

Do up a fresh cut in the blood : keep it wet with hot drops, and it will soon get well.

WARTS.

Apply caustic, or wash the wart with milk-weed.

WEAK NERVES.

Drink freely of scullcap tea. It is the very best and safest of remedies.

A LIST OF SIMPLES,

AND OF SUCH MEDICINAL PREPARATIONS AS EVERY FAMILY OUGHT TO KEEP ON HAND, READY FOR PRIVATE USE.

SENNA.—Dose, a tablespoonful of the leaves steeped for a child.

HOT DROPS.—Dose, tablespoonful for a child.

SWEET TINCTURE OF RHUBARB.—Dose, a tablespoonful for a child.

PENNYROYAL.—For colds.

RED RASPBERRY LEAVES.—For canker, dysentery, etc.

WHITE LILY ROOT.—For canker, etc.

SLIPPERY ELM.—For poultices and for a drink.

MULLIN LEAVES.—For poultices and fomentations.

WINE IPECAC.—Dose, to act as an emetic, fifteen drops, repeated every fifteen minutes till it operates; for an adult, a teaspoonful repeated as above.

SWEET OIL.

SYRUP SQUILLS.—Dose for child, half teaspoonful.

AVENS ROOT.—An astringent and tonic.

CASTOR OIL.—Dose, for an adult, a tablespoonful; for a child, teaspoonful.

CAMPHOR.—Dose, a teaspoonful.

COMPOSITION.—Dose, a teaspoonful.

CRANESBILL.—For canker.

PAREGORIC.—Dose for a child, five to twenty drops.

LOBELIA, OR BLOOD ROOT TINCTURE.—Dose, a teaspoonful for a child.

WORMWOOD —For bruises and worms.

SAGE.

THOROUGHWORT.	VALERIAN.
CATNIP.	BURDOCK LEAVES.
SPEARMINT.	HOARHOUND.
HORSE-RADISH LEAVES.	YARROW.

The doses of medicine recommended for an adult may be varied to the age of the patient, according to the following rule; Two-thirds of the dose for a person from fourteen to sixteen; one-half from seven to ten; one-third from four to six; one fourth, to one of three years old; and one-eighth to one of a year old.

In the recipes, or prescriptions, where it is not convenient to obtain all the articles specified, others of the same nature may be substituted.

LIQUID MEASURE.

A Pint   contains   Sixteen Ounces.
A Teacup   "   A Gill.
A Wineglass   "   Two Ounces.
A Tablespoonful "   Half an Ounce.
A Teaspoonful   "   Sixty Drops.
Four Teaspoonfuls are equal to one Tablespoonful.

DRY MEASURE.

A Tablespoonful contains Four Drachms, or Half an ounce.
A Teaspoon   " One Drachm.
A Teaspoon   " Sixty Grains.

SIGNS USED BY PHYSICIANS IN WRITING THEIR RECIPES.

lb. denotes a pound,
gr. a grain.
R. recipe.
ana, of each alike.
Coch., a spoonful,
P. Æ, equal quantities.
ss., half of anything.
iss., one and a half of any-thing.
q. s., sufficient quantity.
q. pl., much as you please.
O, a pint.
M, 60th part of fluid drachm.

j., one of anything.
ij., two of anything.
iij., three of anything.
iv., four of anything.
x., ten of anything.
xij., twelve of anything.
f., prefixed to *dr.* or *oz.* denotes fluid drachm or ounce.
gtt., a drop.
Pugillas, as much as can be held between the thumb and finger.

MEDICAL DICTIONARY OF TERMS.

ACRID, caustic, biting.
ATTERATIVE, establishing healthy functions.
ANODYNE, easing pain, quieting.

ANTI-BILIOUS, correcting the bile.

ANTI-LITHIC, preventing the formation of gravel or stone.

ANTI-SCORBUTIC, good against scurvy.

ANTI-SEPTIC, preventing mortification.

ANTI-SPASMODIC, relieving spasms.

APERIENT, opening, mildly laxative.

AROMATIC, spicy, fragrant.

ASTRINGENT, binding, contracting the fibres.

BALSAMIC, mild, healing.

CARMINATIVE, expelling wind.

CATHARTIC, purgative, cleansing the bowels.

DEMULCENT, mollifying, lubricating.

DEOBSTRUENT, resolving viscidity, correcting the secretions.

DIAPHORETIC, producing insensible perspiration.

DISCUTIENT, dissolving, discussing.

DIURETIC, increasing the discharge of urine.

EMETIC, causing vomiting.

EMOLLIENT, softening.

EPISPASTIC, blistering.

ERRHINE, producing discharge at the nostrils.

EXPECTORANT, producing expectoration.

HERPETIC, curing diseases of the skin.

NARCOTIC, producing stupor, causing sleep.

NERVINE, strengthening the nerves.

PECTORAL, relieving diseases of the chest and lungs.

REFRIGERANT, cooling.

RUBEFACIENT, producing heat and redness of the skin.

STIMULANT, exciting action.

STOMACHIC, producing action of the stomach.

STYPTIC, preventing bleeding.

SUDORIFIC, causing sweat.

TONIC, strengthening.

VERMIFUGE, expelling or destroying worms.

POULTICES

A good poultice may be made of crumbs of bread boiled with milk, or sweet oil, or spring water.

Brown sugar and soap make a good poultice, or salve, for a boil.

Four ounces of white lily roots, a pound of figs, and four ounces of meal or bean flour, boiled together with as much water as will cover them, make an excellent poultice for swellings and suppurating sores.

A good poultice for ordinary occasions may be made of bread boiled in milk.

For cancers and running sores, a grated carrot, boiled quite soft, makes a good poultice.

Salad leaves well boiled make a poultice that relieves acute pain.

A poultice of flax-seed, or chamomile flowers boiled with the tops of wormwood, make an excellent poultice for inflammations.

A *senapism*, or stimulating poultice, is made by using vinegar instead of water, and the addition of garlic, mustard, horse-radish, etc., to crumbs of bread, or to flour.

CASTOR OIL MADE PALATABLE.

Boil castor oil with twice its quantity of milk, and sweeten it with sugar. Let it cool. Children will not refuse it.

TO MAKE LEECHES TAKE HOLD.

To make leeches take hold on the spot required, take a piece of white paper, cut small holes in it where you wish them to bite, lay this over the place, and put the leeches on the paper. Not liking the paper, they will take hold of the skin where it appears through the hole.

THE TONGUE.

A white fur on the tongue attends simple fever and inflammation. Yellowness of the tongue attends a derangement of the liver, and is common to bilious and typhus fevers. A tongue vividly red on the tip and edges, or down the centre, or over the whole surface, attends inflammation of the mucous membrane of the stomach or bowels. A white velvety tongue attends mental disease. A tongue red at the lips, becoming brown, dry and glazed, attends typhus state.

SEA-SICKNESS.

Make some green tea, strong, with just as much sugar in it as will make it palatable, and bottle it up. When sickness begins to come on, take a cupful; and if that does not prevent the vomiting, let the stomach be completely emptied; take the same quantity, more or less, as the stomach is able to receive; repeat it two or three times, and a restoration will take place.

SECURITY AGAINST LIGHTNING.

Silk is the most useful covering for the body lightning cannot pass through a dry silk handkerchief, so decidedly a non-conductor is it. Hence, if worn next the skin, the air cannot absorb the electricity of the human body. Damp air is a conductor of electricity—dry air is a non-conductor; hence, a dry place is the safest retreat.

IMPORTANCE OF WELL VENTILATED APART-MENTS.

A man consumes or spoils more than one gallon of air in one minute; consequently, all closely confined places must be very unwholesome. Candles and lamps become dim in public assemblies, and this is an indication of the impurity of the air. The perspiration from animal bodies is exceedingly injurious in a confined space. Every room ought to be completely purified, by the opening of the door and windows at least once in the day. A close bed-room is also extremely unwholesome, neither ought the bed be surrounded with curtains.

The fire-place should never be stopped up by chimney boards; but in damp and very cold weather a fire is essential to health, care being taken that the room is not over-heated. Many dangerous colds are caught by those whose lungs are delicate, by changing the atmosphere of a warm and dry sitting-room, for that of a damp and cold bed-chamber.

THREE RULES FOR PRESERVING GOOD HEALTH

1st. Keep the feet warm. 2d. The head cool. 3d. The bowels sufficiently open by your diet.

CONSUMPTION.

This complaint is generally caused by some acute disorder not being removed, and the patient being run down by the fashionable practice, until nature makes a compromise with disease, and the house becomes divided against itself. There is a constant warfare kept up between the inward heat and cold, the flesh wastes away in consequence of not digesting the food, the canker becomes seated on the stomach and bowels, and then takes hold of the lungs. When they get into this situation, it is called a seated consumption, and is pronounced by the doctors to be incurable. I have had a great many cases of this kind, and have in all of them, where there was life enough left to build upon, been able to effect a cure by my system of practice. The most important thing is to raise the inward heat and get a perspiration, clear the system of canker, and restore the digestive powers, so that food will nourish the body, and keep up the heat on which life depends. This must be done by the regular course of medicine, as has been directed in all violent attacks of disease, and persevering in it till the cause is removed.

This complaint is called by the doctors a hectic fever, because they are subject to cold chills and hot flashes on the surface; but this is an error, for there is no fever about it; and this is the greatest difficulty; if there was, it would have a crisis, and nature would be able to drive out the cold and effect a cure. The only difficulty is to raise a fever, which must be done by such medicine as will raise and hold the inward heat, till nature has the complete command. When the patient is very weak and low, they will have what is called cold sweats ; the cause of this is not understood ; the water that collects on the skin does not come through the pores, but is attracted from the air in the room, which is warmer than the body and condenses on the surface. The same may be seen on the outside of a mug or tumbler on a hot day, when filled with cold water, which is from the same cause. It is of more importance to attend to the preventing of this complaint than to cure it. If people would make use of those means which I have recommended, and cure themselves of disease in its first stages, and avoid all poisonous drugs, there would never be a case of consumption or any other chronic disorder.

REMARK.—*Codfish Liver Oil*, is considered almost a specific for this formidable complaint. It will cure in eight cases out of ten. Its application to this disease was discovered a few years since in Germany ; and, so great has been its success, that its use is now sanctioned by the entire Faculty. It is no quack nostrum, but is simply what its name indicates. No consumptive person should be without it a single day, as it is almost certain to effect a cure if taken in season.

REMEDIES FOR POISONS.

It is very important to be familiar with this subject, because poisons are frequently taken by mistake for medicines, and are often so rapid in their effects as to produce death before aid can be called. The stomach pump is unquestionably the best expedient in such cases; but before a physician can be obtained the following antidotes may be used :

FOR CORROSIVE SUBLIMATE.

Give the white of an egg every two or three minutes, or copious draughts of linseed tea, or rice water, or even warm water, with emollient clysters, and warm fomentations to the belly.

FOR OIL OF VITRIOL, TARTARIC, OR PRUSSIC ACID, OR ANY OTHER ACIDS.

Give alkalies, as an ounce of magnesia, in a quart of warm water, a wineglassful every two minutes; soap suds, or chalk and water, will do, if magnesia is not at hand. Tickle the throat to produce vomiting, and drink freely of pearlash or lime-water.

FOR POTASH, OR OTHER ALKALIES.

Drink freely of vinegar, or lemon juice.

FOR ARSENIC.

In solution, drink pearlash water, or chalk and water. If arsenic in powder has been taken, give linseed tea, warm water, milk, water sweetened with sugar or honey, linseed, tickling the throat to promote vomiting.

FOR CANTHARIDES.

Give sweet oil, sugared water, or linseed tea; drink freely to promote vomiting.

FOR SUGAR OF LEAD.

Give Epsom salts, in large quantities, or water with some acid in it, or large draughts of warm water.

FOR OPIUM, LAUDANUM, HEMLOCK, AND OTHER VEGETABLE POISONS.

Drink freely of vinegar or lemon juice. If vomiting has

been occasioned by the poison, and the efforts are still continued, promote it by large draughts of warm water, or thin gruel.

FOR TARTAR EMETIC.

Give strong green tea, oak or willow bark, in large quantities, to dilute and decompose the poison.

In stings from bees or other insects, bathe with salt and vinegar, or sal-ammoniac and vinegar.

In case of poison from the bite of venomous reptiles, apply a poultice of tobacco and vinegar. A lobelia emetic has great effect in expelling the poison.

When poisoned by dogwood, ivy, or swamp sumac, dissolve a quarter of an ounce of copperas (sulphate of iron) in a pint of water, and bathe the part affected.

Where a large quantity of opium or laudanum has been taken, the patient is to be kept in constant motion, on his legs, or by shaking and moving his body, rubbing him at the same time with warm salt or other stimulating applications to rouse the system from torpor.

Olive or sweet oil, mixed with warm milk and water, and drank plentifully until it acts as an emetic, is an antidote to poisons in general.

BITE OF A RATTLESNAKE.

Half a wineglass of olive oil, taken inwardly, is said to be a certain cure for the bite of a rattlesnake and other poisonous reptiles. A little should also be applied to the wound. *Another remedy* is the following;—The roots and branches of plantain and hoarhound, bruised in a mortar, and the juice expressed; of which give one large spoonful as soon as possible. In an hour, if necessary, give another spoonful. Apply to the wound a leaf of tobacco, moistened in rum. This remedy was discovered by a negro, for which his freedom was purchased, and an annuity settled upon him by the general assembly of Carolina.

DROWNED PERSONS.

In attempting to recover persons apparently drowned, the

principal intention is *to restore the natural warmth.* This must be done by rubbing the body with warm cloths, and by warm bricks applied to the stomach and bowels, palms of the hands, and soles of the feet. Camphor, or some strong volatile spirits, must be applied to the nose and temples, and the spine of the back and pit of the stomach rubbed with warm brandy or other spirits. A strong person may blow his own breath into the patient's mouth, as hard as he can, holding his nostrils at the same time. When the lungs are inflated, stop blowing, and press the breast and belly so as to expel the air again. Let the operation be repeated for some time. If the lungs cannot be inflated in this manner, let it be tried by blowing through one of the nostrils, keeping the other closed. To stimulate the intestines, clysters of warm water, with a little salt, and some wine or spirits, must be used. And as soon as it can be made ready, the patient should be put into a warm bath. Until the person shows signs of life, and can swallow, it would be dangerous to pour liquors into his mouth. His lips and tongue may be wet with a feather dipped in some strong spirits, and as soon as the power of swallowing is recovered, a little warm wine or cordial should now and then be given. Assistance must not be discontinued as soon as the patient gives signs of life, as persons have sometimes expired after the first appearances of recovery.

TO PURIFY THE ATMOSPHERE OF A SICK ROOM.

Keep always on the shelf of the washing-stand, or on the mantel-piece or table, or in a corner of the floor, a saucer or small bread pan, or a shallow mug, filled with a solution of chloride of lime in cold water, stirring it up frequently. The proportion may be about a table-spoonful of the powder to half a pint of water. Renew it every two or three days. If the room is large, place in it more than one vessel of the chloride of lime. In stirring it, any unpleasant odor will be immediately dispelled.

On going to sea it is well to take with you one or more quart bottles of this solution, to sprinkle occasionally about your state-room.

TO APPLY AN EYE STONE.

Eye stones are frequently used to extract matter, railroad sparks, and other extraneous substances from the eye. They are to be procured from the apothecaries. They cost but two or three cents apiece, and it is well to get several, that if one does not succeed you may try another. To give an eye-stone activity, lay it for about five minutes in a saucer of vinegar and water, and if it is a good one, it will soon begin to move or swim round in the liquid. Then wipe it dry, and let it be inserted under the eyelid, binding the eye closely with a handkerchief. The eye-stone will make the circuit of the eye, and take out the mote, which, when the eye stone finally drops out, it will bring with it.

OF DEAFNESS.

When deafness is occasioned by an accumulation or hardness of the wax, the ears should be syringed every morning with warm soap and water, till it be removed; and a little wool or cotton worn in them, moistened with two or three drops of camphorated oil of almonds. When it arises from decay of the nerve, electric sparks, a blister behind the ear, and the use of sneezing powder, are the most powerful remedies. When ulceration is the cause, which is known by a discharge of matter, the ulcer should be healed as soon as possible, by syringing the ear every morning and evening with the following lotion, made a little warm:

Take of tincture of myrrh, one drachm; Egyptian honey two drachms; pure water, eight ounces. Mix.

This diseased state of the ear, in which the tympanum is often more or less destroyed, frequently follows the scarlet fever, and is generally very difficult to cure; in consequence of a portion of the tympanum being destroyed, or the surrounding bone of the skull being carious.

A temporary deafness is often produced by slight cold, particularly in children, which frequently goes away in a day or two after the use of a little aperient and sudorific medicine, and avoiding the occasional cause.

Deafness is frequently the consequence of a deficiency of wax, when a liniment that will at the same time soften and gently stimulate the part, will afford considerable relief, if not entirely remove the cause—as the following :

Take of oil of turpentine, two drachms ; oil of almonds, six drachms. Mix. Two or three drops to be instilled into the ear, or applied by means of lamb's wool.

THE EYE—HOW TO PRESERVE THE SIGHT— HOW TO RUIN IT, ETC.

The preservation of the sight is an object of so much importance to every individual, whatever may be his profession or rank in society, that we have thought a few hints in relation to this subject might be productive of beneficial effects.

The blessing of good eye-sight is invaluable. The pleasure of beholding the light of the sun, of walking and riding abroad, guided by the light of the eye, of reading and of seeing one's family and friends, is no small portion of the joy of life ; and yet many there are who greatly abuse their eyes. Persons should learn not only not to abuse their sight, but to use it rightly, and take proper measures to preserve it.

1st. It is well known to the physician that nothing more certainly impairs the sense of vision than debauchery and excess of every kind. The individual, therefore, who would preserve his sight unimpaired, must avoid carefully every species of intemperance. This is an all-important rule, a neglect of which will render every other of but little avail.

2d. A long continuance in absolute darkness, or frequent and protracted exposure to a blaze of light, equally injures the sense of vision.

Persons who live almost constantly in dark caverns or chambers, workers in mines, and prisoners who have been long confined in gloomy dungeons, become incapable of seeing objects distinctly excepting in a deep shade, or in the dusk of the evening. While on the other hand, in various parts of the world, in which the light is constantly reflected from a soil of dazzling whiteness, or from mountains and plains covered with almost perpetual snow the sight of the inhabitants is perfect only in broad daylight, or at noon.

3d. Those, also, who are much exposed to *bright fires*, as blacksmiths, glassmen, forgers, and others engaged in similar employments, are considered by the best authorities as most subjct to loss of sight by cataract.

All brilliantly illuminated apartments have a similar prejudicial effect upon the eyes, though, undoubtedly, not to the same extent. As a general rule, therefore, the eye should never be permitted to dwell on brilliant or glaring objects for any length of time. Hence in our apartments only a moderate degree of light should be admitted; and it would be of considerable advantage, particularly to those whose eyes are already weak, if in place of a pure white or deep red color for the walls, curtains, and other furniture of our rooms, some shade of green were to be adopted.

4th. Reading or writing in the dusk of the evening, or by candlelight, is highly prejudicial. The frivolous attention to a quarter of an hour at the decline of day, has deprived numbers of the perfect and comfortable use of their eyes for many years; the mischief is effected imperceptibly, the consequence is often irreparable.

5th. There is nothing which preserves the sight longer than always using, in reading, writing, sewing, and every other occupation in which the eyes are constantly exercised, that moderate degree of light which is best suited to them; too little strains them, too great a quantity dazzles and confounds them. The eyes are less affected, however, by a deficiency of light than by the excess of it. The former seldom does much, if any, harm, unless the eyes are strained by efforts to view objects to which the degree of light is inadequate; but too great a quantity has, by its own power, destroyed the sight.

6th. The long-sighted should accustom themselves to read with rather less light, and with the book somewhat nearer to the eye than they ordinarily desire; while those that are short-sighted should, on the contrary, use themselves to read with the book as far off as possible. By these means both may improve and strengthen their vision, whereas a contrary course will increase its natural imperfections.

7th. Bathing the eyes daily in cold or tepid water tends to preserve the integrity of their functions; provided, however, the individual does not immediately after such bathing enter a warm room, or unnecessarily exert his sight.

8th. One of the greatest abuses of the eye now prevalent is reading in the cars while they are going upon the railroad. This practice, we are sensible, has been injurious to our own eyes. With a bundle of exchange papers in our pocket, we have frequently felt unwilling to lose so much time as we have been liable to, while passing from the city some eighteen or twenty miles in the country, as has lately been our custom. Hence, to save time, we have resorted to reading, until we have perceived its ill effects. The unsteadiness of the cars, the different degrees of light through which the reader is so suddenly carried, and the constant effort to see, all tend to affect the eye unfavorably. We advise all to avoid reading while riding.

VACCINATION.

As a preventive of the *small-pox*, the vaccine inoculation is now universally practised. This generally produces a very mild and safe form of disease, which continues a few days and then subsides, and leaves the patient ever after free from the fear of small-pox.

RULES FOR THE PRESERVATION OF HEALTH.

1. Avoid as much as possible living near a graveyard in

the warm, damp seasons, they often prove sources of putrid fever.

2. Keep the feet from wet, and the head well defended when in bed.

3. Avoid too plentiful meals.

4. Go not abroad without breakfast.

5. Shun the night air as you would the plague.

6. Let your houses be kept from damps by warm fires.

7. Tender people should have those who lie with them, or are much about them, sound, sweet, and healthy.

8. Nothing conduces more to health than abstinence and plain food, with due labor.

9. For studious persons, about eight ounces of animal food, and twelve of vegetable, in twenty-four hours is sufficient.

10. Water is the wholesomest of all drinks; quickens the appetite, and strengthens the digestion most.

11. Coffee and tea are extremely hurtful to persons who have weak nerves.

12. A due degree of *exercise* is indispensably necessary to health and long life.

13. Walking is the best exercise for those who are able to bear it; riding for those who are not. The open air, when the weather is fair, contributes much to the benefit of exercise.

14. We may strengthen any weak part of the body by constant exercise. Thus the lungs may be strengthened by loud speaking, or walking up an easy ascent.

15. The studious ought to have stated times for exercise, at least two or three hours a day.

16. The fewer clothes any one uses, by day or night, the hardier he will be.

17. The flesh-brush is a most useful exercise, especially to strengthen any part that is weak.

18. Cold bathing is of great advantage to health; it prevents abundance of diseases; it promotes perspiration, helps

the circulation of the blood, and prevents the danger of catching cold.

19. Costiveness cannot long consist with good health ; therefore care should be taken to remove it at the beginning.

20. All violent and sudden passions dispose to, or actually throw people into, acute diseases.

21. The slow and lasting passions, such as grief and hopeless love, bring on chronical diseases.

By observing these few and simple rules, better health may be expected than from the use of the most powerful medicines.

CAUTION IN VISITING SICK ROOMS.

Never enter into a sick room if you are in a violent perspiration (if circumstances require your continuance there for any time), for the moment your body becomes cold, it is in a state likely to absorb the infection, and give you the disease. Nor visit a sick person, especially if the complaint be of a contagious nature, with an empty stomach, as this disposes the system more readily to receive the contagion. In attending a sick person, place yourself where the air passes from the door or window to the bed of the diseased, not betwixt the diseased person and any fire that is in the room, as the heat of the fire will draw the infectious vapor in that direction, and you would run much danger from breathing in it.

MANAGEMENT OF THE SICK ROOM.

RULES.

1. The sick should always be addressed in a gentle voice and conversed with in the most cheerful manner. Their attendants should express sympathy for their sufferings, but endeavor to inspire them with courage and resignation in bearing them.

2. All vials and papers of powders should be carefully labeled, as one medicine may be mistaken for another, and

sometimes poison be administered by neglect of this caution.

3. All unpleasant news should be entirely withheld from, or very *carefully* communicated to, a person who is ill.

4. The chamber should be kept in perfect order, and free from noise and confusion.

5. If the eyes of the patient are not weak, the room should not be darkened, as the rays of the sun, especially of the morning sun, have a vivifying and renovating influence.

6. Wash every article the instant it is used, and do not keep the tables and mantel-piece filled with vials, pill-boxes, etc., for if they are within sight of the patient this practice will annoy him.

7. The room should be well supplied with water, towels, napkins, a slop-pail, saucepans, a couple of bowls and tumblers, several cups, saucers, and wineglasses, several large and small spoons.

8. Pure air contributes not only to the preservation, but to the restoration of health. A sick chamber should be ventilated at least twice a day. The process of ventilation should be as short as possible ; the patient must be well covered, and even his head kept beneath the bed-clothes, if he experiences the slightest sensation of chilliness.

9. The bed-clothing should be changed twice a week, *at least ;* the bed must be made every day, and, if the patient can bear it, twice a day. The bed-clothes should be carried into another room and aired before they are replaced upon the bed.

10. The person of the patient should be kept perfectly clean, and his garments frequently changed. Daily ablutions of the whole person with warm water are very serviceable. The mouth should also be often rinsed.

11. Describe to the physician the patient's minutest symptoms—use no deception in communicating either his mental or his bodily state. Pay strict attention to the physician's directions ; if they are numerous, *note* them down, and obey them *strictly.*

12. The person who has charge of the sick should possess a quiet and even temper, be naturally cheerful, very patient, and disposed to bear with most unreasonable fretfulness and irrascibility.

13. Do not reprove or attempt to argue with a person who is very ill; he can hardly be considered a responsible being, for the mind is not generally in a healthy state when the body is disordered.

WIND INSTRUMENTS.

All these are more or less hurtful to the lungs, which they weaken by introducing too much air, and keeping that organ too long in a state of distension. On this account persons of weak lungs, who play much on the flute, hautboy, or French horn, are frequently afflicted with spitting of blood, cough, shortness of breath, and pulmonary consumption. Blowing these instruments likewise checks the circulation of the blood through the lungs, accumulates it towards the head and disposes such persons to apoplexy.

THE TEETH.

An object very subservient to health, and which merits due attention, is the preservation of the teeth; the care of which, considering their importance in preparing the food for digestion, is, in general, far from being sufficiently culti-vated. Very few persons, comparatively, wash their mouths in the morning, which ought always to be done. Indeed, this ought to be practised at the conclusion of every meal, where either animal food or vegetables be eaten; for the for-mer is apt to leave behind it a rancid acrimony, and the lat-ter an acidity, both of them hurtful to the teeth. Washing the mouth frequently with cold water is not only serviceable in keeping the teeth clean, but in strengthening the gums, the firm adhesion of which to the teeth is of great impor-tance in preserving them sound and secure.

USE OF SPECTACLES.

From whatever cause the decay of sight arises, an attentive consideration of the following rules will enable any one to judge for himself, when his eyesight may be assisted or preserved by the use of proper glasses.

1. When we are obliged to remove small objects to a considerable distance from the eye, in order to see them distinctly.

2. If we find it necessary to get more light than formerly, as, for instance, to place the candle between the eye and the object.

3 If, on looking at, and attentively considering a near object, it fatigues the eye and becomes confused, or if it appears to have a kind of dimness or mist before it.

4. When small printed letters are seen to run into each other, and hence, by looking steadfastly on them, appear double or treble.

5. If the eyes are so fatigued by a little exercise, that we are obliged to shut them from time to time, so as to relieve them by looking at different objects.

When all these circumstances concur, or any of them separately takes place, it will be necessary to seek assistance from glasses, which will ease the eyes, and in some degree check their tendency to become worse ; whereas, if they be not assisted in time, the weakness will be considerably increased, and the eyes be impaired by the efforts they are compelled to exert.

AIR.

Nothing is more pernicious than the air of a place where a numerous body of people are collected together within doors ; especially if to the breath of the crowd there be added the vapors of a multitude of candles, and the consumption of the vital air by fires in proportion. Hence it happens, that persons of a delicate constitution are liable to become sick or faint in a place of this kind. These ought to avoid, as much as possible, the air of great towns; which is peculiarly hurtful to the asthmatic and consumptive, as it is likewise to hysteric women and men of weak nerves. Where such people cannot always live without the verge of great towns, they ought, at least, to go out as often as they can into the open air, and, if possible, pass the night in the wholesome situation of the suburbs.

VENTILATION OF HOUSES.

The great attention paid to making houses close and warm, though apparently well adapted to the comfort of the inhabitants, is by no means favorable to the health, unless care be taken every day to admit fresh air by the windows. Sometimes it may be proper to make use of what is called pumping the room, or moving the door backward and forward for some minutes together. The practice of making the beds early in the day, however it may suit convenience or delicacy, is doubtless improper. It would be much better to turn them down, and expose them to the influence of the air admitted by the windows.

For many persons to sleep in one room, as in the ward of a hospital, is very hurtful to health; and it is scarcely a less injurious custom, though often practised by those who have splendid houses, for two or more to sleep in a small apartment, especially if it be very close.

RIDING AND WALKING

For preserving health, there is no kind of exercise more proper than walking, as it gives the most general action to the muscles of the body; but, for valetudinarians, riding on horseback is preferable. It is almost incredible how much the constitution may be strengthened by this exercise, when continued for a considerable time.

EXERCISE AFTER MEALS.

Exercise is hurtful immediately after meals, particularly to those of nervous and irritable constitutions, who are thence liable to heartburn, eructations, and vomiting. Indeed, the instinct of the inferior animals confirms the propriety of this rule; for they are all inclined to indulge themselves in rest after food. Exercise should be delayed till digestion is performed, which generally requires three or four hours after eating a full meal.

READING ALOUD.

This is a species of exercise much recommended by the ancient physicians; and to this may be joined that of speaking. They are both of great advantage to those who have not sufficient leisure or opportunities for other kinds of exercise. To speak very loud, however, or exercise the voice immediately after meals, is hurtful to the lungs, as well as to the organs of digestion.

DISEASES OF INFANTS AND CHILDREN.

INTRODUCTION.

It requires much attention and experience to treat successfully the diseases of infants and children. Yet the treatment of infantile diseases is simple and tolerably certain; the careful observation of a judicious mother will generally suggest those remedies best adapted to the purpose.

The following chapter, however, will be found very valuable, and is such as every family should possess. The remedies proposed are simple and perfectly safe, and, if followed out, will generally prove effective.

GENERAL RULES.

When children first discover symptoms of disease, it may be known by their being more fretful and troublesome. This is evidence of a disordered stomach, which will continue to grow worse unless relief is given. The first thing to be done is to keep them warm, and use every means to cause perspiration. Give an emetic to clear the stomach—say a little tincture of ipecac, or lobelia. If there be great heat and dryness of the skin, wash the body all over with pearlash; mix three quarters of an ounce to three gills of warm water.

This will open the pores and reduce the heat. Let the child have a plenty of warm drink. After the emetic has operated, give a dose of castor oil. In many cases the oil may be given instead of the emetic. This course will very rarely fail to remove diseases and invigorate the health, without doing any injury to the constitution.

ACIDITY, OR SOUR STOMACH

Magnesia, given in food, purges, and at the same time corrects, the acidity, and thus carries off the cause. Where there is griping, rub a little brandy or any spirit on the bowels warm before the fire. If anything be given internally, let it be a little peppermint, anise, checkerberry, and the like.

APHTHÆ, OR THRUSH.

These are little whitish ulcers affecting the mouth, tongue, throat, and stomach. It is difficult to apply remedies in this disease to young children. The nurse may rub the child's mouth with a little borax and honey, to which a little burnt alum may be added sometimes, keeping the bowels open with magnesia.

CHOLERA INFANTUM.

This disease prevails during the summer, and attacks children from a week after birth till two or three years old. It is attended with vomiting, purging of green or yellow matter, of slime, or of blood; attended with pain, swelling of the belly, and heat of the skin, growing worse toward evening. In this disease, the stomach and bowels must be evacuated, and afterward give charcoal and magnesia, or the latter alone. When there is much irritation, injections of flaxseed tea, with a little laudanum, will give ease. Fomentations to the bowels and abdomen are useful. The removal of children to the country, abstaining from fruit, the use of flannel, and the cold bath, are means prescribed for prevention.

CROUP.

As this is a desperate disease, and one which, if neglected, will surely result in death, active measures should be immediately pursued. Let no time be lost in giving an emetic ; immerse the feet in warm water, and put a poultice of yellow snuff, mixed with goose oil, upon the stomach—sweet oil will answer. Apply a number of thicknesses of flannel, wet it in hot water, over the windpipe, as hot as it can be borne. Change as often as it cools. Place onion poultices upon the feet when taken from the water. This course, if persevered in, will cure in ninety-nine cases out of a hundred.

CONVULSIONS, OR FITS.

These generally proceed from overloading the stomach and bowels with crude, indigestible food. Sometimes they precede an eruption, as chicken-pox, measles, etc,, and from cutting teeth or tight clothing. If costive, give the child a clyster, afterwards a gentle vomit, and keep the body open by small doses of magnesia or rhubarb, and give a dose occasionally of some warming preparation, as peppermint, or anise-seeds, steeped and sweetened. If fits proceed from the pain of teething, a little paragoric may be administered, or a tea of valerian, or the skullcap herb.

ERUPTIONS, OR HUMORS.

In eruptive complaints, children should be guarded against taking cold. Keep the bowels open with castor oil or magnesia. Every measure should be used to keep the eruptions out upon the skin ; for this purpose, keep the child warm, and give it saffron tea.

GALLING AND EXCORIATION.

Wash the parts frequently with cold water, and sprinkle on some absorbent powder, as burnt hartshorn, chalk, or flesh powder. Washing the parts with water in which a little white vitriol has been dissolved, heals the sores very quick.

CHICKEN-POX.

Let the patient be confined to the bed, kept cool, and take a dose of salts. A little saffron tea may be given. This will generally remove the symptoms.

HICCOUGHS.

A little powder of prepared chalk and rhubarb.

DIARRHŒA AND DYSENTERY.

It may be remarked that, in childhood, the bowels are naturally loose. Then three or four stools a day are natural; in middle age, one; in old people, fewer. Allowances must be made for these differences.

Diarrhœa in infants and children is usually brought out either by too much, or an unsuitable kind of food. To effect a cure, it will be necessary to regulate the diet, and give a dose of rhubarb or magnesia, followed by a little prepared chalk,

MUMPS.

This disease chiefly attacks children, both in summer and in winter, and is supposed to be contagious. Those who have the disorder should be kept still and quiet. A purgative of Epsom salts, or cream of tartar, warm fomentations, and confinement to the house, are all that appears necessary to a cure.

NETTLE RASH.

Let the patient drink saffron tea, and keep the bowels open with Epsom salts—use a light diet. This will remove it.

SNUFFLES.

The bowels must be kept open, so as to remove the matter falling into them from the throat. This may be done by remedies prescribed in *looseness.* Besides purging, it may be necessary to foment the nose, or to apply the volatile. liniment.

TEETHING.

Use castor oil to keep the bowels open, and feed with balm tea. When the pain is severe, relieve the little sufferer by a few drops of paragoric. A pitch plaster should be kept constantly between the shoulders, and renewed once in two weeks. Rub the gums with honey three or four times a day. Let the child have pure air, and wash it every day with cold water.

VOMITING.

When occasioned by too much food, promote the evacuation by an occasional teaspoonful of lobelia tincture. When the food is of too acrid or irritating quality, it must be changed to that of a milder nature. Where this cannot be done, a little magnesia, soda, lime-water, or weak pearlash-water, may be given, to neutralize the acidity.

WHOOPING COUGH.

The principal danger to be guarded against in this complaint is an inflammation of the lungs. It will be proper, therefore, to give slight emetics frequently, of wine of ipecac, or tincture of lobelia, to keep the lungs free. Let the diet be light, and easy of digestion, and the drink pennyroyal, or life everlasting, steeped and sweetened with honey or molasses. Keep the bowels open with rhubarb tincture—a teaspoonful may be given to an infant twice a day, as it may need. Let the feet be rubbed, two or three times a day, with an ointment made by beating an onion, and mixing it with an equal portion of hog's lard. Apply a strengthening plaster between the shoulders. In pleasant weather, let the child have fresh air.

WORMS.

Let the patient fast a day, and then take a dose of pink, followed by a portion of senna. Strong salt-water may be given, or powdered sage and molasses; a mixture of milk and honey is also very good. Above all, let the child have plenty of exercise and free air.

MEASLES.

The principal point in this disorder is to keep out the eruption upon the surface of the body. Let the patient immerse his feet in warm water two or three times a day, and drink plentifully of thoroughwort tea, taking care to be well wrapped in a comforter. so as to produce a copious sweat. Saffron is very valuable; let this and thoroughwort be the only drink. Mustard poultices applied to the feet are very useful. Let the bowels be kept gently open with rhubarb.

WIND AND COLIC.

Flatulency often so prevails as to occasion severe griping pains, perfectly obvious by the infant's screaming, crying, and drawing its knees up.

In such cases, it will be necessary to evacuate the bowels by some gentle laxative—castor oil is best. Where the pains are very severe, it will be best to give a dose of paregoric, and apply a bag of hot brand or chamomile flowers to the bowels.

Children that are partly brought up with the spoon, and who are subject to wind, should always have a few caraway-seeds boiled up with their food.

RULES FOR THE MANAGEMENT OF INFANTS AND CHILDREN.

1. An infant from two to four months old, requires to be nursed about once in three hours.

2. After six months, more solid food may be given.

3. Sweetmeats and confectionery should be given very sparingly to young children.

4. Allow the child to sleep freely without disturbance.

5. Dress the child loosely, and use strings instead of pins.

6. Always keep the child clean and neat.

7. Children should always be vaccinated from six weeks to two months after birth.

8. Never swing or jerk children by the arms, as much mischief is often the result.

9. No child should be kept long in study or other pursuits at a time.

10. Never give a child that for which it cries.

11. Never promise to give when the child is done crying.

12. When children are the most violent, the mother should be the most cool and collected.

ROOTS AND HERBS.

"There are herbs to cure all diseases, though not everywhere known."—DR. RAY.

LIST OF THE MOST COMMON ROOTS AND HERBS, WITH THEIR MEDICINAL PRO- PERTIES POINTED OUT.

COLLECTING AND CURING HERBS, BARKS AND ROOTS.

Herbs that are intended for teas or decoctions should be collected while in blossom, or a little after, on a fair dry day, when the dew is off, and spread thin in the shade, or ex- posed to the sun ;—the former, however, is preferable, as by it they retain their natural hue.   Herbs that are wanted for distilling, should be cut when the seeds are ripe, at which time they yield the most oil.

Barks from the bodies of trees should be peeled in the latter period of their running, which is commonly in July, as they are much thicker and stronger than when they first begin to run.   They may be dried in the shade, or by the sun.   The rough, outward bark, or ross, should be taken off when peeled. *Barks of roots* should be collected early in the spring, or late in the fall, while the sap is in the root, and cured in the same manner.

Roots should be collected in the spring, before the tops begin to shoot forth, or in the autumn, after they are decayed. Those that are large and fleshy should be cut into strips or slices, and strung ; after which they may be exposed to a moderate heat, so that they may dry gradually.

After the *barks*, *roots* and *herbs* are thorougly dried, they should be kept close from the air ; also, when pulverized, particularly those that possess an aromatic quality.

ANGELICA, seeds and roots, good for wind.

AVENS ROOT, astringent and strengthening.

ALDER.—This is an astringent, useful in bleeding at the lungs, or as a wash for ulcers.

BAYBERRY ROOT, astringent, in tea, good for canker, in poultices, to cleanse sores, and makes a good catarrh snuff, finely pulverized.

BLACK BIRCH removes obstructions, good for gravel, made into a tea.

BLACK SNAKE ROOT, or BLACK COHUSH ROOT, good to remove obstructions, taken hot at bedtime.

BUGLE HERB, for bleeding at the stomach and lungs.

BURDOCK SEEDS, steeped, will cleanse the blood, and are good for jaundice.

BLACKBERRY.—This is astringent ;—very valuable in the dysentery.

BLUEFLAG, useful in fevers, or to expel humors from the system. Dose, half teaspoonful three times a day.

CATNIP, good for hysterics, worms and restlessness.

CELANDINE, good for jaundice ; the root, simmered in lard, is good to anoint for the piles.

CLIVERS, OR GOOSE GRASS, good in affections of the kidneys or bladder.

COMFREY, made into a syrup, is good for internal soreness and spitting of blood.

DANDELION ROOT promotes urine and cures liver complaints.

ELDER BARD and *Berries* promote the water and perspiration. Good in dropsy.

ELECAMPANE ROOT, good in powder, with honey or molasses, for a cough.

GARGET ROOT, made into an ointment or poultice, good for sores, cancers, and piles.

GOOSEBERRY BUSH LEAVES, steeped and drank, good for gravel complaints.

GOLDEN THREAD.—This is very useful in bitters: simmered in lard, it makes a good ointment for sore lips, hands, etc.

GOLDEN SEAL.—This corrects the bile, restores the organs of digestion, and promotes a discharge of urine.

HYSSOP makes a good gargle in sore throat, and is good for a cough.

HOPS, in poultice or ointment, eases the pain of cancers and sores.

HARDHACK, useful in diarrhœa and dysentery.

HOARHOUND.—This is valuable, combined with thoroughwort, for coughs, colds, and all lung complaints.

INDIAN TURNIP, the fresh root, simmered in lard, is good for scald-head.

JACOB'S LADDER makes an excellent ointment, simmered iu cream, for sore breast.

LIFE EVERLASTING.—This is the most efficacious of all herbs, in breaking up a long-standing cough, drank in form of tea, and sweetened with molasses.

MOUNTAIN CRANBERY, good in bleeding at the lungs.

MAIDENHAIR, made into syrup, good for coughs and influenza.

MOTHERWORT, the herb or root, procures sleep; allays pain and spasms.

MULLEIN makes a good injection, and simmered in lard, cures the piles, outwardly applied.

NETTLE LEAVES excites the skin, and is therefore good for palsy. A decoction of them is good for bloody urine, and is a powerful styptic.

OAK BARK (the white oak), is tonic and astringent, good to brace and strengthen.

PEACH LEAVES, steeped, will carry off worms, drank as tea.

PIPSISSEWA, or prince's pie, made into tea, is good for rheumatism and scrofula.

PEPPERMINT, valuable for the colic ; to prevent sickness at the stomach, etc.

PLANTAIN, good combined with lard, for the salt-rheum ; its juice will cure the bite of snakes.

PENNYROYAL.—This is a stimulant ; it should always be given to assist the operation of the lobelia emetic.

POPLAR BARK.—This is a tonic useful in bitters.

QUEEN OF TAE MEADOW, or Meadow Sweet ; the root is good for diseases of the kidneys, and obstructions, being a powerful diuretic.

RED ROSE WILOW is a fine tonic and astringent. One pound of the bark, boiled to three quarts, and infused in three pints of port wine, adding four ounces of loaf sugar, makes a good medicine to brace up weakly constitutions, taking a teacupful three times a day.

SAGE TEA, with a little lemon juice added, is a good drink in fevers.

SKULLCAP HERB, made into a tea, allays nervousness and excitement.

SENNA is good in compound laxatives and cathartics.

SHEPHERD'S PURSE eases pain, applied as a poultice, and is a good application for the erysipelas.

SKUNK CABBAGE, the root and seeds are good in asthma, coughs, etc.

SLIPPERY ELM, a good drink in sore throat, dysentery and is the best article known to poultice humors and sores.

SUMACH BERRIES makes a good gargle in sore throat; the bark of the root is good made into an ointment for burns, and into poultices for ulcers.

SWAMP OR TAG ALDER purifies the blood, made into a beer or a decoction.

SAFFRON makes a valuable tea for children afflicted with the measles, chicken-pox, and all eruptive diseases.

SASSAFRAS, steeped in water, is an excellent wash for all kinds of humors.

TAMARAC—the bark is good for bitters in jaundice and liver complaint.

TANSY is good in stranguary, and obstructions of the kidneys.

THOROUGHWORT, drank warm, will vomit, but when drank cold acts as a tonic. It is good cold for indigestion of old people.

THYME is a good tonic and stomachic; strengthens the lungs, relieves shortness of breath, and expels wind from the stomach.

UNICORN ROOT is a powerful strengthener, taking a half teaspoonful in powder, in a gill of warm water, three times a day.

VALEVAIN is good in all nervous affections, a teaspoonful taken twice or thrice a day in water, or peppermint tea.

VERNAIE is good in tea for colds and obstructions, and to expel worms.

WHITE POPLAR BARK makes an excellent bitter for weakness.

WITCH HAZEL bark and leaves, steeped and drank, is good for bowel complaints, bleeding at the lungs and stomach. In a poultice or wash they are good in removing inflammation of the eyes, and in painful tumors.

WILD PARSLEY seeds are a warm and powerful diuretic.

WINTERGREEN tea promotes milk in the breasts, relieves obstructions, and restores the strength after dysentery, etc.

WORMWOOD is good in poultices applied to bruises, and the oil or tea destroys worms.

WHITE LILY ROOT, excellent in poultices, to cleanse sores, and to discuss humors.

YELLOW DOCK.—This is physical and bracing ; valuable in the piles ; it will purify the blood, and expel bad humors from the system.

YARROW.—This is useful in blood-spitting, dysentery, piles, etc.

DECOCTIONS, INFUSIONS AND SYRUPS.

The difference between *decoctions* and *infusions* consists only in the mode of extracting the qualities of various substances, by the use of water more or less heated.

DECOCTIONS are made with boiling water, over a heat which produces evaporation. In this way, substances are decomposed while their medicinal properties are extracted, and their volatile or aromatic virtues are dissipated. By this process, the peculiar properties of many plants may be wasted, and the preparation rendered less efficacious than is made by infusion.

INFUSIONS, OR TEAS, are made by pouring water, either hot or cold, upon the substance after being bruised, and steeping it a proper time in a covered vessel, before it be poured or strained off for use. When any articles possessing volatile qualities are to be used in syrups or decoctions, they should be added when the boiling of the other articles is nearly finished.

SYRUPS differ from *decoctions* only in the addition of sweetening and spirits, by which they become more palatable, and will keep longer without fermentation.

It should be recollected that the efficacy of medicine depends much on its freshness and purity ; and that any alteration made by fermentation or freezing renders them not only useless, but very hurtful. The water used in preparing medicine should be soft and pure. Snow-water is purest, and much to be preferred. Next to this is distilled or rain-water; and lastly, spring water, when no better can be had.

SYRUPS are generally prepared in earthern vessels, covered with a paste or crust, and baked in an oven. The quantity of spirits added may usually be about one-fourth, or one-third, of the whole quantity, when prepared, and the sweetening should be sufficient to render it palatable.

HINTS CONDUCIVE TO HEALTH.

TOBACCO—SNUFFING, SMOKING AND CHEWING.

MEDICALLY speaking, are all abominably unwholesome. They are delightful relaxations. Personally speaking (for I have been a snuffer and a smoker), I can bear witness to the great comfort and satisfaction I have derived from them. A cigar, during an evening stroll, is highly agreeable and companionable, but it is habit only which renders it necessary. It is pleasant, I admit, (and ladies do likewise), to catch the whiff of a fine Havana on a frosty night, on an out-door walk. Nor do I object entering a bachelor's crib, where only real tobacco smoking is going on—but a five minutes' stay therein is enough. To those whom smoking causes to spit, it is productive of great depression and considerable nervous irritability; to those who say they swallow their saliva, it is equally pernicious ; to those who are insensible to secretion, it acts locally, and its influence is conveyed by the nervous extremities to the brain. It would appear ill-natured and cynical to forbid a solitary cigar; but in this page I have only to do with its salutariness—I cannot speak in its favor. "I have never suffered from it," may say some one. Well and good ; I do not forbid you taking one, but it surely cannot be wholesome for those who do. Besides, what is agreeable it is very difficult to believe can be hurtful. Nevertheless it may be so ; and smoking, in the majority of instances, I am convinced is so. What is the property of tobacco ?—sedative, stupefying, creative of vomiting, and if swallowed in the form of infusion, poisoning.

Let any man ask himself after spitting and puffing, if he feels better for it ; the reply generally is, " Oh, it is so sooth-ing, it gives rise to such agreeable thoughts—it carries the mind back to the past—it makes a man comfortable even in his troubles. How happy every one appears with a cigar or a pipe in his mouth, from the lord to the basket-woman." A great deal of this may be true, but, on the other hand, the great smoker is generally shaky and nervous, and, like the drinker, never happy but when engaged in his favorite pro-pensity. Of what use is he then to anybody, or even to him self ? None. The little smoker, the occasional smoke breath-er, before he gets through his first, or give him credit for two or three, is left with a dry mouth and a nasty taste—a desire to drink ; and although some will deny that smoking pro-vokes drinking, except coffee or water, few can dispense with grog, ale or wine. Other people it muddles, makes them swimmy, and very disagreeable to talk to. Many men smoke twenty or thirty cigars or pipes in a day, and a young town buck thinks it derogatory to his buckhood unless he can whiff away two or three. To say nothing of the nuisance of smoking, the habit, captivating and socializing as it may be held to be, is decidedly bad—very bad for delicate persons. As to *chewing*, it is an extensive habit. It is so beastly a one that there is little fear of an invalid resorting to it. It is equally pernicious, nay, more so than smoking. Snuffing is sometimes used medicinally, and with great success. Light stimulative snuffs are useful in the affections of the head and eyes, and as a gentle refresher I have no objection to it; but real snuffing, where a man consumes half an ounce daily, and soils half a dozen pocket handkerchiefs in twenty-four hours—for those sort of snuffers awake purposely at night to take a pinch—is, I contend, very enervating, very depressing, except at the immediate moment, and extremely hurtful even to digestion ; for despite all the precaution, the snuff or its juice will get down the gullet. Young men should particularly avoid becoming snuffers; a very short indulgence makes them look ten years older. These habits are very easy to acquire, and very difficult to leave off ; but it is not, as some people say, dangerous to abandon them at the eleventh hour of your life. Mayhap such may not be necessary, but I have known people give up smoking and snuffing, which they had indulged in for years, at a moment's notice, and those people have been my patients, and they have soon found reason to thank me for my advice.

LATE HOURS.

All nature sleeps at night, and why should not man? The great globe, and winds, and waves, move on, 'tis true, and the heart of man beats, and he himself respires, but these things are necessary to keep up the general order. The darkness of night is a simple proof that rest and sleep should be encouraged at that time. Of its necessity man is well aware ; he could not, if he would, do without it. As IT IS, society could not well exist AS IT DOES, did it not encroach upon the hours set aside for repose, but AS IT WAS, our forefathers were wiser, and rising with the lark, retired with the sun. Invalids have little to do with balls, and routs, and evening parties, and persons who value their health will not turn night into day. Ten or eleven o'clock at night should never find delicate persons unprepared to go to bed. It is proverbial, because certified by actual knowledge, that the rest obtained in the early part of the night is more refreshing than that gotten in the morning, Rest is as essential as exercise. The vital energies become exhausted after their due performance, and require repose to regain their strength for the ensuing day. This is a physiological truth ; and if the rest be denied, it becomes an infringement on a law of nature, and that is sure to bring down speedy vengeance. What are the feelings after being up all night? How doubly heavy is the sleep the next night! which, if not taken, the exhaustion becomes an illness. Evils are of two kinds—too much is as bad as too little, and he who retires early should rise early.

It becomes a disease where sleepiness prevails at a time when we ought to be getting up, instead of when going to bed ; but one of the best remedies is to retire early, other things being attended to, nature will do the rest.

Sleeping apartments ought always to be capacious, dry, and well ventilated. The bed should not be too soft, and the bedclothes should be as light as may be consistent with necessary warmth. The inordinate quantity of bed-covering sometimes used has a most relaxing tendency, by promoting excessive perspiration, and by rendering the body over-susceptible to external injurious impressions. Many persons are prone to the pernicious habit of closing the bed-curtains wholly around them,, or else burying their heads under the clothes, and they continue to breathe, during the greater portion of the night, the enclosed atmosphere vitiated by their own respiration ; this is certainly a most unwholesome custom.

The excellence of early rising, and its inspiring influence on both body and mind, have been themes for the poet's song and the sage's sermon. Early rising promotes cheerfulness of temper, opens up new capacities of enjoyment and channels of delight to which the sluggard must be insensible. It increases the sum of human existence, by stealing from indolence hours that would else be utterly wasted, and better still, unquestionably conduces to longevity. All long-livers have been early risers, and—to descend from the poetry of the affair to mere matter of fact—it is remarked by the actuaries of life assurance companies that early rising almost invariably leads to length of days. Now, as the habit of retiring to bed at late hours will hardly admit of early rising, THEREFORE the necessity of refraining from the one in order to secure the advantages of the other. From six to eight hours' sleep are generally held to be sufficient, and no doubt on the average are so. Our sleep is regulated much by the season. In winter, people lie longer, on account, they say, of its being too dark to get up before eight or nine. There is some plausibility in the reason, but the system in cold and dark weather is more prone to sleep than in light sunny times. Invalids need generally plenty of bed rest, but then they should procure it by going early to bed. Persons addicted to late hours plead the parties they form members of as one excuse, and others insist that the evening or night are the only times they have for relaxation. This is all very reasonable for such so constituted, but notwithstanding, late hours are unwholesome. Moon and star-gazing are bad for delicate persons. There is more health and strength to be found in the practice of seeing the sun rise, than in looking at it at any other part of the day. In fact, I know of no feeling equalling in delight that of basking or strolling about, unshaded by housetops or any other earthly canopy than the blue sky in the first hours of the morning sun.

OF EXERCISE AND FRESH AIR.

Exercise and fresh air should be inseparable. They were born with us, but man built houses to shut out the air and lock himself in! And it would appear, in proportion to our advance in civilization, we are setting at defiance the elements of health and longevity. We are absolutely beginning to be more careful of the dead than of the living: we are concocting cemeteries out of town for our defunct relatives, but excluding air and space in our city habitable buildings for ourselves. It is true, here and there is an attempt to widen a street, but the new buildings are becoming approximated instead of distanced. Man, in a state of nature, had to seek his food; to hunt for it; to scramble for it; and hence the difference between the stature and health of the wild Indian and the civilized man. Now, a man need not stir from his couch, for a meal. Look at the difference between the active mechanic, the artisan, even to the ill-fed Irish laborer, and compare him to the confined clerk, the shop man, or the indefatigable stay-at-home of a master, and the evidence of one's eyesight must proclaim in favor of the former—must proclaim that exercise, with moderate sustenance, contributes more to health than high feeding, indolence, and every other enjoyment.

A pensive man, absorbed in his own thoughts, looking from his own window, little dreams of what a tissue of moving atoms he is composed. His blood is traveling onward perpetually; fluids are being deposited on surfaces and again absorbed; his heart is continually beating; his lungs expanding and contracting; and even the viscera have their folds in incessant motion. His very structure adapts him for locomotion; and the composite movements alluded to are mainly dependent upon that locomotion for their healthy persistence, and yet, like a tired horse, how loath he is to stir. What a subject to dilate upon! It is a science in itself. There is nothing still in nature but man (comparatively), and he is called restless. How many of our diseases are attributable to inactivity and confinement.

That exercise and fresh air are essential and salutary—that they are invigorative—that they afford strength and power—that they beget and preserve health—who can deny? That, on the contrary, indolence and confinement sicken the heart, sear the mind, impoverish the body, and shorten life, there cannot be a single doubt. What, then, is it that makes men prefer the latter, or, if not prefer it, yield to it? Necessity? In some degree it is, but in a greater degree it is either indolence or ignorance, perhaps both. The moment a man gets comfort around him, he prefers his ease, his "OTIUM CUM DIGNITATE," and there is a spirit of misappropriation present in young men's minds that leads them to seek relaxation of another, rather than a healthier kind. The theatres, the taverns, the town rendezvous, etc., have attractions more powerful than the morning stroll in the high roads and the fields, and if the one be indulged in the other cannot be availed of. Exercise and fresh air are essential for the due performance of every function of life. By their aid digestion is effected, the proper action of the bowels and skin sustained, sleep secured, a clear head acquired, and life preserved.

Now, with regard to exercise on a more extended scale. To those who have it in their power to avail themselves of it at all times, to those blessed with equipages, they have, indeed, a powerful means of collecting health at every jaunt.

Of all kinds of exercise, walking is the most natural—horse-riding the most delightful, and also the most advantageous, inasmuch as a greater distance can be got over—a greater variety of air be respired, at the cost of positively more exercise, and less fatigue; besides, the country can be reached, which is no easy matter to accomplish on foot. Your horse should be a sure-footed one—over whose neck you can trust the reins to hang—one who will trot, walk or canter. If carriage riding be preferred, or be more convenient, or the only sort of conveyance attainable, pray let it be an open one, else riding for the benefit of the air is ridiculous. In traveling, always select the outside—people only take colds by fearing them; an umbrella, or a great coat, will always keep off the wet. The time of taking exercise should be between meals, neither immediately upon, nor just before one. The amount must rest on the time that can be spared—distance is less an object than time. A valetudinarian should be out in the open air as many hours as possible during the day, and the man in health, to keep so, should at least be on foot or in the stirrups three or four hours daily. The feeble plead inability to get about, and the indolent will justly tell you, exercise doth not agree with them; but the habit of inactivity once broken, it is astonishing how luxurious exercise becomes. Weak parts become strong, and health and strength are acquired every day.

By exercise abroad, not only do diseases of the body give way, but also those of the mind. A fit of blue-devils is invariably cured by a ride on horseback—there are so many things to engage the attention when seated on a cheerful, sprightly pony, and passing by different objects, that new currents of thought are driven through the mind despite the greatest determination to be sad. Independently, when mounted, of the benefits arising from motion—from mental employment, and the necessary attention to keep one's seat, the lungs are having a feast of their daintiest relish, as we find ourselves carried "over the hills and far away ;" the blood becomes purified, and whizzes to its uttermost confines; and the rider, in a short time, feels in reality a new man. It is something to fancy we have no life within us, but it is another to know we have life under us. Exercise cures constipation, corpulency, nervousness, and all forms of indigestion. A simple evidence of the importance of exercise is to be found in the majority who are busily engaged during the week, and who take what they call rest on Sunday—that is to say, who do not go out all that day. There are many who neither dress nor shave on a Sunday, but eat and drink, and sleep. Without appealing to any one in particular, for they include rich as well as poor, I may ask, at least whether the Sunday indolence does not make the Monday a less agreeable day than the Saturday ? The extra feeding has a great deal to do with it, but the want of the usual excitement of business (the exercise of the mind), and the usual bustling about (the exercise of the body), are not uninfluential. Day promenading is more beneficial than walking about in the night air. In wet weather, when out door exercise is scarcely available, pacing the passage with windows open is a good substitute. A man may walk many miles in his own chamber. Gymnastic exercises are recommendable—the use of the dumb-bells—skipping—games of ball—battledoor and shuttlecock—in fact, any pursuit that keeps the body active. Friction with the flesh-brush is no bad imitation of exercise.

What has not fresh air, or, as it is called, when quitting the crowded city, change of air, effected! How many has it not snatched from the jaws of death! How many has it not saved from the tedious pilgrimage of sickness, and spared from desolate loneliness! The apparently consumptive, the melancholy hypochondriac, and the waning and harassed dyspeptic, has it restored to former lifefulness and joy. The first gush revives the expiring breath. Bedridden invalids have been known to rise and walk the day following a removal into the country. Apart from local peculiarities and advantages, fresh air is in every instance useful. These are not mere rhapsodies, but eulogies which the recollections and daily experience of all can substantiate.

The present facilities for obtaining fresh air far exceed those of former times, indeed even only of ten years back; and he must be regardless or very apathetic of his own health, who does not now and then avail of them to get a sniff of the country. The railroads, omnibuses, and steamboats, are boons, despite their monopolies, nuisances, and dangers, that while they have their annoyances, which we every day are holding up to censure, we ought to be charitable toward, and trust to time for improvements.

The best time for riding for health, enjoyment of the country and for the purposes of exercise, is certainly in the morning before breakfast when the season will admit of it; say from six till eight or nine in the morning. Despite the objections to getting up early, the horror which some people have of it, and the many real hindrances, let the experiment be but made, and the temptation to repeat it will be very strong; besides the quietude, freedom from annoyances on the roads, the air is so much fresher, purer, and more delightful than at any other time of the day. Pray try it. If starting out upon an empty stomach destroy the pleasure, take a small cup of coffee and a biscuit or rusk, or biscuit or rusk only, or a crust of bread.

LIEBIG'S THEORY ON LIFE, HEALTH, AND DISEASE.

How often does an invalid find himself bemoaning over his condition, wondering within his own mind what can be the matter with him! If he have a watch that stops, or gets out of order, he takes it to the maker, and is contented to learn that it wants cleaning, or that the spring is broken, and he leaves it with the artificer to effect the necessary reparation ; but when ill himself, notwithstanding his doctor may tell him he has rheumatism, or indigestion, or that he is hypochondriacal, and that, like his watch, he wants cleansing and freshening up, and undertakes to do the same for him, still he is not so easily satisfied. If not righted within a few days, he gets impatient, and ponders over malady— *What is rheumatism ? what is indigestion ? and what is hypochondriacism ?* If the recent invalid thinks in this manner, how much more does the conjecture worry the confirmed invalid—he who has been ailing for time—not weeks and months only, but years ; he who is so feeble as to be scarcely able to stand—whose heart beats ready to burst on the slightest exertion and excitement—whose breath appears denied him—although in the prime of life! How natural is it that such a person should exclaim, "Woe is me!" and that he should like to know what really *is* the matter with him—what, in fact, his disease is, and why he should be singled out as the sufferer, when he sees younger and older comrades free from similar annoyances. The category may be extended still further, and in his wanderings and wonderings he at last seeks to know, *What is life ? And why should he not ?*—the problem is not so unsolvable. It certainly is as well to have some reasons for the faith which is within us ; and it surely is consolatory to ascertain, if we cannot find out what life really is, at least how it is to be preserved ; if not what pain actually be, at least what produces it ; and if the philosophy of death be inexplicable, let us push our inquiries, which c an be resolved, as to what retards its approach.

The solutions to the inquiries of what is life and what is disease, may do more—they may teach principles; and if the explantaion, which I am about to offer, be intelligible and correct, the truth and utility of the code presented, that all may reach the top of "threescore and ten," will be strongly and easily impressed upon the least reflective mind.

It is one thing to know *what* tends to the maintenance and preservation of health, but another to know the why and wherefore; and it is presumed it will considerably strengthen the mind of the timid invalid or the skeptical valetudinarian, if it can be shown *why* gross, inappropriate, or insufficient feeding be injurious, and *wherefore* fresh air, exercise, and rest, should be such a curative for the ailments of mortality, and a preservative for the healthy man.

Addressing my work in a home phraseology for the homely purpose of advising such as may not be chemically learned in the different properties of food and drink, and also those who may not have made the study of their economy a feature to this time, it might almost appear that the present chapter, seemingly leaning to metaphysical theories, is superfluous, that I and my book are attempting to carry our readers out of their depth; but I will rely upon the combined sagacity of my friends and myself to avoid such a fatal immersion. I am not about to promulgate any novel doctrine of my own coinage, nor one that shall insist upon fallacies in past times, but it would exhibit great remissness in the author of such an article as this professes to be, were he to withhold (which, if he did, might be construed into "that he did not know") from the public what is passing as recognized notions among his own professional contemporaries on this very important and interesting subject—principles not only influencing how to avoid disease, but how to cure it. Shakspeare has familiarized us with the seven ages of man, rom the cradled child to toothless decrepitude; but the tenure of life is held upon the same terms with the infant at the breast as the old man at seventy, namely, by feeding and breathing. The value of fresh air, careful living and exercise, were appreciated in the days of the " bard for all time."

The same materials and combinations would have formed gas and steam a thousand years ago, that yield them now, and the principles of life have not altered since the creation. but it has fallen to the lot of modern times to give the new reading to their *modus operandi,* or economy in detail.

To Liebig, of Glessen, the leviathan in chemistry of the present century, are we mainly indebted for the prevailing theory ;—

1st. It is, that the human body is determined in its configuration by a property inherent with its existence, denominated *vis vitæ,* or *vital force,* (or say *life itself,* if preferred), but of which, beyond the truth of its presence, we are ignorant.

2dly. That our existence is dependent upon chemical operations ;

3dly. That the human body is its own laboratory, wherein it generated its own heat ;

4thly. That it is constantly consuming and giving *off* its own elements ; and

Lastly. That it derives a renewal of the same from the nourishment supplied to it, and the atmosphere by which it is surrounded.

This is all plain sailing ; amounting, in reality, that we live by eating, drinking, and breathing, which everybody can understand. But the phenomena about to be named, exhibit much originality of thought, and when understood, are strikingly evident.

The living human body is reducible, like all other matter, to its elementary principles : and as it is always undergoing waste or decomposition, it will soon consume itself, or, vulgarly speaking, die of inanition, were it not for the supply from without.

Liebig therefore says, that as a living body cannot form its own elements, they can only be derived from the food which contains them. The known elementary substances in all nature number between fifty and sixty, nearly a fourth of which are discovered in the human body.

The principal elements inhabiting the corporeal substance of man, and of which we have chiefly to do with in these details, are Oxygen, Hydrogen, Carbon, Nitrogen, therefore all food not containing especially these four elements in combination is innutritious; and as nitrogen holds the more prominent place in the animal economy, as contributing to the formation of every part of the human body, no food amalgamates with the blood that does not possess it; hence the distinction between food called

NITROGENIZED, or Nutritious,	and	NON-NITROGENIZED, or Innutritious.
This class includes bread, meat, and all vegetables, the latter containing though in a less degree, a corresponding bulk of bread and meat, the elements of the organized body.		This class includes, to the wonderment, perhaps, of a great many, such, especially, who have imbibed the notion that we could not do without them, namely:—fat, gum, sugar, *wine*, *beer*, *spirits*.

Nitrogen, or *azote*, enters into every organic or living substance. Fat and water contains no nitrogen, and yet they are component parts of the animal body; but they are not considered *organized* or *living substances*.

Nitrogen, therefore, is indispensable for the development, growth, nutrition, and renovation of all living parts; consequently, it is only nitrogenized food that is capable of forming blood, and of contributing to the organized structures. Liebig gives to such food the name of *elements* of nutrition.

Non-nitrogenized food does not enter into the composition of blood, or contribute to animal life, but it is essential to health, as furnishing *carbon* and *hydrogen*, the oxydation of which develops heat; in fact, without the continual supply of non-nitrogenized food, there would not be a sufficiency of carbon to check the influence of the oxygen upon the other elements of the body, and consequently we should die as in starvation—be literally burnt to death. Liebig calls non-nitrogenized food—elements of respiration. This explanation may appear to justify the imbibition of wine, beer, and spirits—but they exert another influence—they are locally mischievous taken to excess, and produce disturbance of action, creating irritation that breaks up the equilibrium of vital force presently to be described, and which is, in fact, disease; besides, also, there are other sources of carbon less destrucrive and more abundant, at less consumption, than wine, beer, or spirits. It will be remembered that in the preceding pages they have been considered merely as *stimulative*, not *nutritive*. The vital force is the property that only determines the division of the body into legs and arms, but resists powerfully all alterations which caprice or accident may provoke; for obesity and leanness (both forms of disease) do occur. Heads can be flattened, as is done in some wild countries, noses and ears can be lengthened, and feet can be obstructed in their development, as we see among the Chinese; but these changes are all at the cost of natural resistance. We cannot turn a man into a horse, although we may impose upon him the labor of one!

It is *vital force* which propels the blood in its circulatory round throughout the body, which distributes the various secretions through their various ramifications, which provokes the exchange of the old materials in the reparation of the body for the new, which, in fact, regulates every voluntary or involuntary movement; and this *vital force* furthermore is influenced (within its own sphere) by the same laws which regulate all nature, such as gravitation, attraction, and repulsion, from the falling of a stone to the stumble of that glorious fabric—man!

The *materials* of life are held together by chemical cohesion and resistance. The principal phenomenon is *combus-*

tion, which operation is perpetually, more or less, going on, by the *carbon* of the food and the *oxygen* of the atmosphere.

Carbon is the essential constituent of every living or organized tissue, both vegetable and animal; and Liebig supposes that an adult man consumes nearly a pound daily. The same *carbon* is disposed of, after having been *burnt* in the body, in its contract with oxygen, and escapes in equal quantity, except that unconsumed, and which goes to form fat, by the excretions, and principally by the exhalation from the lungs in the *form* of carbonic acid gas.

Oxygen abounds in all nature—the air we breathe, the water we drink, and the food we consume, all contain it. No function of life, or operation in nature, could exist or be fulfilled without it; it is oxygen which rusts iron, which tarnishes quicksilver, and which oxydizes other metals. It is the combination of oxygen that kindles the fire in the grate that illuminates our rooms, that contributes to the warring of the elements. Earth, water, air, and fire, would lose their identity without it; these are familiar examples. We could not live independently of it, nor are we able to breathe any atmosphere divested of it.

The following is the theory of animal heat;—Wherever a union of oxygen and carbon takes place, in whatever part of the body it may be, combustion ensues, and heat is thereby evolved.

Hence the warmth of the body is kept up according to our consumption of carbon, and the amount of oxygen we inhale, or otherwise consume. In cold and clear weather, oxygen abounding in proportion to the rarefaction of the atmosphere, the greater is the combustion and consequent abstraction of the carbon; hence, also, the greater necessity for its supply, and consequently, the greater appetite we experience to induce us to furnish the bodily fuel. This explains why the Esquimaux are such great feeders; and it furthermore proves that food and exercise are better and more permanent generators of warmth than clothing.

The fact can be attested by the feelings after a meal in the coldest weather; a simple illustration of the office of exercise is by provoking the circulation of the blood through benumbed fingers, which immediately glow with warmth, on being excited. Oxygen accompanies the circulation throughout the body, but where it is not freely distributed, which it is not when the equilibrium of the vital force is disturbed, as in cold fingers, the combustion alluded to does not, or only very feebly, take place, because the distribution of the oxygen thereto is retarded, but the moment the circulation recovers itself, then the combustion goes on as usual, and warmth is restored.

The body, like any other substance, has a tendency to accommodate itself to the temperature of the surrounding medium. It becomes cool, or increases in warmth accordingly; and hence the necessity of adapting the diet to preserve a uniformity of temperature, such as is consistent with health.

Clothing is merely an equivalent for food. In proportion to artificial warmth, the less is our appetite.

Liebig adds, if we were to go naked, and were exposed, as in savage life, to extremes of cold and fatigue, we should be able to consume immense quantities of whale blubber and tallow candles by the pound, or drink almost *ad libitum* brandy and train oil without bad effects, because the carbon and hydrogen thereby consumed would only meet the demand of the absorbed oxygen.

Thus does he explain the injury of over and depraved feeding. An American arrives in a hot climate—loses his appetite, and stimulates his stomach by spices and other hot provocatives; he eats as usual, but he does not get rid of it; or a Londoner may commit the same folly of overloading his system at home; the quantity of carbon accumulates; in the one instance, the temperature of the atmosphere forbids exercise, or does not allow a sufficient amount of oxygen to keep the quantity of carbon in subjection; and in the other, the love of ease and corporeal indulgence constitute similar hindrances. Disease in both instances ensues.

In America, these errors from excess of carbon are more prevalent in summer. In winter, the excess of oxygen prevails, and hence diseases of the lungs; a strong reason why persons prone to consumption should be generously supported in the cold months.

Regularity of living should not comprise the same weight and quantity of food daily, whether the day be fine or dry, or cold and clear, or warm and foggy, or whether exercise be taken or not; because under these circumstances the amount of oxygen does not correspond with the supply of carbon, for, as it has been observed, the oxygen prevails in cold and clear weather, and more is consumed in exercise than in indolence; and the oxygen would then be in excess, whereas in damp weather, with indolent habits, it would be insufficient.

It has been calculated that a man receives about two pounds of oxygen daily; the same amount is given off again, whether he receives food or not, in combination with a part of his body, and accordingly, if he take no food, each day he must diminish in weight until all the consumable materials are disposed of. The duration of life under these circumstances is modified by the quietude observed, the state of the atmosphere, and the presence of water. On water alone persons have lived twenty days.

In starvation, not only is the fat consumed, but every other part of the body which is soluble goes to supply the imperative demands of the oxygen, taken in through the lungs; the muscles shrink and lose their contractibility, the brain itself at last yields to the intruder, and undergoes the process of oxydation, and delirium, mania, and death, close the scene. Decay is the result of a similar union with oxygen.

In all chronic diseases, death is produced by the same cause—the chemical action of the atmosphere.

Man and all other animals are exposed at every period of

their lives to the unceasing and destructive action of the atmosphere. With every breath he expires a part of his body, every moment of his life he produces carbonic acid, the carbon of which his food must replace, or *he dies!*

THE FOLLOWING IS THE SUMMARY AND INFERENCES OF THE LIEBIGIAN THEORY.

The man derives his support from food analogous in elementary principles to his own composition.

That he is continually undergoing wear and tear, or, in other words, wasting away on the one hand, and supplying the consumption on the other, so that when in health and at maturity, no diminution or increase in his weight is observed.

So continuous is this change going on, that every movement is the result of an alteration of structure—not a finger is raised, a glance taken, a thought given birth to, without a change—without a wear and tear of the material wherein abides the function. In proportion to the intensity of the feeling or movement, so is the change in the organization. It then can easily be conceived how injurious must excess of any one manifestation of human life be, much more when many are combined, whether such be fatigue of body or abuse of mind. Hence the seeming fact of many men looking old at mid-life, and others, who have been careful, looking younger than they really are.

In stating that every word, thought, or deed, involves a consumption of material is only re-echoing what hitherto physiologists calculated upon taking place in cycles of three years, namely—an entire change in every particle of the human body—so that we retain at the expiration of that time not an atom of our former self. This is very probable when we reflect upon the constant, though necessary metamorphosis of structure or tissues we are subjected to in the scheme being detailed. It is the vital force that preserves our positive facial identity.

Liebig defines health to be a perfect equilibrium of all the functions of the body—where the balance between waste and supply is faithfully kept up; which, to our modern and homely way of thinking and expressing ourselves, is as much as to say, a man is in health when he is well. Disease, of course, is the opposite condition to this, where the equilibrium is disturbed, when there necessarily follows some change of structure, however small. The positive disorganization may not be easily recognizable, if at all—but it must occur. Every atom of the body has its office, and its function depends upon its property, and where is there a particle without one?

A ripple in the silent pool from the falling of a pebble extends its circles to its confines, in relation to the force of the agitation, and so it is with the dissemination of disease.

Health may be likened to a summer's day—disease may be compared to a shower or a storm, and the mischief and danger depend upon the violence and permanence of either. Notwithstanding the figurative language, this flourish about a definition—the comparison is a simple one, and when admitted, leads a man to think where the evil lies, and what it is; thus, then, do we arrive at the understanding of the problem just given. Disease, like the pebble thrown in the pool, extends its disturbance far and wide, and hence the shock of an upset stomach to the whole system, or a gouty toe to the generation of fever—by sympathy, which is the exercise of a law, as the ripple on the water.

The practice of medicine hitherto certainly has had the odium of being considered more or less entirely empirical; but not a medicine is administered now whose operation and influence are not pre-ascertainable, and where a doubt exists, it is because we do not reflect, rather than we cannot find out.

Liebig seems to attribute all diseases to the disordered condition of the blood; and, consequently, we are to infer that the onus of a distemper lies in the food we take, the air we breathe, or the external worldly or the moral circumstances which influence the condition of that fluid ; and he further intimates that the cure, therefore, of disease rests less on the chemical properties of drugs than the dieting, nursing, and general regimen, on which the creation of healing blood depends. The *chemical* treatment of disease is rather of a circumscribed nature, being confined to the supply of those elements which enter into the composition of the blood; thus have we recommended the inhalation of oxygen or vital air, as it is called, the internal exhibition of iron, sulphur, lime, soda, iodine, etc.; all others act on the principles of counter-irritants.

The leading elements of the body have been stated to be oxygen, hydrogen, nitrogen, and carbon; this reiteration is imperative to enforce the importance of the following fact ;— of these elements, be it remembered, the nitrogen is *the* important inhabitant of the organized structures. Although the other three enter into the composition of man, they only fulfill the purposes of fuel to the vital fire ; the carbon not consumed is stored up for future occasion in appropriate cells, and is denominated fat. The nitrogen that becomes displaced by the new food in the ordinary rule of change passes off by the kidneys and glandular system, or else supplies the place of carbon when that element is deficient, as in the progress of starvation. Liebig considers the brain and nerves to be composed of a somewhat higher organization than that which enters into the formation of the other structures of the body, and that they are less easily arranged. All the more important glandular secretions are, at the expense of the nitrogen, the sole support of animal life, and hence, where those secretions are usually profuse, as in the irregularities previously alluded to, it needs no ghost to point out the fearful consequences, and how and in what manner such drainages act, to the prejudice of those essential portions of our bodies, the brain and nerves ; hence we have the disordered and impaired intellect of early life ; hence the faulty state of our bodily and mental sensations; hence the debility—for what is strength but the full tone of healthy organization, and how can there be tone, when the organization is imperfect? What mars the sound of a cracked bell but its fracture? What robs the musical chord of its full vibratory intonation but laxity in its tension? And what is debility but incapacity for the muscle to lift its weight, the stomach to furnish its solvent juice, or the brain to be the harbinger of our will and desire? The excesses of gourmandism, drinking, smoking, and other exhaustive practices destroy the vital structure, not only by the consumption of its elements, its nitrogen especially, but by impending the acquisition of oxygen and loading the system with carbon, which accounts for congested livers, diseased respiration, disordered kidneys, and the whole host of diseases abridging or making life miserable.

Of the importance of the other, besides the four leading elements, the physiologist is fully alive. Iron is detected in the blood—phosphorous in the nervous system—lime in the bones and membranes—potass and soda in the secretions, all of which severally play their part.

Notwithstanding the objections which the common-sense man, the hater of all "outlandish names," he who would "call water water, and fire fire," may have to the new vocabulary of terms, to him so mysterious (for as well might an Englishman object to the French and German being different to his native tongue, as to deny to chemistry a language of its own), still a little reflection will reconcile him to his new world of ideas, and the impression will be the more lasting and effective when he thinks in his own tongue and construes properly the translation I am attempting to give. That man thrives only on elements analogous to those in his self-composition, merely signifies that he should live on nutritious food. Butter, sugar, wine, beer, and spirits, although called *non-nitrogenized* food, are still known as they are called, and though fattening, palatable, and universally consumed, are *not nutritious;* and the last three, seemingly strengthening, because stimulating, still in themselves they are not nourishing. They may be strictly called medicinal condiments. Hence, again, not only is innutritious food unwholesome, not only are excesses in indulgences, in pleasures as they are called, in the overstraining of our appetites, and consequently various powers of life, prejudicial, but equally so are the penalties we impose upon ourselves for such transgressions, namely, the penalty of physic-taking, and when, like the other evils just enumerated, overdone. By physic-taking, I apply it in its usual sense—the habit of resorting on nearly all occasions to strong purgative medicines. The weakness and faintness so rapidly consequent upon diarrhœa, or bowel complaint, is well known : the frequent, and to some people who take physic all their lives, the continual drainage kept up (such individuals never experiencing a solid evacuation), must be evident, and more so when it is told that each operation is at the expense of not merely the feastings and gorgings of yesterday, but of the principal elements of life—each muscle, each nerve, each sense, gives up a portion of its individual self. Again, the ostensible purpose of such remedies is to dislodge the excess of carbon, but what is the use of so doing if the re-supply be immediately at hand ?—the hurtful nature of such violent excesses, of one day draining the system, and the next day filling it to repletion, must be apparent to all who think of it—and the individual, guilty of such ways, lives but too soon to find it out. By the continuance of purgation, at last more carbon is thrown off than received, and the waste of the body then is kept up, at the expense of the nitrogen. A coat worn in all weathers can not last so long as one well taken care of ; and it is preposterous to suppose that the body does not wear out—it is true, it is made to last, with care, the often-quoted term of three score and ten, and more, but, like the coat, if subjected to undue vicissitudes it cannot possibly exist half its time.

The practice of giving purgative medicines in almost every disease, is a leading feature in physic—medical men resort to it—some make it their hobby—the public seem intuitively to imitate them. The poor man flies to his dose of salts, while he who is disinclined for such and similar drinks, swallows some quack pill. Purgatives are the bases of nearly all the quack medicines. Occasional purgation is indispensable; but how much better would it be to withhold the excess poured into the system, and to suffer nature to get rid of its natural quantity in the natural way! Physic (purgative) is, at best, when even properly and skilfully administered, but a necessary evil.

Ill health assumes many very formidable aspects, and the moment a man falls ill, he loses courage, and flies to physic; it is a popular saying, that a stitch in time saves nine; but then finding relief once, he resorts to it again and again, and having discovered, as he fancies, the remedy, he returns to the cause of his disease.

The folly of taking physic indiscriminately (quack medicines, for instance) is so glaring, that no man in his senses would risk the danger. Surely, the proper person to repair a watch is not the dress-maker, and how can any one dare to say that this or that medicine will cure all disorders, any more than the milliner would insist that she was the proper person to mend a broken spring of a chronometer or the wheel of a stage coach? The principles of physic may be learned by the divine, as well as music by the amateur; but principles without practice seldom lead to perfection, and the dabblers in physic, the pill-mongers, and the nostrum-vendors, are sad outrages upon the present state of society.

Finally, to recapitulate. The body consists of elements, derivable only from food, analogous to itself in elementary composition.

The main structures of the body—the blood, the brain, and nervous system, and the substantiality of man—are made up of nitrogenized atoms. Other elements are present, such as oxygen, hydrogen, and carbon; but they are principally designed to form the fluids of the body, and to preserve its heat. Their undue proportion constitutes disease. Their equalization rests upon the supply and their combustion; judgment and the will can regulate the former, and fresh air and exercise the latter. The administration of physic is a science; judiciously exercised, the due and proper proportion of the elements of the body can be preserved; obnoxious ones can be removed, and those necessary, furnished.

The treatment of ill-health by diet and regimen, is really very simple, ay, and very beautiful.

There is no doubt but that, owing to diet and regimen, we are indebted for all those qualities that make man the noble fellow he is. The clear head, the strong arm, the bright eye, the fair skin, and the due universal energy, are we bound to give credit for, to the care a man takes of himself, supposing the notion to be followed out from parent to son; and we may depend upon it, in like manner have we to thank ourselves for feeble and enervated health, for listless and tamed subjection, and for indifference, at last, to our actual existence.

The inferences to be gathered from Liebig's theory are, that we should rather support than debilitate—that we should refrain rather than overfeed; and the main and most effective proposition contained in it, is, that we should study " How to live,"—that we should really eat and drink upon principle, as we would fill any other office in life. The stores are so abundant for our delight and downright enjoyment, that the selection to secure health is not confined to those which are insipid or tasteless. Man may even be luxurious—be an epicure, and yet gain health and strength at every meal. The hurtful things in this life are not those which are the nicest, but which the vitiated taste of man and the novelty of enjoyment provoke.

If my reader have journeyed with me thus far, I shall be content if I have even excited in him a curiosisy to extend the inquiry concerning himself. The theory of Liebig involves a subject that, when more generally understood, cannot fail to be as generally appreciated. The chemistry of man, if investigated, will be more likely to enable him to "know himself," as the Scripture adviseth, than all the closet meditations which logicians or moral philosophers can advise upon.

There is in this country a disinclination to attach the full importance to organic or physical health, lest the idea savor or seem to encourage the atheistical doctrines of materiality; but the surmise is false. The modifications of light are owing to the medium through which it is transmitted, and the manifestations of the mind are in like manner marked by the organization which exhibits it.

It may well be said, how fearfully and wonderfully are we made : but complicated and mysterious as the whole fabric seems to be, yet how beautiful is the arrangement! The ingenuity of man could not suggest a single improvement! Not a fibre, or vein, or artery, have we superfluous—not an atom is wanting.

REMARKS ON WARM BATHING.

Reader, did you ever take a warm bath ? The question may be libelous, and yet no more than asking you whether you have ever been to Paris. Formerly, the latter was an adventure, and a remarkable one in our history ; and scarcely less so was the former. There was, however, some justifiable excuse for not bathing; bathing-houses were few, and bathing was expensive ; consequently a general tepid wash was rarely indulged in, as we grew beyond the nursery Saturday nights' ablutions. But let us move the original question, and if the answer be in the negative, let me suggest the experiment. *Take one.* Apart from its cleanly properties, its moral virtues, and its salutary tendency, it has a strong inducement in the personal comforts which it affords. Supposing you never took one, to induce you to do so, fancy for a moment the delight of warmth. Standing with your back to the fire is proverbial ; warming our hands before the blazing coal is a luxury in cold weather ; shaving in hot weather—what a pleasure ! Taking also our memory for our last cold ; was not half the cure of it effected by the hot foot-bath by which the shrivelled skin, the bound head, and the lazy back-ache, were resolved into soft and refreshing sleep ? Now fancy the entire body immersed, neck high, in a warm bath. Even the dumb must speak in its praise. First, we will consider it as a luxury ; secondly, a remedy ; lastly, a duty.

Enjoyments are better appreciated by contrasts. Take, for instance; arriving at the end of a journey, " nipped to the nose," fingers cold as icicles, toes senseless as marble, teeth chattering upon a still tongue, and the body trembling, shivering, and fluttering, like a poor dog rescued from drowning, and withal exhausted by, most likely, wakefulness, possibly wet and fatigue ; imagine or recollect all these phenomena, and then remember the elysium of a hot bath, if you happen to have entered one ; or, if such a fact cannot be recalled, should the like feelings ever assail you again, in justice to my commendation, *try one*. It surpasses the toasting before the kitchen fire ; an oven bears no comparison to it, and bed is a sorry rival. Such a state of things as half-freezings, and similar sufferings, are highly dangerous ; and a cold caught one day often sees the victim confined in a week. A hot bath, taken at the fitting moment, arrests the threatened invasion, dissolves the rigid members, reanimates nose, fingers, and toes, and sends the blood merrily on to every extremity, where ten minutes before it was a stranger, and composes the body in a state of thankful and grateful ease, and sends death about his business. This is not a mere fanciful sketch by a bath proprietor, but a positive and undeniable truth ; and a warm bath aptly taken has, in hundreds of instances, and thousands too, averted and cured illness that bitter experience tells have proved fatal for the want of one. A cold is the most accessible of all complaints in this variable climate; neglected, it leads to the most fatal. *A warm bath is the readiest, cheapest, quickest, best, and most certain cure.* I am not the only authority for the assertion. Every traveled man of forty can attest it; "*Probatum est!*" Now, setting aside this rhapsody on the best way of warming ourselves, and of killing a cold, the reader may desire to know what medical men think of the virtues and usefulness of warm bathing. That it is conducive to health; that it absolutely is the best substitute for exercise and physic, when the former can scarcely be had, and of the latter there be too much already swallowed, is indisputable. That it equalizes the circulation of the blood; renders the skin supple and moist; promotes free perspiration, and relieves the body from a layer of thick, obstructive accumulation of scurf and oleaginous surfacial deposit, and so proves salutary, giving thereby an impetus to absorption and secretion, is also a great fact, and, therefore, it is most wholesome and wise, on not too frequent occasions, to avail of it.

A man calling himself in health, to keep himself so, should certainly take a warm bath once a week throughout his life; certainly a fortnight should not pass without one. Let the skeptic try the experiment, and, in addition to improved feelings, the great one of knowing his entire body to be clean, and spotless, and wholesome, will be such a comfort, that a misery is in store if the practice be omitted. The effect of a warm bath to a person in health, is highly delightful. The sensations during the process are exquisite, and afterwards no less so. The liberty of motion, the pleasurable and agreeable diffusion of warmth, and the perfect ease during the indulgence, have no parallel. The flexibility of the joints, the freedom of respiration, the improved tone of nervous feeling in mind and body, intellect being brighter, and every faculty livelier—memory, thought and idea at command, after the bath—are notorious truths known to the patron of the warm ablution. The next view may be the virtues of warm bath-

ing in illness, in severe cases, or to a person (for these obser-
vations apply to both sexes, and, of the two, with perhaps
greater right to the ladies) in delicate, dyspeptic, or nervous
health. First, the bath allays all pain, and removes all, not
positively inflammatory—and even in these cases is highly
serviceable under proper advice ; it quiets all nervous irritability ; promotes general perspiration ; quickens and yet softens the circulation, overcoming thereby obstructions in
deep-seated parts, and allowing an easy and regular flow of
blood throughout its course. Warm bathing also acts bene-
ficially on the kidneys and urinary organs ; it helps the bowels, and stomach, and liver, giving new life to each, the action of each being thereby healthily excited ; it consequently
promotes digestion, and contrary to the popular fear of a
warm bath, weakening, it in reality strengthens the system ;
and furthermore, in opposition likewise to the apprehension
that a warm bath is dangerous, as being liable to give cold
afterward, it, I unhesitatingly declare, fortifies you against
one. Colds are only taken when the bath exhausts, when it
is taken too hot, or the bather has been too long in it, or he
incautiously submits himself to draughts, or may linger about
in the cold and damp air, and so "take a chill" on coming
out of one. In all cases of restlessness—the fidgets—in hy-
pochondriasis, better known as low spirits—general bodily
and mental depression—the warm bath is most useful ; it
tranquilizes the whole system, induces a good night's rest,
soothes excitability, stills an irregular and fluctuating pulse,
and calms a turbulent mind. As a matter of health and duty, the bath is imperative ; as one of ease, and comfort, and
enjoyment, and lastly, of cleanliness, incomparable ; if omitted from distrust, in the first instance, folly ; if from
dilatoriness or indolence, or on the score of trouble or expense, unpardonable.

The usual temperament of a warm bath is ninety-eight
degrees, but according to the object in view, it can be modified and borne at the pleasure of the bather ; if taken for

mere refreshment and cleanliness, the above heat will prove very agreeable and suitable for the purpose; if suffering from cold or other indisposition and perspiration be desirable, one hundred degrees will be found effective, and ten minutes are quite long enough to remain in it; if the stay be much protracted, exhaustion follows, and the effect is hurtful. The French people accustom themselves to pass a full hour in the warm bath, but the practice is relaxing, and indeed enervating. The best time for taking a bath is before a meal, or some time after one. The morning is most favorable for invalids, because the body is fresh and able to encounter any little extra fatigue; but the bath is equally serviceable at all periods of the day, morning, noon, or evening, and those persons whose engagements are imperative during what are called business hours, must not plead "the fear of taking cold after sunset" as an excuse for the omission. Indeed the apprehension of taking cold (which prevails to a popular degree) after a warm bath under any circumstances, is quite erroneous; for, in fact, instead of predisposing a person to a catarrh or a rheumatic attack, or in plain language, a cold, the bath absolutely helps to stave one or either of the others off. The absolute effect of a hot bath is, that it stimulates, arouses and keeps up the circulation, thereby diffusing warmth throughout the frame, which renders it invulnerable to the dreaded evil; and if a man do not suffer that excitement to subside, and do not linger about in the cold or damp air but proceed briskly on his way, he will derive the double benefit of feeling stronger and better, if possible, than before, and of enjoying the refreshment of the immersion. A bath may be taken safely in the "bitterest" and coldest weather. Foggy and damp, and wet days are the least favorable for the indulgence. In the summer the bath is most essential, for the skin having double duty to perform, it urgently requires to be kept cleanly lest any obstruction to the perspiration should ensue. If the bath be wanted for a specific purpose, and the illness be one of uncertainty, or beyond the comprehension of the invalid, a medical opinion had better be had; but I am not speaking "*fee*-prospectively," for, invaluable as professional guidance must be admitted to be, on all and every occasion especially if it be good, I am an advocate that common sense should tell, not only "when to run for the doctor," but when to do without him, and, therefore must leave my readers to discriminate for themselves. Great as the pleasure, delight, and salubrity of a warm bathing is, there is a time and a season for all things. I have observed that for cleanliness and comfort, and health, a warm bath may be taken once a week, or once a fortnight at least, but for special purposes, one may be taken daily for a time, or twice or thrice a week; but the practice must not degenerate into such frequency as to enervate and enfeeble, which, like any other practice carried to excess, it will do. All that I can add is, that the warm bath is a most excellent adjunct in the cure and maintenance of health. It rarely disagrees, but its services are manifold, and the introduction of baths for the poor is a noble national donation, and will doubtless tend to the extension of the practice of ablution; for cleanliness is a speaking advertisement, and carries with it the comforts, agreeable feelings, and permanent health which warm bathing can so effectively administer.

ON VAPOR, SULPHUR, FUMIGATING, AND OTHER BATHING.

Vapor bathing is an immense luxury and a vastly powerful remedial agent. Its story is soon told. The bather is closeted in a chamber, like a tent, which is furnished with fragrant steam, which quickly surrounds the body, and soon causes great but bearable warmth that ends in profuse perspiration. The feelings on the occasion are most delightful; a vapor bath has been fancifully compared to "Mahomet's seventh heaven." It is needless to go into long details here; but I may briefly enumerate the many complaints, vapor fumigating, heated air, or other medicated bathing, triumphs over. The various baths of this kind are to suit special local diseases and the constitutions of particular individuals ; but they had all better (the baths) be taken (more or less) under medical surveillance. First and foremost it may be stated that few skin complaints yield without the use of the bath. Some of the more inveterate kinds admit of no other remedy. All chronic painful affections, such as exist in the bones, joints especially, the broad muscles of the back, the thick muscles of the buttocks, thighs, constituting lumbago, rheumatism, neuralgia, etc., all more or less modifications of the same malady, are ameliorated and cured by medical bathing. The vapor bath is an almost infallible cure for a cold. This and the warm bath may honestly be called the hot-water cure. It is greatly useful in chronic affections of the kidneys, in nervous affections of the various parts of the body—tic douloureux especially—and also as a great renovator of health, inducing a healthy action upon the circulation, provoking the proper functions of the liver and digestive organs, the skin, and all the various secretions. Steam bathing constitutes a system in itself, and is worthy of every reliance and attention on the part of the profession and the public; but theory will help very little either party. I have witnessed the effects of bathing on a very large scale, both in England, and at the " Hospital St. Louis " in Paris, where I saw many hundreds of cures of skin and other diseases effected by bathing ; and I, therefore can confidently affirm that bathing such as I have enumerated, and its many modifications, must be seen to be understood, when it will be found to be a great medical agent, and to supersede a vast deal of the drugging and physicking poor human mortality is driven to have recourse to.

ON COLD BATHING.

This part being professedly a guide to health, it would be very incomplete, having introduced the subject of warm

bathing, did I not say a word or two on its friendly antago-
nist, cold bathing ; for, strange to say, although apparently
of such a dissimilar nature, its tendency and usefulness are
the same. " The cold-water cure" has made a great stir in
the world ; and it is ridiculous to suppose, notwithstanding
the prejudices against it among certain medical men and
others who know nothing about it, that it is a mere chimera,
when thousands of people recover and live to tell of the
service it has rendered them. No matter whether the cure
has been effected by temperate living and by country exercise, certain it is, invalids who have employed cold bathing
in conjunction, as far as they can judge by their feelings, and
as far as observers can declare from personal knowledge—
certain it is that cold bathing, either local or general, is a
highly important remedy, and that by its means the parties
in question have got well. Physic, without the observance
of careful living, exercise, and fresh air, and other such ad-
juncts, would do very little alone ; but the credit is usually
given to the medicine, and why should not the bath be as
fairly treated ? *The cold shower bath, the douche bath*, where
a large stream of cold water is forcibly directed to particular
parts of the body, have severally their patrons. The *sitz
bath*, similar to the common hip bath, but not so deep, is
really a great agent in diseases of the pelvic viscera, or organs contained in the lower part of the abdomen, and in
nervous affections, pains, and debility of the neighboring
structures, female complaints, etc. *The cold plunge bath*,
although taken, perhaps, more for pastime than health,
yields both. Mark the color and glow of the bather after a
jump-in, a short swim, and a quick dressing ;—consult his
feelings the remainder of the day and he will tell you the
bath strengthens him, cheers his spirits, gives him a freshness of feeling unattainable by any other means ; that, in
fact, he longs for the next morning to give him his next immersion. Why do people congregate by the seaside and
there venture among the sportive waves, allowing the foam-

ing sea to engulph them, were they not convinced they derived benefit from the practice? Young and old, after a sojourn, even though it be brief, at the coast, return home renovated and replenished with healthful and happy looks, and the majority will speak with rapture of the benefits of sea-bathing. Indeed, the fact is incontrovertible. Of course, cold bathing, in all its forms, requires some little prudence in its indulgence. It is not wise to remain in too long, nor can it be done with impunity any more than in the warm bath (two errors of frequent happening), and therefore certain rules should be observed as a guidance; for instance, except an immediate reaction follows the immersion, the shock of the bath leaves behind a chill which may end in a severe cold, or establish rheumatism, or set up fever or general irritability, and it may thereby weaken instead of strengthening the bather. It is therefore prudent to jump in, move about for a couple of minutes, come out and dress, and then walk about to keep up the excitement.

The best time for bathing is the morning, either before or after breakfast—before, if strong enough, or an hour after breakfast; if the former time prove not so salutary, cold bathing tells its effects very speedily; if it disagree, the sensations will bespeak as much; if on the contrary, the desire to repeat it will predominate. The bath should never be taken on a full stomach; and it is unwise to compel young people to bathe against their inclinations. Diffidence may be overcome, but dread, if defied, may produce illness.

Bathers must in all instances be guided by their feelings, when and how often they may take the baths; but they may safely venture every or every other morning. The cold shower bath may be taken every morning all the year round, and some people take the same evenings also, and with benefit. The sitz and douche had better be taken under medical guidance. The temperature (for that varies, owing to weather, situation, etc.) must be studied. Some weak systems cannot command a wholesome and prompt reaction from a *very* cold bath, and therefore the bath should be changed for a tepid; but the ordinary cold bath in the summer season, as at the sea, is about the most agreeable and safe. In conclusion, cold water, whether in tub, stream, or sea, is one of those beneficent gifts Nature has bestowed on man for his own use, and, if employed with careful consideration, affords the end in view—universal good,—and cannot but elicit from every thankful mind the homage and gratitude due to the great and benevolent Author of its source.

EVERY LADY'S COOK-BOOK.

EASY SYSTEM OF CARVING.

Every person standing at the head of a family should be well informed upon the general principles of carving, without which, it will be impossible to perform the honors of the table with propriety. An attention to the following rules will enable any one to perform this branch of domestic duty with facility and despatch.

Rule 1. In carving, your knife should be light and sharp, and it should be firmly grasped.

2. The dish should be situated near the carver, so as to render the task easy.

3. Fish requires very little carving; it should be carefully helped with a fish-slice, which prevents the flakes from being broken.

4. To carve a turkey, fix the fork firmly on one side of the thin bone that rises in the centre of the breast; the fork should be placed *parallel* with the bone, and as close to it as possible. Cut the meat from the breast lengthwise, in slices of about half an inch in thickness. Then turn the

turkey on the side nearest you, and cut off the leg and wing; when the knife is passed between the limbs and the body, and pressed outward, the joint will be easily perceived. Then turn the turkey on the other side, and cut off the leg and wing. Separate the drum-stick from the leg-bones, and the pinions from the wings; it is hardly possible to mistake the joint. Cut the stuffing in thin slices, lengthwise. Take off the neck-bones, which are two triangular bones on each side of the breast; this is done by passing the knife from the back under the blade part of each neck-bone, until it reaches the end; by raising the knife the other branch will easily crack off. Separate the carcass from the back by passing the knife lengthwise from the neck downward. Turn the back upwards and lay the edge of the knife across the back bone, about midway between the legs and wings; at the same moment place the fork within the lower part of the turkey, and lift it up; this will make the back-bone crack at the knife. The croup, or lower part of the back, being cut off, put it on the plate, with the rump from you, and split off the side-bones by forcing the knife through from the rump to the other end.

Remark.—The choicest parts of a turkey are the side-bones, the breast, and the thigh-bones. The breast and wings are called light meat; the thigh-bones and side-bones dark meat. When a person declines expressing a preference, it is polite to help to both kinds.

5. A goose is carved nearly as a turkey, only the breast should be cut in slices narrow and nearly square, instead of broad, like that of a turkey; and before passing the knife to separate the legs and wings the fork is to be placed in the small end of the leg-bone or pinion, and the part pressed close to the body, when the separation will be easy. Take off the merry-thought, the neck-bones, and separate the leg-bones from the legs, and the pinions from the wings.

Remark.—The best parts are the breast, the thigh bones, and the flesh parts of the wings.

6. A sirloin of beef should be managed thus:—Place the curving bone downward upon the dish. Cut the outside lengthwise, separating *each slice* from the chin-bone with the point of the knife. The tenderloin is on the inside; it is to be cut crosswise.

7. A saddle of mutton is the two loins together, and the back-bone running down the middle to the tail. Slices are to be cut out parallel to the back-bone on either side.

8. In a leg of mutton, the knife is to be entered in the thick, fleshy part, as near the shank as will give a good slice. Cut towards the large end, and always to the bone.

9. A fillet of veal is the thick part of the leg, and is to be cut smooth, round, and close to the bone.

Remark.—Some prefer the outside piece. A little fat cut from the skirt is to be served to each plate.

10. In carving a pig, if the pig be whole, cut off the head and split it in halves along the back-bone. Separate the shoulders and legs by passing the knife under them in a circular direction.

Remark.—The best parts are the triangular piece of the neck, the ribs, legs and shoulders.

REMARKS UPON COOKING UTENSILS, THEIR USES, ETC.

Metallic utensils are quite unfit for many uses, and the knowledge of this is necessary to the preservation of health.

The metals commonly used in tne construction of cooking utensils, are silver, copper, brass, tin, iron, and lead. Silver is preferable to all others, because it cannot be dissolved by any of the substances used as food. Copper and brass are both liable to be dissolved by vinegar, acid fruits, and pearlash. Such solutions are highly poisonous. Neither acids nor anything containing pearlash should be suffered to remain in vessels of this kind, more than an hour.

Iron is one of the safest metals for the construction of culinary utensils. Some articles of food, such as quinces, orange peel, artichokes, etc., are blackened by remaining in iron vessels, which, therefore, must not be used for them.

Leaden vessels are very unwholesome, and should never be used for milk and cream if it be ever likely to stand till it becomes sour. They are unsafe also for the purpose of keeping salted meats.

The best kind of pottery-ware is oriental china, because the glazing is perfect glass, which cannot be dissolved, and the whole substance is so compact that liquid cannot penetrate it.

Acids and greasy substances penetrate into unglazed wares excepting strong stone-ware ; or into those of which the glazing is cracked, and hence gives a bad flavor to anything they are used for afterwards. They are quite unfit, therefore, for keeping pickles or salted meats. Glass vessels are infinitely preferable to any pottery-ware.

Wooden vessels are very proper for keeping many articles of food, and should always be preferred to those lined with lead. It is useful to char the insides of wooden vessels before they are used, by burning wooden shavings, so as to coat the insides with a crust of charcoal.

There is a kind of hollow iron-ware lined with enamel, which is superior to every other utensil for sauces or preserves ; indeed, it is preferable for every purpose.

Whatever contaminates food in any way, must be sure, from the repetition of its baneful effects, to injure the health.

MANNER OF SETTING DISHES ON TABLE.

1. Soup, broth, or fish, should always be set at the head of the table ; if none of these, a boiled dish goes to the head where there is both boiled and roasted.

2. If there be but one principal dish it goes to the head of the table.

3. If three, the two small ones to stand opposite nigh the foot.

4. If four, the biggest to the head, the next biggest to the foot, and the two smallest dishes on the sides.

5. If five, you are to put the smallest in the middle and the other four opposite.

6. If six, you are to put the top and bottom as before, and the two small ones opposite for the side dishes.

COOKERY OF MEATS.

ROAST BEEF.—The sirloin is considered the best for roasting. Spit the meat, pepper the top, and baste it well while roasting with its own dripping, and throw on a handful of salt. When the smoke draws to the fire, it is near enough; keep the fire bright and clear. From fifteen to twenty minutes to the pound, is the rule for roasting.

BEEF BOILED.—The round is the best boiling piece. Put the meat in the pot, with water enough to cover it; let it boil very slow at first—this is the great secret of making it tender—take off the scum as it rises. From two to three hours, according to size, is the rule for boiling.

BEEF STEAK.—The inside of the sirloin makes the best steak. Cut about three quarters of an inch thick—have the gridiron hot, put on the meat and set it over a good fire of coals—turn them often. From eight to ten minutes is the rule for broiling.

ROAST PORK.—Take a leg of pork and wash it clean—cut the skin in squares—make a stuffing of grated bread, sage, onion, pepper and salt, moistened with the yolk of an egg. Put this under the skin of the knuckle, and sprinkle a little powdered sage into the rind where it is cut; rub the whole surface of the skin over with a feather dipped in sweet oil. Eight pounds will require about three hours to roast it.

The SHOULDER, LOIN or CHINE, and SPARE-RIB are roasted in the same manner.

PORK STEAKS.—Cut them off a neck or loin; broil them over a clear fire, turning them often—pepper and salt them while broiling—when done, put them in a plate and add a piece of butter.

BROILED HAM.—Cut the ham in thin slices. If the ham is too salt, soak before broiling in cold water—then take care to dry them—fry a few eggs and serve an egg on each slice of ham.

FRIED SAUSAGES.—Put a little butter in a frying-pan; as soon as it is melted, put in the sausages and turn them often —fry them over a slow fire; when they are done brown drain off the fat and serve them.

TO MAKE SAUSAGE MEAT.—Take two pounds of lean meat to one of fat pork; chop fine, and mix it with two teaspoonfuls of black pepper, one of cloves, seven of powdered sage, and five of salt.

ROAST MUTTON.—The loin, haunch, and saddle of mutton and lamb must be done the same as beef. All other parts must be roasted with a quick, clear fire; baste it when you put it down, and dredge it with a little flour, just before you take it up. A leg of mutton of six pounds will require one hour to roast before a quick fire.

ROAST VEAL.—In roasting veal pursue about the same course as in roasting pork. Roast before a brisk fire till it comes to a fine brown color; when you lay it down baste it well with good butter, and when near done, with a little flour.

In roasting, time, distance from fire, basting, and a clear fire, are the first articles which require a cook's attention.

DIRECTIONS FOR BOILING.

For all sorts of boiled meats, allow a quarter of an hour to every pound; be sure that the pot is very clean, and skim it well, for everything will have a scum rise; and if it boils down, it makes the meat black. All sorts of fresh meat are to be put in when the water boils, but salt meat when the water is cold.

TO BOIL EGGS.—Try the freshness of eggs by putting them into a pan of cold water. Those that sink the soonest are the freshest.

Never attempt to boil an egg without a watch beside you. Let the water boil before the eggs are put in. In three minutes an egg will boil soft; in four, the white part is completely cooked; in ten, it is hard enough for a salad.

POULTRY AND GAME.

To roast fowls the fire must be quick and clear. If smoky, it will spoil both their taste and looks. Baste frequently, and keep a white paper pinned on the breast till it is near done.

TURKEY.—A good sized turkey should be roasted two hours and a half or three hours—very slowly at first. If you wish to make plain stuffing, pound a cracker or crumble some bread very fine, chop some raw salt pork very fine, sift some sage (and summer-savory, or sweet marjoram, if you have them in the house, and fancy them), and mold them all to gether, seasoned with a little pepper. An egg worked in makes the stuffing cut better.

BOILED TURKEY.—Clean the turkey, fill the crop with stuffing, and sew it up. Put it over the fire in water enough to cover it; let it boil slowly—take off all the scum. When this is done it should only simmer till it is done. Put a little salt into the water, and dredge the turkey with flour before boiling.

ROAST DUCKS AND GEESE.—Take sage, wash and pick it, and an onion; chop them fine, with pepper and salt, and put them in the belly; let the goose be clean picked, and wiped dry with a cloth inside and out; put it down to the fire and roast it brown. Ducks are dressed in the same way. For wild ducks, teal, pigeons, and other wild fowl, use only pepper and salt, with gravy in the dish.

ROAST CHICKEN.—Chickens should be managed in roasting the same as turkeys, only that they require less time. From an hour to an hour and a half is long enough.

BOILED CHICKEN.—A chicken should be boiled the same as a turkey, only it will take longer time—about thirty-five minutes is sufficient. Use the same stuffing, if any, and serve it up with parsley or egg sauce.

BROILED CHICKEN.—Slit them down the back and season with pepper and salt ; lay them on a clear fire of coals, the inside next the fire till half done ; then turn, and broil to a fine brown color. Broil about thirty-five minutes.

BOILED PIGEONS.—Boil them about fifteen minutes by themselves ; then boil a piece of bacon ; serve with slices of bacon and melted butter.

Pigeons may be broiled or roasted the same as chickens, only cover the breast with thin slices of fat bacon. When nearly done, remove the bacon, and dredge with flour, and baste with butter. They will cook in about half an hour.

MEAT GRAVIES.

BEEF GRAVY.—The gravy which flows from the meat while roasting is the best. Remove the fat and sediment, and season with a little salt. If too thin, dust a spoonful of brown flour.

Veal gravy is made in the same manner, only adding a small piece of butter.

SAUCE FOR A FOWL.—Stew the neck and gizzard with a small piece of lemon peel, in about a cupful of water ; then take the liver of the fowl, and bruise it with some of the liquor ; melt a little good butter, and mix the liver and the gravy from the neck and gizzard gradually into it ; then give it a boil up and pour it into your dish.

SOUPS AND BROTHS.

BEEF SOUP.—Take three pounds of beef cut in small pieces, four quarts of water, and two tablespoonfuls of sifted bread ; season with pepper, salt, turnip, onions, and one head of celery, cut fine. Stew all together four hours.

VEAL SOUP.—Take four pounds of the knuckle of veal, and two gallons of water ; let it simmer away to two quarts, strain, and season it with pepper, salt, mace, and thicken as you like with a tablespoonful of flour, kneaded with a little butter.

PEA SOUP.—To a quart of water add a quart of dry peas, and let them soak over night, then boil them in the same water about half an hour. Then change the water, and add a pound of salt pork; boil till they are all soft, season with salt, pepper, and onions.

OYSTER SOUP.—Take a pint of oysters and stew them five minutes in their own liquor; then pound the hard part of the oysters with the yolks of three eggs boiled hard. Mix this with the soup, with salt, pepper and nutmeg, and let it boil again fifteen minutes.

CLAM SOUP.—Boil half a peck of clams about fifteen minutes, then take them from the shells and clean and wash them. Have ready the stew kettle, and fry three or four slices of salt pork, crackers, potatoes, etc. Season each layer with pepper, add a little thickening of flour and water, strain the clam water, and cover all over and let it stew about an hour; take care that it does not burn.

FISH.

There is a general rule in choosing most sorts of fish; if the gills are red, the eyes full, and the whole fish firm and stiff, they are fresh and good : if, on the contrary, the gills are pale, the eyes sunk, and the flesh flabby, they are stale.

BOILED CODFISH.—Cod fish should be boiled over a slow fire, and skimmed frequently. Season the water with salt, and be sure that there is sufficient water in the kettle to cover the fish. Garnish it when served up with parsley.

HALIBUT.—Halibut should be cut up into slices of four pounds each, and may be baked or fried. The skin on the back must be scored. When *baked*, use a sufficient quantity of butter to keep it moist. If *boiled*, lay it in the kettle on a strainer, cover it with salted water, boil it slowly half or three-quarters of an hour, and skim it well. Garnish it with horse-radish, serve it with melted buter. To *fry* halibut, cut it in slices less than an inch thick ; and with this as all other fish, take care to have plenty of butter, lard, or oil in the pan, and that it be hot before the fish is put in.

FISH CHOWDER.—Fry a few slices of salt pork, dress and cut the fish in small pieces, pare and slice the potatoes and onions, then place them in the kettle, a layer of fish, then of the fried pork, potatoes, onions, etc., seasoning each layer with salt and pepper. Stew over a slow fire thirty minutes.

VEGETABLES.

In boiling vegetables, always let the water boil before putting them in, and continue to boil until done. Do each kind by itself when convenient.

TURNIPS should be pared or scraped before boiling. If very large, cut them in halves or quarters; boil from forty minutes to one hour. If you mash them, press the water out first.

BEETS should be washed clean, but never cut or scraped. Boil from forty minutes to two hours ; then put them, one at a time, into a pan of cold water, and slip the skin off with your hand as quickly as possible.

CARROTS may be cut if too large. Boil from thirty minutes to an hour and a half.

PARSNIPS should be boiled from twenty minutes to one hour.

ONIONS are best boiled in milk and water, from twenty to thirty minutes.

STRING BEANS should be boiled from one hour to an hour and a half. Take them out as soon as done, and pour cream or milk over them.

SHELLED BEANS require from half an hour to an hour's boiling.

GREEN CORN should be boiled from twenty to forty minutes.

GREEN PEAS should always be boiled alone, in as little water as possible, twenty minutes.

ASPARAGUS.—Boil the same as peas. Toast slices of bread, lay them in a dish, spread the asparagus over them, and pour cream over the whole. Some first boil and thicken the cream.

WINTER SQUASH.—Cut it in large pieces, and boil it from twenty to forty minutes in a small quantity of water. When done, take it up in a large dish or wooden bowl, pare it, and press the water out with a small plate, and mash smooth.

SUMMER SQUASH should be boiled whole, and need not be pared at all. If large, take out the seeds after it is done.

CABBAGE AND DANDELIONS should be boiled from thirty to sixty minutes in plenty of water. The latter should be washed in three or four waters. Take them out of the water each time, and not pour it from them.

If salt is used in greens or cabbage, it should be put in while they are boiling.

BEET TOPS AND SPINACH should be boiled about twenty minutes, in a small quantity of water.

BOILED POTATOES.—Old potatoes are better to have the skin cut off the seed end, and better still to be pared and put into cold water two or three hours before boiling. Do not boil them in the same water. When a fork will pass through them easily, pour off the water, and hang the kettle over the fire again, uncovered, until the potatoes are quite dry. Some squeeze each one lightly in a dry cloth.

BAKED POTATOES.—Wash and wipe them before putting them in the oven. Bake from twenty minutes to an hour and a half.

BEANS AND PEAS should be cooked in soft water. Soak them over night, and then put them over the fire in fresh water, and let them cook very slowly, if you wish to bake them, or they will break to pieces. Change the water two or three times while they are softening. Salt them, and bake them in a deep pan. If baked in a brick oven, they are better to stand in three or four hours. The water should cover them by an inch when they are set in.

FRUITS, JELLIES, ETC.

Acid fruits should be cooked in bright tin, brass or bell metal, and poured out as soon as they are done. Brown earthern vessels should never be used, as they are glazed with white lead, a poison which very readily unites with an acid.

STRONG APPLE SAUCE.—Boil down new, sweet cider, till it is as nearly thick when cold as molasses. Pare and quarter your apples, and put them into some hot syrup. Cover and do them over a slow fire until tender. Put some molasses with the syrup, unless a part of the apples are sweet. This will keep good through the winter.

BOILED PEARS AND APPLES.—Boil them whole in a small quantity of water, until they begin to soften : then add a little sugar or molasses, and finish.

RASPBERRY JAM.—Weigh equal quantities of fruit and sugar. Put the fruit into a preserving pan, and mash with a silver or wooden spoon. Let it boil up, then add the sugar. Stir it well.

STRAWBERRY JAM is made the same as raspberry.

CURRANT JELLY.—Put the currants into a jar, and set them in a kettle of hot water until they become soft, so that you can mash them easily and express the juice. Strain it, and allow a pound of sugar for every pint. Boil them together slowly, skimming well, until it becomes ropy.

CRANBERRY JELLY.—To one quart of berries, put one pint of water and one pint of sugar, and let them boil half an hour without stirring ; then take off the jelly with a spoon, and what remains makes good sauce.

PRESERVES.—A pound of fruit to a pound of sugar is the rule for preserves.

PRESERVED CITRON.—Pare and cut open the citron ; clean all out except the rind ; boil till soft. To a pound of citron add one pound of sugar, and a lemon to each pound; put the sugar and lemon together, and boil it till it becomes a syrup, skimming it well; then put the syrup and cinnamon together, and boil it an hour.

BREAD, PUDDINGS, PIES, CAKES, ETC.

TO MAKE GOOD BROWN BREAD.—Take one quart of Indian meal and three pints of rye meal; put it into a pan, turn a half cupful of molasses and two teaspoonfuls of ginger into it. Take some saleratus and dissolve it in warm water, enough to mix the meal rather soft; let it remain in the pan to rise over night. When light enough, put into pans and bake it. Bread made thus will not sour so quick as when yeast is put into it.

TO MAKE A CHEAP AND HEALTHY BREAD.—Take a pumpkin and boil it in water until quite thick; then add flour so as to make it dough.

TO MAKE LOAF BREAD, HOT BREAKFAST CAKES, BUCK-WHEAT CAKES, ETC., *superior to anything of the kind before produced.*—Mix dry, and well rubbed together, two teaspoonfuls of cream of tartar, with one quart of flour; then dissolve three-fourths of a tablespoonful of super carbonate of soda in a sufficient quantity of *sweet* milk; mix the whole together, and bake immediately. If water be used instead of milk, add a little shortening.

DYSPEPSIA BREAD.—Three quarts of unbolted wheat meal, one quart of soft water, one gill of yeast, one gill of molasses, and a teaspoonful of saleratus.

BAKER'S GINGERBREAD.—Three-fourths of a pound of flour, one quart of molasses, one-fourth of a pound of butter, one ounce of saleratus, and one ounce of ginger.

BISCUITS.

SODA BISCUIT.—Take one quart of flour, two teaspoonfuls cream of tartar, one teaspoonful salt, one of saleratus or soda, small piece of butter for shortening. Mix with water.

MUFFINS.—A quart of milk, two eggs, two spoonfuls of yeast, two pounds of flour, a lump of butter size of an egg —which is to be melted in the milk—and a litile salt ; the milk is to be warmed, and the ingredients added. Let it rise, and then turn the mixture into buttered pans, and bake to a light brown.

PUDDINGS.

RULES TO BE OBSERVED IN MAKING PUDDINGS.

1. For boiling puddings there should be a tin form, or a muslin bag. The former should have a closely-fitting cover : the latter should first be dipped in boiling water, and then well floured on the inside, to prevent the pudding sticking to the cloth ; the tin form should first be rubbed over with suet or butter, before putting in the pudding.

2. Tie batter puddings very close.

3. Bread puddings, or those made of corn meal, should be loose, as they swell very much in boiling.

4. The water must be boiling when the pudding is put in.

5. The pudding, if boiled in a bag, must be turned frequently while boiling, otherwise it will stick to the pot.

6. There must be enough water to cover the pudding, and the water must be kept boiling all the time.

7. If boiled in a tin, do not let the water reach the top of it. When the pudding is done, give whatever it is boiled in one sudden plunge into cold water, and turn it out immediately. If it is not to be served soon, lay the cloth in which it was boiled over it. It is best to serve as soon as turned out.

8. Baked puddings, bread, Indian meal, or custard, require a moderate heat. Batter or rice, a quick oven.

BAKED INDIAN PUDDING.—Scald a quart of milk, and stir in seven table-spoonfuls of Indian meal, a teaspoonful of salt, a teacup of molasses, and a table-spoonful of ginger or cinnamon. Bake three or four honrs. If you want whey, you must pour in a little cold milk after it is all mixed.

BAKED RICE PUDDING.—Swell a coffee-cup of rice, add a quart of nice milk, sweeten it with brown sugar, and bake it about an hour in a quick oven.

PLUM PUDDING.—Pound six crackers, and soak them over night in milk enough to cover them ; then add three pints of milk, four or five eggs, one-half pound of raisins, and spice it with nutmeg ; sweeten it with sugar and molasses. Bake about two hours.

CUSTARD PUDDING.—Take five eggs to a quart of milk, sweetened with brown sugar or molasses ; spice with cassia or nutmeg ; a little salt. Bake fifteen or twenty minutes.

BATTER PUDDING.—Beat up from four to six eggs with a quart of milk ; add a little salt, and flour enough to make it pour with ease. Boil three quarters of an hour.

TAPIOCA PUDDING.—Pick and wash a coffee-cupful of tapioca, and pour upon it a pint of boiling milk. After standing half an hour, add another pint of cold milk, with sugar, and raisins if you like.

STEAM PUDDING.—Pare and slice ten or twelve apples ; put them in a kettle with a little water, say a gill, make a crust the same as for soda biscuit, and cover the apples : close the kettle so that no steam can escape. Cook in about twenty minutes. Eat with sauce. This is a very cheap, wholesome, and agreeable pudding.

SAUCES AND CREAMS FOR PUDDINGS.

1. Take equal quantities of sugar and molasses, boil them together, and stir in a little flour.

2. Take the juice of an orange, a cup of sugar, and the same of good cream.

3. Good sour cream, made very sweet with sugar, with or without seasoning, makes excellent sauce.

4. Beat two eggs well, then add a cup of stewed apples and a cup of sugar. Beat all well together.

PIES.

MINCE PIES.—Take one quart of wheat or rye bread, and one quart of sour apples, after they are chopped fine, one pint of sugar-house molasses, one pint of cream or milk, one pint of chopped raisins, two large spoonfuls of cinnamon, one teaspoonful of salt, the juice of six lemons, and the rind of one grated.

APPLE PIES.—Peel and stew the apples, mash them fine, with sugar, a little butter and grated nutmeg, or lemon peel; bake in a rich crust and quick oven, but not hot enough to scorch.

CUSTARD PIES.—Allow six or eight beaten eggs to a quart of milk, and sweeten with sugar. Do not bake them too much. It is a good plan to put the crust on the plates, prick and bake them, before pouring in the custard.

CRANBERRY TARTS.—Put two pounds of sugar into two quarts of cranberries, wet with water and stew them until done. When wanted for use put them on a puff-paste crust.

SQUASH PIES.—Boil and sift the squash, and make them exactly like pumpkin pies.

CARROT and sweet potato pies are made in the same way with crackers; eggs or rice should always be used with them.

CAKES.

RULES TO BE OBSERVED IN CAKE-MAKING.

1. In making cakes, if you wish them to be pleasing to the eye as well as the palate, use double-refined white sugar; although clean brown sugar makes an equally good cake.

2. None but good sweet butter should be used for cake-making; if the butter should be a little salt it will do no harm. Butter in the least degree rank or strong will spoil any cake.

3. Cake mixture cannot be beaten too much.

4. An oven, to bake well, must have a regular heat throughout.

5. An earthen basin is the best for beating eggs or cake mixture in.

6. To ascertain whether a cake is done, if it is a small one, take a broom splint and run it through the thickest part; if it is not done, there will be some of the dough sticking to it; if done, it will come out clean.

7. Cakes to be kept should be folded in a linen napkin, and put in a stone jar.

SUPERIOR INDIAN CAKE.—Take two cups of Indian meal, one tablespoonful of molasses, two cups of milk, a little salt, a handful of flour, and a little saleratus; mix thin, and pour it into a buttered bake-pan, and bake half an hour.

NUT CAKE.—Take one pound of flour, one quarter of a pound of butter, same of sugar, five eggs, and spice to your taste.

SEED CAKE.—One teacup of butter, two cups of sugar, rubbed into four cups of flour; mix with milk hard enough to roll; half a teaspoonful of saleratus; seeds to your taste.

SPONGE CAKE.—Sift one pound of flour and one pound loaf sugar; take the juice of one lemon, beat ten eggs very light, mix them well with the sugar, then add the lemon and flour. If baked in a pan, two hours is necessary.

LOAF CAKE.—Take two pounds of flour, half pound of sugar, a quarter of a pound of butter, three eggs, one gill of milk, one half teacupful of sweet yeast, cloves and nutmeg for spice.

POUND CAKE.—One pound of flour, one pound of sugar, one of butter, ten eggs, rose water and nutmeg.

WEDDING CAKE.—Take four pounds of flour, three of butter, three of sugar, four of currants, two of raisins, two of eggs, one ounce of mace, and three nutmegs; a little citron and molasses inproves it. Bake about three hours.

DEPARTMENT OF SICK COOKERY.

In making porridge, always wet the flour or meal in a part of the water; boil the remainder, and stir the thickening into it, and when it is sufficiently cooked, add the milk, and let it boil up once. Wheat meal will boil in three minutes, Indian meal and ground rice in six or eight minutes.

COMMON MILK PORRIDGE.—Three or four spoonfuls of wheat meal, or Indian meal and flour, one pint of water, and one quart of milk.

GRUEL.—Indian rye, oat and wheat meal and rice, are used for gruel. Wet two or three spoonfuls with water, and stir it into a quart of boiling water, and boil until they are well cooked. Indian meal should boil full half an hour.

BEEF TEA.—Cut a pound of good beef into thin slices; simmer in a quart of water twenty minutes; after it has once boiled and been skimmed, season it if you wish, and add salt.

BEEF GRUEL.—Take two pounds of lean beef, five quarts of water simmered down to three quarts; add half a cup of rice and a little salt. Veal or mutton is prepared the same way.

Weak persons may take eggs in the following manner. Beat an egg very fine, add some sugar and nutmeg; pour upon it a gill of boiling water, and drink it immediately.

A VERY SUPPORTING BROTH AGAINST ANY KIND OF WEAKNESS.—Boil two pounds of loin of mutton, with a very large handful of celery or an onion, in two quarts of water to one. Take off part of the fat. Any other herbs or roots may be added. Take half a pint three or four times a day.

SIPPETS, WHEN THE STOMACH WILL NOT RECEIVE MEAT. —On an extremely hot plate put two or three slices of stale bread, and pour over them some gravy from beef, mutton, or veal, with which no butter has been mixed. Sprinkle a little salt over them.

RICE CAUDLE.—Boil a quart of water, and pour into it a teacupful of ground rice, mixed with a little cold water; when of a proper consistence, add sugar, lemon peel, and cinnamon. Boil all smooth.

DRINKS FOR THE SICK AND CONVALESCENT.

LEMON WATER, A DELIGHTFUL DRINK.—Put two slices of lemon, thinly pared, in a teapot, a little bit of the peel, and a bit of sugar, or a large spoon of capillaire ; pour in a pint of boiling water, and stop it close two hours.

APPLE WATER.—Cut two large apples in slices, and pour a quart of boiling water on them, or on roasted apples; strain them after they have stood two or three hours, and sweeten lightly.

A REFRESHING DRINK IN A FEVER.—Put a little tea-sage, two sprigs of balm, a *little* wood-sorrel, into a stone jug, having first washed and dried them; peel thin a small lemon, and clear from the white ; slice it, and put a bit of the peel in ; then pour in three pints of boiling water, sweeten and cover it close.

YEASTS.

In summer, bread should be mixed with cold water ; in damp weather, the water should be tepid ; and in cold weather, quite warm. If the yeast is new, a small quantity will make the bread rise. In the country, yeast cakes are found very convenient, but they seldom make the bread as good as fresh, lively yeast.

POTATO YEAST.—Boil potatoes soft, peel and mash them, and add as much water as will make them of the consistence of common yeast ; while the potatoes are warm, put in half a teacupful of molasses, and two table-spoonfuls of yeast. Let it stand near the fire until done fermenting, when it will be fit for use.

HOP YEAST.—In two quarts of water boil a handful of hops, strain, and pour the liquor hot upon half a teacupful of wheat flour. When about milk-warm, add a teacupful of yeast. Let it ferment, will be ready for use and may be bottled.

TEA, COFFEE, ETC.

TEA.—Scald the teapot with boiling water, then put in the

tea. Pour on the water—it must be boiling hot—and let the tea steep about two minutes. A teaspoonful of tea to a person is the rule.

DELICIOUS COFFEE.—Grind the coffee just before making. Allow about two spoonfuls to a person. Put it in a basin, and into it an egg, yolk, white, shell and all. Mix it up with the spoon to the consistence of mortar; put warm, not boiling water, in the coffee-pot; let it boil up and break three times; then stand a few minutes, and it will be as clear as amber, and the egg will give it a rich taste.

COCOA SHELLS.—Let the shells be soaked over night, then boil them in the same water in the morning. They are considered nutricious and healthy, and are very cheap.

PICKLES AND CATSUPS.

Kettles of block tin, or lined with porcelain, are the best for pickling. Iron discolors the acid, and the verdigris, produced by the vinegar on brass, copper, or bell-metal, is extremely poisonous. If, after keeping the pickles any time, you discern any symptoms of their not keeping well, boil them over again with fresh vinegar and spice. The jars in which pickles are kept should always be full enough of vinegar to cover the pickles. Vinegar for pickles should only boil five or six minutes.

A method of pickling cucumbers, which is good, is to put them in salt and wa er as you pick them, changing the salt and water once in three or four days. When you have done collecting your cucumbers for pickling, take them out of the salt and water, turn on scalding hot vinegar, with alum and salt in it.

TO PICKLE VEGETABLES.—Soak them for about one day in brine, then drain them, put them into bottles, and pour on them boiling vinegar until quite covered. Cork immediately.

TOMATO PICKLES.—Take one peck of tomatoes gathered green, and one third as many peppers, soak them in co water twenty-four hours; cold sharp vinegar enough to cover, with one ounce of bruised cloves to a gallon of vinegar. Tomatoes pickled in this way will keep one year.

PEPPERS.—Take those that are fresh and green, soak them in salt and water eight or nine days, changing the brine each day, and keeping them in a warm place. If they are not wanted very fiery, make a slit in them and extract the seeds.

TOMATO CATSUP.—Take six pounds of tomatoes, and sprinkle with salt; let them remain a day or two, then boil, and press through a coarse sieve or colander. Put into the liquor half a pint of vinegar, cloves, pepper, ginger, and cinnamon; boil them one third away. Bottle tight. It should be shaken before being used.

CHOICE MEDICAL COMPOUNDS

VALUABLE TO EVERY FAMILY.

The following recipes may be relied upon as being genuine, they have been often proved, and never disappointed the expectations of any one.

WORM ELIXIR.

Take one ounce saffron, one ounce aloes, one ounce myrrh; steep the myrrh four days in half pint rum or brandy, then add the saffron and aloes.

Dose.—Give a teaspoonful once a month to children, and they will never be troubled with worms.

OPODELDOC.

Take common white soap three ounces; camphor one ounce; oil of origanum half an ounce; alcohol one pint. Cut the soap and dissolve it in the alcohol, in which the other articles have been previously dissolved, and cool it in wide-mouthed vials for use.

PAREGORIC.

Take opium one drachm; flowers of benzoin one drachm; camphor two scruples; oil of anise one drachm; licorice one ounce; spirits one quart.

Dose.—A teaspoonful for an adult; half, for a child two years old.

GRAND FAMILY SANATIVE.

Gum aloes half an ounce; rhubarb one ounce; ginger one ounce; myrrh one drachm; cayenne pepper one teaspoonful; spirits one quart. Steep twenty-four hours, then add a tea-cupful of sugar, and half a pint of water.

Dose.—Take from one to two large table-spoonfuls half an hour before eating. Good for dyspepsia and all derangements of the stomach, in children or adults.

HEART-BURN LOZENGERS.

Take prepared chalk four ounces; crab's-eyes prepared two ounces; bole ammoniac one ounce; make into a paste with dissolved gum arabic.

SEIDLITZ POWDERS.

Fold in a paper one drachm of Rochelle salts; in another paper a mixture of twenty grains of tartaric acid, and twenty-five grains of carbonate of soda. Dissolve their contents in separate tumblers, not half full of water, then pour the one in the other. Drink while foaming.

SODA WATER.

Take one third of a teaspoonful of carbonate of soda, and half that quantity of tartaric acid, loaf sugar to make it pleasant. Dissolve the soda first, and drink while it foams.

ALL-HEALING SALVE.

Take equal parts of rosin, beeswax, sweet oil; melt and mix, stirring until cool. This is a good healing salve for all common sores; but if a more healing remedy is needed, add to this when almost boiling hot, two pounds of red lead; when almost cold, add half an ounce of pulverized camphor. This should be spread thin, and renewed once or twice a day.

RHEUMATIC TINCTURE.

Take camphor two drachms: gum guaiacum one ounce; nitre one ounce; balsam Tolu two drachms; spirits one quart; mix well.

Dose.—Half a teaspoonful in a little water three or four times a day.

SPASMODIC, OR CRAMP TINCTURE.

Take four ounces of camphorated spirits; four ounces of essence of peppermint; half an ounce of spirits of ammonia; one teaspoonful of cayenne pepper, and two of ginger.

Dose.—According to age and urgency of disease; say tablespoonful at first, and a teaspoonful every half hour afterward, till the pain abates. Dilute with a little water.

DYSENTERY AND DIARRHŒA CORDIAL.

Take rhubarb one ounce; saleratus one teaspoonful; pour on them a pint of boiling water. When cold, two teaspoonfuls of essence of peppermint.

Dose.—Teaspoonful once in fifteen minutes, till the symptoms abate.

VOLATILE LINIMENT.

Take one ounce of spirits of ammonia or hartshorn, and add sweet oil until it is as thick and looks like cream. This is good for an external application in all swellings and inflammations.

BALSAM OF HONEY.

Take of balsam of Tolu two ounces; gum storax two drachms; opium two drachms; honey eight ounces. Dissolve these in a quart of spirits of wine. This balsam is very useful in hoarseness, and allaying irritations of the lungs. It will often cure a cough that is alarming.

TOOTH-ACHE PASTE.

Take gum of opium, gum camphor, and spirits of turpentine, equal parts; rub them in a mortar to a paste. Put **in** the hollow of the tooth. This, it is said, will cure and prevent from ever aching.

PLASTER FOR WHITE SWELLINGS.

Melt together in an iron ladle, or earthen pipkin, **two** ounces of soap and half an ounce of litharge plaster. When nearly cold, stir in a drachm of sal ammoniac, in fine powder; spread upon leather, and apply to the part affected.

DYSPEPTIC BITTERS.

Take four ounces of golden seal, two ounces of bitter root, four ounces of poplar bark, four ounces of peach-meats ; add two quarts of water and two quarts of gin. Good in dyspepsia, weakness of the stomach, etc.

Dose.—Two thirds of a wineglass before eating.

TINCTURE OF LOBELIA.

This is made by putting two ounces of the dried herb and seeds together, in a pint of common gin. Let it stand a week, when it will be fit for use. For children, from one to two teaspoonfuls is a dose ; and for adults, from a half **to** a whole wineglassful, always repeating the dose every fifteen or twenty minutes, till it vomits. A little warm saleratus water will promote the operation of it, whenever desired.

HOT DROPS.

This is made by adding three fourths of a pound of best gum myrrh, pulverized, and one ounce of African cayenne, to one gallon of alcohol, or fourth proof brandy.

COMPOSITION.

Take one pound of bayberry bark, eight ounces of ginger, two ounces of cloves, two ounces of cayenne, and mix them well together.

SWEET TINCTURE OF RHUBARB.

Rhubarb, in coarse powder, two ounces; licorice root one ounce; fine white sugar two ounces; new rum, three pints. Digest in a warm place one week, then strain.

Dose.—For an adult, from a half to a whole wineglassful.

NERVE OINTMENT.

Neatsfoot oil a gill; spirits of turpentine one ounce; beef's gall one ounce; brandy half a pint. Simmer till mixed, and bottle for use. It is excellent for rheumatism, and perishing or contracted limbs.

LINIMENT.

Of most excellent kind, is made by incorporating two ounces of camphor; six ounces of spirits of wine; and then adding two ounces spirits sal ammoniac, and two drachms oil of lavender.

STOMACH PLASTER FOR A COUGH.

Take beeswax, Burgundy pitch, and rosin, each an ounce; melt them together in a clean pipkin, and then stir in three quarters of an ounce of common turpentine, and half an ounce of oil of mace. Spread it on a piece of sheep's leather, grate some nutmeg over the whole plaster, and apply it quite warm to the region of the stomach.

PULMONIC SYRUP.

Take six ounces of comfrey roots and twelve handfuls of plantain leaves; cut and beat them well; strain out the juice, and, with an equal weight of sugar, boil it up to a syrup. This is said to be an infallible cure for coughing blood.

TO REMOVE FRECKLES.

Take two ounces of lemon juice, a half drachm of powdered borax, and one drachm of sugar; mix together, and let them stand in a glass bottle for a few days; then rub it on the hands and face occasionally.

INDIAN RECIPES.

These recipes have been collected with great care, and are alone worth double the price of the paper and this book.

A CERTAIN CURE FOR A COMMON COLD.

Boil a common-sized turnip, put it into a saucer, and pour upon it half a cup of molasses, and let it stand fifteen minutes; then turn off the syrup, at the same time squeezing the turnip so as to express its fluid. The syrup to be drank warm on going to bed.

CURE FOR THE LOCKJAW.

Bind upon the wound, and in close contact with it, a common cent, or any piece of copper. It will give immediate relief. Tarnished copper is the best.

DROPSY ON THE CHEST.

Take a quarter pound of dried milk-weed, cut small; pour on it a quart of boiling water; simmer to one pint; when cool, add a pint of best Holland gin; pour both liquor and roots into a decanter, cork it tight, and let it stand twelve hours.

Dose.—For an adult, half a wineglassful every three hours, day and night. If it nauseate too much, the dose may be varied. Effect seen in three or five days. This has been repeatedly tried, and was seldom known to fail.

CURE FOR A WEAK STOMACH AND DYSPEPSIA.

Take a demijohn half full of wild cherries, and fill up the demijohn with pure *old Jamaica spirits*. Take half a wineglassful twice a day. Use no sugar, as it destroys the tonic properties of the cherries. This preparation has accomplished wonders in restoring the sick.

SORE THROAT.

Inhale through a tunnel the steam of hot vinegar, in which sage leaves have been steeped.

A MEDICINE TO CURE INWARD ULCERS.

Sassafras root bark, two ounces; coltsfoot root, two ounces; bloodroot, one ounce; gum myrrh, one ounce; winter bark, one ounce; socotrine aloes, one ounce; steep them in two quarts of spirits, and drink a small glass every morning.

FOR THE BILIOUS COLIC.

Take West India rum, one gill; West India molasses, one gill; of hog's lard, one gill; and the urine of beast one gill. Simmer well together. This composition will seldom fail of performing an effectual cure for life.

FOR A HECTIC COUGH.

Take three yolks of hens eggs, three spoonfuls of honey, and one of tar; beat well together; add one gill of wine. Take a teaspoonful three times a day before eating.

REMEDY FOR WEAKNESS IN THE URINE VESSELS.

Steep two ounces of good red bark in one quart of wine for twenty-four hours; let the patient drink a tablespoonful if two or three years old; if older, a little more.

SALVE FOR A BURN.

Take wild lavender, the green of elder bark, chamomile and parsley, and stew them in fresh butter; strain off, and add to it beeswax, rosin, and white diachylon, equal parts.

A CURE FOR GRAVEL IN THE BLADDER OR KIDNEYS.

Make a strong tea of the herb called heart's-ease—drink plenty. Or, take the root of Jacob's ladder, and make a very strong tea, and drink plenty. It is a certain remedy.

FOR THE RATTLES IN CHILDREN.

Take bloodroot, powder it, give the patient a small teaspoonful at a dose; if the first does not break the bladder in half an hour, repeat again three times. This has not been known to fail curing.

CURE FOR THE ITCH.

Take half a pound hog's lard, four ounces spirits turpentine, two ounces flour sulphur, and mix them together cold. Apply it to the ankles, knees, wrists, and elbows, and rub it in the palms of the hands, if there be any raw spots. Apply a little three nights when going to bed.

CURE FOR CORNS ON THE FEET OR TOES.

Take white-pine turpentine, spread a plaster, apply it to the corn, let it stay on till it comes off of itself. Repeat this three times.

FOR THE DROPSY.

Half a pound of blue-flag root, same of elecampane root, boiled in two gallons of fair water to one quart, sweetened with one pint of molasses. Let the patient take half a gill three times a day before eating.

A CURE FOR THE FLYING RHEUMATISM.

Prince's pine tops, horseradish roots, elecampane roots, prickly-ash bark, bittersweet bark off the root, wild-cherry bark and mustard seed—a small handful of each; one gill of tar water into one pint of brandy, or in the same proportion. Drink a small glass before eating, three times a day.

CURE FOR THE SALT-RHEUM.

Take swamp sassafras bark, boil it in water very strong, take some of the water and wash the part affected; to the remainder of the water add hog's lard, simmer it over a moderate fire till the water is gone. Anoint the part affected after washing. Continue four days. Never fails of a cure.

A CURE FOR BLEEDING AT THE STOMACH.

Take a pound of yellow dock root, dry it thoroughly, pound fine, boil it in a quart of sweet milk, and strain off. Drink a gill three times a day. Take also a pill of white-pine turpentine every day, to heal the vessels that leak.

HOUSEWIVES', OR FAMILY RECIPES.

THESE RECIPES HAVE ALL BEEN PROVED.

1. To Wash White Merino Shawls.—Wash the shawl in fair suds made beforehand, rub no soap on the shawl, rinse in clear warm water, with two changes if you please; then take a solution of gum Arabic, and add to it warm water till you think it will produce a little stiffness like starch when dry. Press with a moderately hot iron, before quite dry, laying a clean cotton or linen cloth between the iron and the shawl.

2. To Cleanse Black Veils.—Pass them through a liqor of beef's gall and water; then take a small piece of glue, pour boiling water on it, and pass the veil through it; clay and frame it dry, and it will be as beautiful as new.

3. To Clean Britannia or Silver.—Simple whiting, powdered and moistened with alcohol, is the best article ever used.

4. To Destroy Red Ants.—Crack shagbark walnuts, and lay them where you wish to collect them, and then wet the cracks where they come with corrosive sublimate.

5. To Take Out Grease Spots from Silks, Cotton, or Woolen.—Pulverize fine new pipe-stems or pipes, lay it on the spots, put a brown paper, when you can, under the cloth, and one over the powder, set on it a warm iron, and it will extract all the grease, if it remains sufficiently long.

6. To Clean Bedticks, However Badly Soiled.— Apply Poland starch, by rubbing it on thick with a wet cloth. Place it in the sun. When dry, rub it in with the hands;

repeat it, if necessary. The soiled part will be as clean as new.

7. TO PREVENT LAMPS FROM SMOKING.—It is very often difficult to get a good light from a lamp, and yet keep it from smoking; but if the wick is first soaked in strong vinegar, and then thoroughly dried, this annoyance will be prevented. Still, the wick must not be put up too high.

8. TO TAKE MILDEW OUT OF LINEN.—Take soap and rub it well; then scrape some fine chalk, and rub that also in the linen. Lay it on the grass; as it dries wet it a little, and it will soon come out.

9. TO TAKE STAINS OUT OF MAHOGANY.—Spirits of salts, six parts; salts of lemon, one part. Mix, then drop a little on the stains, and rub them till they disappear.

10. TO RESTORE COLORS TAKEN OUT BY ACIDS.—Sal-volatile or hartshorn will restore colors taken out by acids. It will not harm the garment.

11. TO SET COLORS FAST IN CALICO AND OTHER GOODS.—Ox's gall will set the color of any goods, whether silk, woolen, or cotton. Dissolve one tablespoonful of gall in a gallon of warm water, and wash the article in it, without soap. The gall is a cheap article, and a bottle of it should be kept by every family.

TO MAKE A VARIETY OF COLORS.

GENERAL RULES.

I. The materials should be clean, rinsed with soap, and entirely wet, that they may not spot.

II. Light colors should be steeped in brass, tin, or earthern, and if set at all, with alum.

III. Dark colors should be steeped in iron, and set with copperas.

12. GREEN.—For every pound of yarn or cloth add two and a half ounces of alum, and one pound of fustic. Steep in the strength, but not boil; soak the cloth until it comes to a good yellow color; then throw out the chips, and

slowly add indigo in proportion to the green you wish to obtain.

13. ROSE.—Steep balm blossoms in earthen or tin ; add a small quantity of alum to set the color.

14. STRAW.—Steep saffron blossoms in water, in earthen or tin. Set it with alum.

15. SKY BLUE.—Twelve or sixteen drops of the blue composition, to be had at the druggists, poured into a quart bowl of soft warm water, will dye a great many articles. If you want a deeper color, add a few drops more of the composition. If you wish to color cotton goods, put in pounded chalk to destroy the acid, which is very destructive to all cotton. Let it stand until the effervescence subsides, and then it may be safely used for cotton as well as silk. The old colors should be all discharged by soap or a strong tartaric acid water, then rinse.

16. NANKEEN.—The simplest way is to take a pailful of lye, to which put a piece of copperas half as big as a hen's egg. Boil in copper or tin kettle.

17. LILAC.—Take a little pinch of Archil, and put some boiling hot water upon it ; add to it a very little lump of pearlash. Shades may be altered by pearlash, common salt, or wine.

18. SLATE.—Tea grounds, boiled in iron vessels, set with copperas, makes a good slate color. To produce a light slate color, boil white maple bark in clear water, with a little alum. The bark should be boiled in a brass utensil. The goods should be boiled in it, and then hung where they will drain and dry.

19. ROYAL PURPLE.—Soak logwood chips in soft water until the strength is out, then add alum, a teaspoonful to a quart of the liquor. If this is not bright enough, add more alum. Rinse dry. When the dye is exhausted, it will color a fine lilac.

20. RED.—Steep balm blossoms in water, in earthen or tin, and vary the shade with a decoction of logwood.

21. BLACK.—Boil logwood in cider or vinegar, in iron ves-

sels. One pound of logwood to one pailful of water ; add a little copperas to set the color.

22. SOFT SOAP.—Ten pounds of potash mixed in ten gallons of warm water, over night ; in the morning boil it, adding six pounds of grease; then put it in a barrel, adding fifteen gallons of warm water.

23. HARD SOAP.—One pound of salt of soda, two pounds of hard soap, five quarts of water ; boil down to three quarts ; let it stand until cold, then cut it in slices to dry.

24. LABOR-SAVING SOAP.—Take two pounds of sal soda ; two pounds of yellow bar soap, and ten quarts of water. Cut the soap in thin slices, and boil together two hours; strain, and it will be fit for use. Put the clothes in soak the night before you wash, and to every pail of water in which you boil them, add a pound of soap. They will need no rubbing; merely rinse them out, and they will be perfectly clean and white.

25. TO PRESERVE CHEESE.—Cover them carefully with paper put on with flour paste, so as to keep out the air. In this way they may be kept free from insects for years. Keep them in a cool, dry place.

26. TO DESTROY BEDBUGS.—Rub the bedsteads well with lamp oil; this alone is good, but to make it more effectual, get a sixpence worth of quicksilver and add to it. Put it into all the cracks around the bed, and they will soon disappear. The bedsteads should first be scalded, and wiped dry, then put on with a feather.

27. TO CLEANSE FOUL CASKS.—Fill them with meal, or bran, and water, and let them stand till fermentation takes place ; it will entirely cleanse them without expense, as the mixture is afterward better food for swine than before.

28. TO PRESERVE HAMS.—Hams, after being well salted and smoked, may be preserved sweet a year by packing them down in oats.

29. METHOD OF CLEANING CHINA.—Mix a little pearlash, or potter's clay, or soda, with your water, and it will give them a bright appearance.

SECRETS AND PATENTS IN THE USE-FUL ARTS REVEALED.

To prepare a Transparent Paper for Drawing.—Have one or several sheets of fine and very thin paper, and rub them over with oil or spirits of turpentine, mixed in double the quantity of the oil of nuts. To cause the paper to imbibe this mixture, dip a sponge or feather in it, which you will pass on both sides of the paper, and let it dry.

When you want to use it, lay it on a print. Then, with a brush, a pencil, or a pen, pass over all the strokes, lines and turns of the design laid under. You may even thus learn to shade with neatness, if you wash that same design, while fixed on the original print, with India ink.

By practising often you may learn to draw very neatly, and even with boldness. This method will certainly prove very useful and entertaining for those who have not the patience to learn in the common way.

To take off instantly the Copy of a Print.—Make a water of soap and alum, with which wet a cloth or paper, lay it on a print or picture, and pass it once under the rolling press, and you will have a very fine copy of whatever you shall have laid it upon. Some other powerful pressure will produce the same result.

A Varnish to prevent the Rays of the Sun from passing through Window or other Glass.—Pound gum adragant into powder, and put it to dissolve for twenty-four hours in whites of eggs well beaten, Lay a coat of this on your glass with a soft brush, and let it dry.

To make a Cheap Green Paint for Walls.—Take

four pounds of Roman vitriol, and pour on it a teakettleful of boiling water ; when dissolved, add two pounds of pearl-ash, and stir the mixture well with a stick until the effervescence cease ; then add a quarter of a pound of pulverized yellow arsenic, and stir the whole together. Lay it on with a paint-brush, and if the wall has not been painted before, two or even three coats will be requisite. If a pea-green is required, put in less, and if an apple-green, more of the yellow arsenic. The cost of this paint is less than one fourth of oil color, and the beauty far superior.

A STRONG PASTE FOR PAPERING ROOMS, AND OTHER USEFUL PURPOSES.—Take wheat flour, and mix with it a fourth, fifth or sixth of its weight of powdered resin or rosin ; and when it is wanted still more tenacious, mix with it gum arabic, or any kind of size. Stir the whole in enough water to make a very thin batter. which is boiled until it is of a viscid consistence.

TO MAKE PAINT WITHOUT WHITE LEAD AND OIL.—Take two quarts of skimmed milk, two ounces fresh slacked lime, and five pounds of whiting. Put the lime into a stone-ware vessel, pour upon it a sufficient quantity of milk to make a mixture resembling cream ; the remainder of the milk is then to be added ; and lastly the whiting is to be crumbled and spread on the surface of the fluid. in which it gradually sinks. At this period it must be well stirred in, or ground as you would other paint, and it is fit for use. You may add any coloring matter that suits the fancy.

It is to be applied in the same manner as other paint, and in a few hours it will become perfectly dry. Another coat may then be added, and so on until the work is completed to your liking. This paint is of great tenacity and a slight elasticity, which admits of being rubbed hard, even with a coarse woolen cloth, without being injured in the least.

It has little or no smell when wet, and when dry is perfectly inodorous. It is not subject to be blackened up by sulphurous vapors, and it is not injurious to the health, all which qualities give it a decided preference. The above will cover twenty-seven square yards once over.

TO MAKE WATER OIL, FOR PAINTERS.—Take eight pounds of pure unslacked lime, add twelve quarts of water; stir it and let it settle, turn it off gently, and bottle it; keep it corked till used. This will mix with oil, and, in proportion of half, will render paint more durable.

THE BEST SHAVING SOAP EVER INVENTED.—Take four pounds white bar soap, one quart rain-water, one half pint beef's gall, one gill spirits turpentine. Cut the soap into thin slices, and boil five minutes after the soap is dissolved; stir while boiling; color it with one half paper vermilion; scent with what you like; use the oil instead of essence. Seventy-five cents worth of materials will make seven dollars' worth of soap.

WHITE SPRUCE BEER.—Three pounds of loaf sugar; five gallons of water, with enough of essence of spruce to give it a flavor; a cup of good yeast; a little lemon peel, if you choose; and when fermented bottle it up close. It is a delightful beverage in warm weather.

IMPERIAL GINGER POP.—Take cream tartar one pound; ginger one and a half ounce; white sugar seven pounds; essence lemon one drachm; water six gallons; yeast half a pint. Mix. Tie the cork down.

VOLATILE SOAP, FOR REMOVING PAINT, GREASE SPOTS, ETC.—Four table-spoonfuls of spirits of hartshorn, four table-spoonfuls of alcohol, and a table-spoonful of salt. Shake the whole well together in a bottle, and apply with a sponge or brush.

POWDER FOR REMOVING SUPERFLUOUS HAIR.—Powdered quicklime two parts; sulphuret of arsenic one part; starch one part. Mix in fine powder, and keep in a close vessel.

FRENCH ROSE POMATUM.—White wax one pound; lard three pounds; suet three pounds. Melt, and when partly cold, stir in rose-water one pint; ottar of rose forty drops. The appearance of this pomatum is much improved by giving it a pink color.

To make a powder, by which you may write with Water.—Bruise to a powder a handful of galls, half an ounce of vitriol, an ounce of gum arabic and gum sandrick. Mingle them finely sifted together, then rub your paper with a little of it, laid upon cotton wool; and, having smoothed it, take water and write upon the paper; then suffering it to dry, it will be black.

Cheap and excellent Blue Color for Ceilings, etc. Boil slowly for three hours, a pound of blue vitriol, and half a pound of the best whiting, in about three quarts of water; stir it frequently while boiling, and also on taking it off the fire. When it has stood till quite cold, pour off the blue liquor; then mix the cake of color with good size, and use it with a plasterer's brush in the same manner as whitewash, either for walls or ceilings.

Common Small Beer.—A handful of hops to a pailful of water; a pint of bran, and half a pint of molasses; a cup of yeast and a spoonful of ginger.

Root Beer.—Take a pint of bran, a handful of hops, some twigs of spruce, hemlock or cedar, a little sassafras, or not, as you have it; roots of various kinds, plantains, burdock, dandelions, etc.; boil and strain; add a spoonful of ginger and molasses to make it pleasant, and a cup of yeast. When you want it soon, let one bottle stand where it is warm, and the rest will work cold. This for a gallon.

For Indelible Ink.—To four drachms of lunar costic in four ounces of water, add sixty drops of nutgalls made strong by being pulverized and steeped in soft water. The mordant which is to be applied to the cloth before writing, is composed of one ounce of pearlash dissolved in four ounces of water, with a little gum arabic dissolved in it. Wet the spot with this, dry and iron the cloth, then write.

For Red Marking Ink.—Half an ounce of vermilion, one drachm of salt of steel, finely levigated with linseed oil to a proper consistency.

Ink Powder for immediate Use.—Reduce to powder ten ounces of gallnuts, three ounces of green copperas, two ounces each of powdered alum and gum arabic. Put a little of this mixture into white wine, and it will be fit for immediate use.

TO MAKE INK FOR MARKING LINEN WITH TYPE.—Dissolve one part of asphaltum in four parts of oil of turpentine; add lampblack or black lead in fine powder, in sufficient quantity to render of proper consistence to print with type.

UNSURPASSABLE BLACKING.—Put one gallon of vinegar into a stone jug, and one pound of ivory black well pulverized, a half pound of loaf sugar, a half ounce of oil of vitriol, and six ounces of sweet oil; incorporate the whole by stirring.

TO MAKE COLOGNE WATER.—Take a pint of alcohol, and put in thirty drops of oil of lemon, thirty of bergamot, and half a gill of water. If you desire musk, or lavender, add the same quantity of each. The oils should be put in the alcohol and shook well before the water is added. Bottle it for use.

ESSENCES.—An ounce of oil to one pint of alcohol is about a fair proportion. Let them be well shaken together.

TO MAKE SARSAPARILLA MEAD.—One pound of Spanish sarsaparilla; boil five hours, so as to strain off two gallons; add sixteen pounds sugar and ten ounces of tartaric acid; one half wineglass of syrup to one half pint tumbler of water, and one half teaspoonful of soda powder, is a fair proportion for a drink.

LEMON SYRUP.—Take one pound of Havana sugar, boil it in water down to a quart, drop in the white of an egg, and strain it. Add one quarter of an ounce of tartaric acid; let it stand two days; shake it often. Four drops of oil of lemon will much improve it.

TURKISH ROUGE, TO GIVE A BEAUTIFUL COMPLEXION.—Get three cents' worth of alkanet chips at any druggist's; tie them in a gauze bag, and suspend it in a glass vessel containing a half pint of alcohol. When it comes to the right color, take out the alkanet. This is a superior rouge; it will not rub off, and is in noways injurious to the face.

COMPOSITION FOR LUCIFER MATCHES.—Take four parts glue, dissolve, and when it is hot, add one part phosphorus, and sift in a few spoonfuls of whiting, to bring it to the proper thickness. This is the identical receipt from which the N. E. Friction Match Company's matches are made.

TO REMOVE WRITING INK FROM A PRINTED PAGE.—Add one-half part red oxide lead to three parts muriatic acid; pour it on the page, and immediately wash it off with water.

TO PREPARE GUN COTTON.—Mix in a glass vessel one part (weight) pure nitric acid, with two parts (weight) concentrated sulphuric acid. With this mixture saturate, for ten minutes, finely carded wool cotton; then with a glass rod press the cotton so as to remove as much of the acids as possible, after which it must be washed with rain water until all the acid taste is removed; then carefully dry, and it is ready to "go off."

Much care must be used both in preparing and using this vegetable lightning. Must not let much of the acids get on the hands—it bites badly. All the materials should be of the best quality.

A WATER-PROOF GLUE.—Melt common glue in the smallest possible quantity of water, and add by drops linseed oil that has been rendered drying by having a small quantity of litharge boiled in it; the glue being briskly stirred when the oil is added.

TO STAIN HARPS, VIOLINS, OR ANY OTHER MUSICAL INSTRUMENT.—*A Crimson stain.*—Take one pound of ground Brazil, and boil it in three quarts of water for an hour; strain it, and add half an ounce of cochineal; boil it again for half an hour gently, and it will be fit for use. N. B.—If you would have it of the scarlet tint, boil half an ounce of saffron in a quart of water, and pass over the work previous to the red stain. Observe, the work must be very clean; and of air-wood or good sycamore, without blemish. When varnished it will look very rich.

For a Purple stain.—Take a pound of chip-logwood, to

which put three quarts of water; boil it well for an hour; add four ounces of pearlash, and two ounces of pounded indigo, and you will have a good purple.

For a fine Black.—When black is required in musical instruments, it is produced by japanning, the work being well prepared with size and lamp-black; take some black japan (from the varnish maker's) and give it two coats, after which varnish and polish it.

A fine Blue stain.—Take a pound of oil of vitriol in a glass bottle, in which put four ounces of indigo, and proceed as before directed in dyeing.

A fine Green stain.—Take three pints of strong vinegar, to which put four ounces of the best verdigris ground fine, half an ounce of sap-green, and half an ounce of indigo.

For a bright Yellow.—There is no need whatever to stain the wood, as a very small bit of aloes put in the varnish will make it of a good color, aud has the desired effect.

TO STAIN BOX-WOOD BROWN.—Hold your work to the fire that it may receive a gentle warmth, then take aqua-fortis, and with a feather pass over the work till you find it change to a fine brown (always keeping it near the fire); you may then oil and polish it.

TO MAKE VARNISH FOR VIOLINS, ETC.—Take half a gallon of rectified spirits of wine, to which put six ounces of gum sandrach, three ounces of gum mastic, and half a pint of turpentine varnish; put the above in a tin can, in a warm place, frequently shaking it until it is dissolved; strain it and keep it for use. If you find it harder than you wish, add a little more turpentine varnish.

TO MAKE COURT-PLASTER.—Dissolve isinglass, suspend your silk on a wooden frame by tacks, apply the glue with a brush, and let it dry; repeat it, and when dry cover it with a strong tincture of balsam of Peru. This is the real English court-plaster. It is pliable, and never breaks. The more common is covered over with the white of egg and dried.

MISCELLANEOUS RECIPES.

To Make the Hair Curl.—At any time you may make your hair curl the more easily by rubbing it with beaten yolk of an egg, washed off afterward with clear water, and then putting on a little pomatum before you put up your curls; it is well always to go through this process when you change to curls after having worn your hair plain.

Oil for the Hair.—A very excellent ready-made oil for the hair, which answers all common purposes, is made by mixing one part brandy with three parts of sweet oil. Add any scent you prefer; a selection can be got at the druggist's.

To Prevent the Hair from Falling Out —One of the most efficacious methods of preventing the hair falling out is to moisten it occasionally with a little fresh, strong beer. It also keeps the hair in curl. When first used it is apt to render the hair dry, but a small quantity of bear's oil will remove this objection.

Black Ball.—Melt together, moderately, ten ounces of bayberry tallow, five ounces of beeswax, one ounce of mutton tallow. When melted, add lamp or ivory black to give it a good black color. Stir the whole well together, and add, when taken from the fire, half a glass of rum.

To Render Cloth Wind and Rain Proof.—Boil two pounds of turpentine, and one pound of litharge in powder, and two or three pints of linseed oil. The article is to be brushed over and dried in the sun.

White-wash that will not rub off.—Mix up half a pailful of lime and water, take half a pint of flour and make a starch of it, and pour it into the white-wash while hot. Stir it well and it is ready for use.

FEATHERS.—It is said that tumbled plumes may be restored to elasticity and beauty by dipping them in hot water, then shaking and drying them.

ICY STEPS.—Salt strewed upon the door-steps in winter will cause the ice to crack, so that it can be easily removed.

TINCTURE FOR DISEASED GUMS.—Take Peruvian bark coarsely powdered, one ounce, and infuse it for a fortnight in half a pint of brandy. Gargle the mouth at night with a teaspoonful of this tincture, diluted with an equal quantity of rose water.

SHAVING SOAP.—A very nice soap for shaving is made by mixing a quarter of a pound of Castile soap, one cake of old Windsor soap, a gill of lavender water, the same of Cologne water, and a very little alcohol. Boil all these together until thoroughly mixed.

RED BOTTLE WAX.—Common resin, four pounds; tallow, one pound; red lead, one pound. Mix with heat. Any coloring matter may be substited, if other colors are wanted.

TO CURE FRECKLES.—Take two ounces of lemon juice, a half drachm of powdered borax, and one drachm of sugar. Mix together, and let them stand in a glass bottle for a few days; then rub it on the hands and face occasionally.

CERTAIN CURE FOR ERUPTIONS, PIMPLES, ETC.—Having in numberless instances seen the good effects of the following prescription, I can certify to its perfect remedy. Dilute corrosive sublimate with the oil of almonds, apply it to the face occasionally, and in a few days a cure will be effected.

TO PERFUME CLOTHES.—Take cloves, cedar and rhubarb, each one ounce; pulverize and sprinkle it in the chest or drawer. It will create a beautiful scent, and prevent moths.

INFLAMED EYES, very painful, as every afflicted son of Adam knows, may be cured in a week, and the eyes made perfectly strong, by using a decoction of elder flowers and laudanum. Add three or four drops of the laudanum to a small glass of the tea, and let the mixture run into the eyes three or four times a day.

To BLACKEN THE EYELASHES.—The simple preparations for this purpose are the juice of elder-berries, burnt cork, and cloves burnt at the candle. Another means is, to take the black of frankincense, resin, and mastic. This black will not come off with perspiration. It is also equally as good for the hair of the head.

CHEAP WHITE HOUSE PAINT.—Take skim-milk two quarts, eight ounces fresh slacked lime, six ounces linseed oil, two ounces white Burgundy pitch, three pounds Spanish white. Slack the lime in water, expose it to the air, and mix in about one-fourth of the milk; the oil, in which the pitch is previously dissolved, to be added a little at a time; then the rest of the milk, and afterwards the Spanish white. This quantity is sufficient for thirty square yards, two coats, and costs but a few cents. If other colors are wanted, use instead of Spanish white other coloring matter.

To POLISH STOVES.—Mix powder of black-lead with a little common gin or alcohol, and lay it on the stove with a piece of linen rag; then take a dry but not hard brush, dip it in some of the dry black-lead powder, and rub it to a beautiful brightness.

CONFECTIONERY.

To CLARIFY SUGAR FOR CANDIES,—To every pound of sugar put a large cup of water, and put it in a brass or copper kettle, over a slow fire, for half an hour; pour into it a small quantity of isinglass and gum Arabic, dissolved together. This will cause all impurities to rise to the surface; skim it as it rises; flavor according to taste. All kinds of sugar, for candy, are boiled as above directed. When boiling loaf sugar, add a tablespoonful of rum or vinegar, to prevent its becoming too brittle while making.

COMMON TWIST, OR COUGH CANDY.—Boil three pounds of common sugar and one pint of water, over a slow fire, for half an hour, without skimming. When boiled enough, take it off; rub the hands over with butter; take that which is a little cooled, and pull it, as you would molasses candy, until it is white; then twist or braid it, and cut it in strips.

CANDIED LEMON OR PEPPERMINT, FOR COLDS.—Boil one pound and a half of sugar in a half pint of water, till it begins to candy round the sides; put in eight drops of essence; pour it upon buttered paper, and cut it with a knife.

FRUIT CANDIED.—When the fruit is preserved, take it from the syrup, dry it in an oven, then dip it in sugar boiled to candy weight, and dry it again.

FINE PEPPERMINT LOZENGES.—Best powdered white sugar, seven pounds; pure starch, one pound; oil of peppermint to flavor. Mix with mucilage.

SAFFRON LOZENGES.—Finely powdered hay saffron, one ounce; finely powdered sugar, one pound; finely powdered starch, eight ounces. Mucilage to mix.

ICING FOR CAKES.—Beat the whites of two small eggs to a high froth; then add to them a quarter of a pound of ground or powdered sugar; beat it well until it will lie in a heap; flavor with lemon or rose. This will frost the top of a common sized cake. Heap what you suppose to be sufficient in the centre of the cake, then dip a broad-bladed knife in cold water, and spread the ice evenly over the whole surface.

STRAWBERRY ICE CREAM.—Take a pint of picked strawberries, rub them through a sieve with a wooden spoon; add four ounces of powdered sugar and a pint of cream.

ORNAMENTAL FROSTING.—For this purpose have a small syringe, draw it full of the icing, and work it in any design you fancy. Wheels, Grecian border or flowers, look well or borders of beading.

FRUIT AND FRUIT TREES.

HOW TO KILL BORERS IN TREES.—Rub hard soap into every place in the tree that seems wounded by them; it will effectually destroy them. Strong lye made of potash swabbed on, is equally good—one pound to a gallon of water.

APPLE TREE.—Prune the decayed limbs, and rub the trunks with a hard brush, then paint with a mixture of soft soap and sulphur; strew lime under the trees and around the trunk. This course will destroy the worms and improve the quality of the fruit and grass, and will prevent the trees from decay. Five gallons of soap to one of sulphur.

PEAR.—This tree dies of a disease called the fire-blight. It occurs in summer; the leaves, from the extremities of the branches, for two or more feet, appear as if scorched. This should be cut off a foot or more from the diseased part, and immediately buried. When this is practiced the evil is arrested.

PEACH.—These trees do best in elevated situations; when the soil is unfavorable on hills, it should be improved; cold, wet or spongy soil is unfavorable. When peach trees begin to languish, remove the soil around them, and supply its place with charcoal; it will produce a sudden renovation and improve the richness of the fruit. Prune in the extremities of the branches of bearing trees, two feet, in July every year. This will keep the tree full of bearing buds and healthy wood. Trees that have the yellows must be removed, as the disease is contagious. Graft them in September. Peach trees may be preserved from the ravages of the worms, by freeing the diseased part from earth, and gum, and spreading over it a thin coat of common hard soap, and filling up with fresh soil. It must be repeated every season, and as it is dissolved by the rain, it descends to the roots, and causes it to grow vigorously, besides destroying insects and eggs, and cleansing the bark. Several hundred trees may be done in a few hours. It is equally good for other fruit.

PLUM.—This tree is becoming much affected with the "*black gum*," caused by an insect. Cut off the diseased part without delay, and burn it. This will preserve it.

QUINCE.—This is a beautiful tree when in blossom, and when the fruit is ripe it is highly ornamental. It is easily raised from cuttings or layers taken from the tree in April, and planted in a shady place, and the soil enriched, which will keep it from sudden drought. Also water occasionally. They might grow in any part of the country with suitable care.

BRIEF HINTS FOR TRANSPLANTING.—Previous to laying out an orchard or fruit garden, the soil should be manured and pulverized to a great depth. It should be made sweet, that the nutriment which the roots receive may be wholesome; free, that they may be at full liberty to range in quest of it; and rich, that there may be no defect in the food.

If orchards are made from meadows or pasture lands, the ground should be improved as much as possible by manuring, trenching, ploughing, etc. At the time of planting, let the holes be dug somewhat larger than is sufficient to admit the roots in their natural position, and of sufficient depth to allow of a foot of rich and pulverized mold to be thrown in before the trees are planted.

In transplanting trees, they should not be placed more than an inch or two deeper than they were in the nursery beds, and the earth intended for filling in should be enriched and well pulverized by mixing in some good old manure; and if any leaves. decayed brush, or other refuse of a farm are attainable, let such be used around the trees in filling, taking care that the best pulverized mold is admitted among the fine roots. The trees in planting should be kept at ease, and several times shaken so as to cause an equal distribution of the finer particles of earth to be connected with the small fibres of the roots; and when completely levelled, let the ground be well trodden down and moderately watered, which should be repeated occasionally after spring planting, if the weather should prove dry.

TREES AND PLANTS should always be carefully packed at the nursery, for the protection of the roots and limbs, as well as for convenience in transportation.

To Kill Weeds in Gravel and Brick Walks.—Keep them moist with brine a week in the spring, and three or four days in the fall, and it will prevent their growing.

PARLOR PLANTS.

1. Plants which have bloomed through the summer, *will* rest during the winter. To remove them from the heat and dust of the parlor—to place them in a dry, light, warm cellar, will certainly conduce to their entire rest ; and the parlor will lose no grace by the removal of ragged stems, falling leaves, and flowerless branches.

2. *Very little*, if any, water should be given to plants thus at rest.

3. When the plants are wanted to bloom in the parlor late in the winter, it is often better to let them spend the fore part of the winter in the cellar or pit.

4. All plants which are not growing, or for whose growth your parlors are not suitable, should be put into the cellar, and should there be allowed to stand over in a state of rest.

5. According to your accommodations, select a *few* vigorous, symmetrical, hearty, healthy plants for the window. *One plant*, well tended, will afford you more pleasure than twenty half nurtured.

6. *There can be no such thing as floral health without fresh air and enough of it.* This must be procured by frequent ventilation.

7. It is found that plants have the property of correcting bad air within a few hours, when they are exposed to the light of the sun ; but that, on the contrary, during the night, or in the shade, they corrupt the common air of the atmosphere. Hence it is a dangerous practice to have shrubs in an apartment that is slept in.

8. To restore frozen plants, dip them in cold water till they are thawed, then set them in a moderately warm place. They will often die down to the roots, but sprout again ; frequently, they only shed their leaves.

9. The practice of watering plants by the roots—that is, pouring water into dishes in which the pot sits—is highly improper. It should always be poured upon the surface, that it may filter through and refresh the fibres of the plant.

FLOWERS.—Flowers may be preserved fresh in tumblers or vases by putting a handful of salt in the water, to increase its coldness. If put under a glass vase, from which the air is entirely excluded, they will keep a long while.

CANARY BIRDS.

GENERAL DIRECTIONS.—To keep canaries healthy, the cage should be washed as often as once in two weeks, and oftener cleaned. French lettuce or cabbage may be given them in July and August ; plantain is also good,—it may be given in hot weather three times a day. Lettuce seed and plantain seed is also good to be given as food, mixed in a small pot. In hot weather they should have clean water in pans once a day, to wash and bathe in, which greatly refreshes them. A piece of cuttlefish bone or sand should be in the cage, to keep them in a healthy condition. Their fountains should be filled, and the water fountains changed every day. The bird-seed is a mixture already prepared, to be used as it is. Sponge cake may be given occasionally, and crackers and sweet apples ; worms are also good ; but food containing salt is injurious.

HOW TO DISTINGUISH THE MALE FROM THE FEMALE.— To distinguish the male from the female, it is observed that a streak of bright yellow may be noticed over the eyes and under the throat ; his head is wider and longer, and in general is much higher colored ; his feet, too, are larger. They also begin to warble first, which is often at a month old. They are quicker, more taper, and sprightlier than the hens. If the hen lays, take out the egg and substitute an ivory or wooden one, as they then will hatch all at the same time.

LADIES' AND GENTLEMEN'S POLITE TEACHER.

1. A LETTER of introduction, note of invitation, or reply, should always be enclosed in an envelope.

2. A letter of introduction should always enclose the card and address of the person introduced.

3. Notes of invitation should always be sent in the name of the lady of the house.

4. Invitations should be answered within two days.

5. Notes of invitation should not be sealed.

6. Figured and colored paper is much used ; pure white paper, with gilt edges, is more strictly in good taste.

7. It is considered a mark of respect to commence a letter towards the middle of the page.

8. Printed cards should be used when the party is large.

9. All letters should be sealed and superscribed as in the following example. It gives room for the post-mark without defacing the superscription :

```
MISS ANN STONE,

        BOSTON,

                MASS.
```

MODELS OF INVITATION CARDS AND NOTES.--The usual form is simply :

Mrs. —— requests the pleasure of Mr. and Mrs. ——'s company on Thursday evening at 8 o'clock.

Separate notes should be sent to the sons and daughters, if their company is wished.

The answer should be as follows :

Mr. and Mrs. —— accept with pleasure Mrs. ——'s invitation for Thursday evening next.

If a refusal is sent, it should be expressed thus :

Mr. and Mrs. —— regret that it will not be in their power to accept Mr. and Mrs. ——'s invitation for Thursday evening next,

The date should always be put at the bottom of the note on the left hand side.

HOW TO ADDRESS A LADY.—We address a married lady, or widow, as Madam, or by name, as Missis or Mistress Jones. In answering a question, we contract the Madam to ma'am, as "yes ma'am—no ma'am—very fine day, ma'am."

A young lady, if the eldest of the family, unmarried, is entitled to the surname, as Miss Smith, while her younger sisters are called Miss Mary, Miss Julia, etc. The term "Miss," used by itself, is very inelegant.

LANGUAGE OF THE FINGER RING.—If a gentleman wants a wife, he wears a ring on the first finger of his left hand.

If he is engaged, he wears it on the second finger.

If married, he wears it on the third finger.

If he never intends to get married, he wears it on the fourth finger.

When a lady is not engaged, she wears a hoop or diamond on her first finger.

If engaged, she wears it upon the second finger.

If married, she wears it upon the third finger.

If she intends to remain a maid, she wears her ring upon her fourth finger.

Thus, by a few simple tokens, the passion of love is expressed.

RULES OF CONVERSATION.

1. Address yourselves to the capacity of those to whom you speak.

2. Direct your conversation to such subjects as you know to be agreeable to the company.

3. Good humor and wit is the charm of conversation.

4. It is not impolite to laugh, in company, when there is anything amusing going on.

5. Nothing is more annoying than to be frequently interrupted in conversation.

6. Contradiction is the greatest rudeness any person can be guilty of.

7. Whispering in company is highly improper.

8. Never attempt to take the lead in conversation.

9. It is not good taste for a lady to say, " Yes, *Sir*," and " No, *Sir*," to a gentleman.

10. Due deference should always be paid to the aged.

DRAWING.

YOUNG PEOPLE'S PRIMARY INSTRUCTION IN THE ART OF DRAWING.

1. The apparatus required to teach drawing is very inexpensive. Let each pupil be provided with a slate, and a slate-pencil cut to a point; also a small piece of sponge, wherewith to wipe and clean the slate when necessary.

A sheet of paper, and a softish black lead-pencil, may be adopted in preference to a slate and slate-pencil, but they are less economical, and therefore need not be used till an advance has been made in the lessons.

In some schools where rigid accuracy is enforced, a boy somewhat advanced in his lessons stands at the black-board, and from the book in his hand copies a figure upon it. The pupils in their seats observe the motions of his hand, and, following him slowly and according to their best judgment, they copy the figure from the board upon their slates.

2. The principle of this practice, which we wish to see adopted and followed, is, first, to teach the art in the simplest possible manner and at the least expense; and, second, to give freedom of hand or execution. The child, it will be observed, commences with the slate and slate-pencil, and having got over the initiatory difficulties and gained a little confidence, he is promoted to the board. Here copying figures in the first instance, and afterwards working from his improved taste and imitative faculties, he acquires a free,

bold style of delineation, without which the power of drawing remains stiff and spiritless.

3. To commence, in whatever manner, place the pupil fairly before his slate, and cause him to draw perfectly straight lines. The lines must be drawn with the hand alone, that is, without any assistance from squares or rulers. The lines should in this easy manner, but with as much steadiness as possible, be drawn horizontally, perpendicularly, and obliquely ; in short, in all directions that may be thought proper; and their accuracy may be tested with the instruments.

Being tolerably perfect in straight lines, we advance to bends or curves. Explain that all lines whatsoever, used in drawing, are either straight or curved. or a modification of either ; and point out how much more beautiful is the appearance and effect of a curve, in comparison with a straight line.

4. We now come to the drawing of objects, beginning with those of the simplest forms. In these and other figures it will be observed that some of the lines are thin and others thick, the thin lines indicating the parts of the object which are in the light, and the thick ones indicating those which are in the shade. Point out how it is possible to represent a solid object—such as a block of stone or a house —on a flat surface, by means of a due mixture or arrangement of thin and thick lines or marks, and by giving some of them an inclination in a particular direction.

5. There are examples of exercises in the drawing of familiar objects or utensils. This usually yields much pleasure to the beginner, and excites his imagination to discover objects which he may sketch in a similar style. Let this fancy be liberally indulged. Desire him to draw the outlines of a cup, vase, drinking-glass, basin, book, hammer, axe, desk, chair, nail, candlestick, box, etc. Having drawn them in a front view, then put them in a different attitude so as to express an end, a side, a corner, or any other point of view. Drawing of objects in this manner from nature, and not from

paper, may be called a great step in advance, and is really the practical commencement of the art.

While about this stage of advancement, and while the mind is awakening to the power of expressing objects by means of various lines of a light and dark character, invite attention to the method in which a person is able to draw a subject from its appearance or from memory. It may be done in something like the following terms :—

When we see, for example, a chair standing on the floor, we observe its shape or figure, its line of back, seat, legs, and all other parts about it. We then take a pencil, and bending the mind intensely on the form of the chair, try to define all the lines of the object on the paper or board. The more perfectly that the hand can obey the direction of the mind, while bent in thought on the object, so will the drawing be more true in all its details.

6. Plant and flower drawing is a valuable branch of the art, and is particularly suitable for females. The course of instruction should not be confined to a few objects merely, but be extended to exercises on all the elegant objects of this kind which are ready at hand. Any flower growing in a pot on the window-sill, any tree or bush that presents itself, or any shrub or blade from a garden, may be copied. On the correct imitation of these objects from nature is founded the art of designing carvings in architecture and carpentry, mouldings for plaster-work, and patterns for lace, paper-hangings, carpets, and other objects of taste.

7. From plants we proceed to the sketching of animals, such as dogs, cats, swine, rabbits, horses, goats, sheep, birds or other creatures which are familiar to observation, and of which a few examples are given. Next, the pupil may advance to the drawing of faces and human figures, but this only, in a great measure, as an amusement ; for a correct method of delineating these objects in their various forms and attitudes, is not to be gained without the most patient study of models and living figures, and may very properly be delayed till a more advanced period.

8. It is necessary to add, with respect to drawing plans of houses, or maps of fields and countries, that the pupil should be taught to measure and compute dimensisns in height, length, and breadth. This is to be done in the first place by a foot rule, or a diminished scale of inches and fractional parts, prepared for the purpose ; but afterwards, and when a little skilled in these computations, he must learn to *guess*, or measure by the eye, the dimensions of the object on which he is engaged, and then to draw it, preserving the just proportions of the several parts. This is a kind of exercise which will largely contribute to cultivate the perceptive faculties of pupils, and make them useful to themselves in many of the common occupations of life.

9. The first, or purely elementaɪy course of lessons, will properly terminate with exercises in drawing, with the hand alone, a variety of simple mathematical figures, such as circles, squares, parallelograms. These may be tried again and again, to give precision of hand and eye, or till the figures approach so near perfect accuracy in form as to stand the test of measurement by the compasses.

Let the pupil be instructed to avoid any approach to confusion in the designs, to give all the lines with an easy sweeping effect, so as to express what is called *spirit*, and to cultivate, at the same time, simplicity and chasteness.

10. We conclude these brief directions by mentioning, in the most emphatic manner, that, further than mere amusement for the moment, the exercises on this or any other elementary work on drawing, will be of no use whatever, unless the pupil *do the things with his own hand, and seek for originals in actual objects before him.*

Exercises to a reasonable extent on the black-board are absolutely indispensable for giving that *freedom of hand* which we have already adverted to, and for teaching the art of handling compasses, measuring distances, and other matters of practical utility.

YOUNG LADIES' GUIDE.

BEING INSTRUCTION IN EMBROIDERY ON SILK, VELVET, MUSLIN, LACE, MERINO, ETC.

The taste for embroidery is daily increasing, and this species of work is not only ornamental but useful. In the following pages we have given instructions in all the most popular and beautiful modes of embroidering; and have endeavored to express ourselves as explicitly as possible.

EMBROIDERY WITH FLOSS SILK, THREE-CORDED, OR SADDLER'S SILK, CHENILLE, WORSTED, ETC.

1. Floss silk is used to embroider on either silk, satin, merino, or any fine material which does not require washing.

2. To embroider on cloth, fine flannel, or merino, that is to be washed, it is necessary to use three-corded, or saddler's silk.

3. Chenille is sometimes employed in canvass work, but being one of the richest materials used in embroidery, it shows to the greatest advantage on velvet, silk, or satin.

4. Worsted is used principally for embroidery on canvass; but on fine merino, brown holland, and even white muslin, it is equally beautiful. The colors of German worsteds do not fade when washed with soap.

5. A light and simple frame is the most convenient for the above-mentioned species of embroidery. The frame should merely consist of four smooth pieces of light wood, half or three quarters of a yard in length, and quarter of an inch in

thickness, neatly joined together. The frame should then be covered with ribbon or muslin, wound tightly around it. To this muslin the material designed to be embroidered is to be sewed. Square frames are preferable.

6. After the frame has been prepared, the pattern to be embroidered should be drawn. If the material used is silk, or satin, or muslin, or any transparent substance, the pattern may be fastened on the wrong side, hung over a window pane, and traced upon the material with a lead-pencil. When velvet, or cloth, or any dark-colored silk is to be embroidered, the pattern should be drawn on white tissue or blotting paper, and the paper lightly tacked upon the right side of the velvet. The embroidery is to be executed over the paper, and when the work is completed the paper is carefully torn away. Sometimes patterns are drawn on dark materials by means of chalk, but the chalk is apt to rub off.

7. After the pattern is drawn, the work should be sewed into the frame in such a manner as to be perfectly smooth and even. It is not necessary that the frame should be of the same size as the material to be embroidered. If the stuff is wider or longer than the frame, the portion over should be rolled up and covered with white paper. When the article is smaller than the frame, a piece of muslin may be sewed to the stuff so as to make it of the necessary size.

8. For worsted work a rather coarse darning-needle should be used, and for floss silk a fine one. A large round-eyed needle is necessary for chenille and three-corded silk. If the needle is too large, besides being clumsy, it will muke a hole in the work.

9. The stitch for embroidery is very easy. You make a knot at the end of the silk, chenille or worsted, and bring your needle through the material on which you intend to work, from the under side to the upper one. Next, the needle is again put through to the under side, following the pattern, and then put back and brought to the upper side, close to where it came through before, The same process is then repeated, care being taken not to draw the silk too

tight. The stiches should lay slantingly and beside each other. To embroider the stalks of flowers, a stitch very similar to back stitch should be used.

10. The way to embroider in the manner above designated, may be learned without further instruction than those we have already given. The work when once understood is accomplished with great rapidity, and never becomes tedious.

RAISED EMBROIDERY.

This kind of embroidery is extremely pretty in fancy pieces, for working animals, birds, shells, fruits, or flowers, it may be done with either silk, worsted, or chenille. The pattern must be traced and the material framed as usual ; then commence a foundation for the raised parts by working with course cotton or wool, layer upon layer, with long stitches, until the outline of the design is closely approached, paying attention at the same time to the shape of the object. When this is finished, begin the embroidery over it with a long needle, and shade in the usual manner, passing the needle through the whole substance of the foundation, which will the more easily be done should it be formed of wool.

Flowers, such as roses, on a very reduced scale for sprig work may be beautifully and easily executed in this description of embroidery. A small round must first be slightly raised with cotton ; then commence the centre of the rose with two or three small French knots, and form the flower by working round them in small stitches, keeping the middle of the darkest shades ; the stitches should partly cross each other, so as to give the appearance of one leaf over another. If skilfully done, the centre of the flower should have the sunken appearance which it has in nature. If worked too large, their beauty and effect will be lost Four shades of silk will be found sufficient.

STITCHES IN EMBROIDERY ON MUSLIN AND LACE-WORK.

1. SATIN STITCH.—This resembles the threads in satin,

and is much used in embroidery. You make a knot at the end of the cotton, silk, or worsted, and bring it through the material on which you intend to work, from the under side to the upper one. Next, the needle is again put through to the under side, at about half an inch distance, and is then put back and brought to the upper side, about half way from the first point, the next stitch is carried to the same distance from the second; again the needle is brought back, and the same process is repeated. In working on a surface, the stitches run in parallel lines to each other, and are taken the lengthway of the figure or subject you are making. They are also of unequal lengths, in order that the ground may be more effectually covered. In the working of drapery, you must be sure to take each stitch the way the threads or grain would naturally fall.

2. BUTTON-HOLE STITCH.—The needle must go in on the wrong side, and be brought out on the right, five threads down. To make the stitch, the needle is passed through the loop, before it is tightened or drawn close.

3. EYELET HOLES.—These are first run round; then a hole is cut out, or made by a piercer, which is the preferable way; and the needle is passed through the aperture, under the inner thread, and you sew round it thickly, so as to entirely conceal it. You may make oval eyelet holes in the same manner, making the opening oval, instead of round.

4. FORMATION OF BARS.—You take four threads of the muslin on the needle, and sew three times over them, passing the needle through the same opening each time, and drawing the four threads as close as possible. Each succeeding four threads are taken up the same way, and thus the required number of bars can be easily formed. The thread in this stitch passes from bar to bar, on the right hand.

3. EMBROIDERY FEATHER STITCH.—Leaves are often worked in this stitch, which is only an elongated button-hole stitch. Its appearance, on a leaf, is very beautiful.

6. GLOVER'S STITCH.—This is the same as button-hole

stitch, only each stitch is taken a little higher up than the one which preceded it.

7. DOUBLE BUTTON-HOLE STITCH.—This is two stitches together then the space for two left unoccupied, then the two button-hole stitches repeated, and so on alternately.

8. HALF HERRING-BONE STITCH.—This is worked the cross way of the muslin; four threads are taken on the mesh at once.

9. LINES.—These are formed by drawing together six threads of the muslin, and sewing over them with fine thread, as close as possible.

10. STRAIGHT OPEN HEM.—This is done by drawing out three or four threads, the selvedge-way of the muslin, and working over the cross threads from side to side, in a kind of zigzag direction.

11. VEINING OPEN HEM.—This is worked in a curve, or other pattern, in which the threads cannot be drawn out. The hem is made by sewing over two threads, taken the angular way of the muslin, and then pursuing the same method with two threads taken the contrary way, and uniting them together as in a straight open hem. The appearance is the same, but the pattern is a curve or other shape.

12. CHAIN STITCH.—This is often employed in lace-work. Make a knot at the end of the cotton, and draw it through to the right side. While you put in the needle, let the end hang loose, and bring it out below, so as to incline a little to the left hand; pass the needle over the cotton, as you draw it out, and this will form a loop; each succeeding one is done in the same manner.

13. PEARLING.—This is a kind of lace edging, not worked with needles, but often used as a finish to embroidery of muslin. It is very pretty, and is sold ready for use.

14. DARNING.—This is, when employed in lace-work, done as follows; It is worked as common darning, but with fine cotton, which is doubled; and in this stitch, the inner edge of flowers is sometimes worked, the centre being executed in

half herring-bone stitch. It looks well; but rows of chain stitch are, in our opinion, preferable.

15. INTERIOR STITCH.—So called because often employed to fill up the centres of leaves in lace-work. The stitch is formed by taking two threads the breadth-way of the leaf, and sewing over them; then leaving a row of one thread, and sewing over two threads as before.

16. EYELET HOLES IN LACE-WORK.—These are not difficult to execute, and when well arranged, have a beautiful appearance. One mesh of the net is left for the centre, and you work round it in button-hole stitch. A great variety of devices may be formed, by a tasteful and judicious disposition of these eyelet holes.

17. SPOTS ON NET.—These, though simple, form an elegant variety in lace-work. To make each spot, the middle is to be passed backwards and forwards, through one hole in the net, and alternately under and over two of the threads of which that hole is formed. These spots must be placed in clusters, but an open mesh must be left between each.

18. TAMBOUR STITCH.—This has a close resemblance to chain stitch. The needle, which has a small hook at the end, and is fixed in a handle of ivory, is put through the material stretched in the frame, on the upper side, and the cotton being held underneath, in the left hand, is put upon the hook and drawn through to the right or upper side, where it forms a loop. Through this loop the needle is again passed, and also through the material, a few threads from the place it passed through before. The cotton is again drawn through, and thus a succession of loops is formed. The pattern is worked entirely in these loops or stitches.

19. These are the stitches most commonly employed, and therefore the most necessary to be known. We have done all in our power to so explain them as to enable our readers to practise them with facility.

EMBROIDERY ON MUSLIN.

A degree of skill which can only be acquired by practice,

is necessary to those who would excel in this branch of the art. The work must, of course, be done by pattern, and very beautiful ones may be purchased at a moderate cost.

The material generally employed in working on muslin is cotton.

The pattern is placed against a window, and drawn with a black lead-pencil on the muslin. To secure accuracy, the muslin should be tacked down to the pattern before the tracing is commenced.

The outlines of the patterns are thus run around with fine cotton, directly over the pencil-marks. Then commence working in the usual embroidery stitch, taking care that the stitches do not lay over each other, but side by side, so as to give the work a smooth and even appearance. A frame is not necessary.

INSTRUCTIONS IN LACE-WORK.

In commencing this delicate and beautiful work, you must place over the net a piece of French cambric, proportionate in size to the subject or device you are intending to work; and under both these the paper pattern is to be placed, and secured by a tack in the edge in its proper position. It is essential to remark, that though the design, as a whole, may be large, yet each part should be smalll; the introduction of large leaves, sprigs, or flowers, would greatly detract from that beauty of appearance, which is so essential to be preserved. Clusters of small flowers, or leaves, are proper ornaments in this elaborately-wrought fabric. Having placed the materials and pattern as directed, the outlines of the design are to be run round with cotton. This sewing must be done twice, and the running thread be sewn over with fine cotton; the sewing to be moderately thick; this will give the extreme edge of each leaf or flower a raised appearance —a point in this work of most essential importance. The cambric is then, with a pair of small and sharp scissors, to be cut off, as near to the raised edge as possible.

The various patterns are so numerous, that it is next to impossible to enumerate them. One beautiful variety is formed by filling up the centres of flowers with insertion stitch; for the mode of doing which, the reader is referred to the chapter on stitches. Leaves and flowers thus filled up have a remarkably neat appearance.

EMBROIDERY IN GOLD THREAD.

This kind of embroidery is usually employed in large and bold designs, as it is never used except in cases where much display and extreme brilliancy are required. The materials made use of as foundation for these costly displays of needle-work are various, according to the taste of the wearer, or the occasion on which they are employed. Crape, India muslin, or some kind of silk, are generally employed, as the best calculated to give the desired effect, and to exhibit the beautiful devices to the best possible advantage. The gold thread should be of a fine and uniform texture, and little or no difficulty will be found in working it. When it is properly made, it is almost as flexible as common thread.

The stitch in which gold thread embroidery is worked is (with occasional exceptions) satin stitch, and, of course, you work by a pattern previously prepared. This must be laid under the material used as a foundation, and which is generally sufficiently transparent to allow it to be seen through it, and the outline of the subject intended to be worked is sewn on in white thread. This done, you commence working in gold thread, or with silver, but this latter is not desirable, as it soon gets black and tarnished.

EMBROIDERY FOR INSERTION.

Embroidery is often done upon muslin, in narrow stripes, for insertion work, and looks extremely pretty. Almost any device, but chiefly foliage and flowers, and sometimes fruit, are proper for this kind of work, and any or all of the various stitches may be introduced with the happiest effect. It is unnecessary to give examples, as they would only tend to confuse and mislead. Every lady must use her own judgment in these cases, and be guided in her choice by the use to which the insertion work is to be applied. In all patterns for this kind of embroidery, there must be a hem stitch on each side of the embroidery, the manner of forming which is fully explained in the following description.

It is done either in a straight line or in a curve. For the first kind you draw out threads to the breadth of a narrow hem, at a little distance from the row of insertion work previously executed. The number of threads thus drawn out should not exceed four, which are to be taken up on the needle, commencing on one side, and these are to be sewn over three times with very fine cotton. The threads are taken and sewn over singly, and when the thread has reached the opposite side, you take up four more of the cross threads and sew them over twice, thus uniting the eight together at the side opposite to that one on which you commenced. Then sew the last four, three times over, as in the first stitch, and the thread will here again be found at the side on which you begin. You proceed in this manner to the end, and the opened hem when thus worked forms a kind of undulating wave, that looks elegant and appropriate.

THINGS TO BE REMEMBERED.

1. In fancy *needle-work* the light of day is especially important.

2. In many departments of fancy needle-work great and unceasing care is requisite, in order to avoid faults which cannot afterwards be repaired. In cloth-work, for instance, be careful not to split the threads of the canvass.

3. During the progress of your work, it is desirable that you keep that portion still untouched covered with tissue paper, or it will otherwise have a soiled appearance.

4. Cut your wools into certain lengths, and put them into elongated papers, or you may wind them on a reel. Each paper should be labelled with its peculiar shade, or it may be numbered.

5. Plaid patterns may be worked from plaid ribbons; and in so doing the choice of elegant *material* will be as attainable as it is multifarious.

6. When beads are introduced they should not be too numerous, or they will give an appearance of heaviness to the work.

7. In using floss silk, it should be cut in short lengths, or it is apt to get round.

HINTS TO YOUNG LADIES.

THE COLOR AND STYLE OF BONNETS, DRESSES, &c., BEST SUITED TO VARIOUS COMPLEXIONS.

EVERY lady should study and determine what dress and hat best becomes her form and complexion. In America there is not the distinction made in the style of dress it is necessary there should be, between a tall and short, or a slender and a thick person, or a dark or light complexion, but all must dress in the latest fashion, however unbecoming it may be.

THE HAT. A delicate, pale complexion should wear a pink lining, but where there is color with it, blue or straw color should be worn. A brunette or dark complexion should wear white lining, with a delicate rose trimming; never black, unless unavoidable. A large person, with prominent features, should never wear a small hat. The reverse with small persons. An extremely red or yellow complexion should not wear high colors. Yellow, lilac, and red are the most trying colors to the complexion: A close cottage is generally becoming, and never considered unfashionable.

2. THE DRESS. Suit the dress to the complexion, the same as the hat. A short figure should not wear so full a skirt as a tall one. Every species of drapery is graceful to a tall figure and may be worn to advantage. Tight sleeves, without trimming, are becoming to full forms, medium height or below it. To a tall, slender figure, with long arms, they are very ungraceful, unless trimmed with folds or drapery.

3. FLOUNCES. Flounces are graceful upon tall persons, whether slender or otherwise, but never upon diminutive ones.

4. TUCKS. Tucks are equally graceful upon both, and never look out of fashion. A couple of wide tucks, which give the appearance of two skirts, are very beautiful for an evening dress, made of delicate materials. Any species of trimming down the front or sides of the skirt, increases the apparent height. Capes are only becoming to persons with falling shoulders, unless made to fit the form.

5. HIGH-NECK DRESSES. High-neck dresses are simple and generally becoming ; upon a very high-shouldered person a low-necked dress is more appropriate. and if the shoulders are only moderately high. the neck may still be covered and the dress finished off about the throat with a narrow piece of lace, instead of a collar. Dresses with loose backs are only becoming upon very fine and slender fingers.

6. EVENING DRESSES. Evening dresses of transparent materials look well when made high in the neck ; but upon very young girls it is more graceful to cut the dresses low, leaving part of the shoulders exposed. A dress should always be made loose over the chest and tight over the shoulder blades. Long sashes fastened in front are more becoming than belts, unless there is much trimming upon the dress. Cuffs or narrow lace at the wrist finish the dress, and give the hands a small appearance. The effect of a well made tournure (or bustle) is to make the waist look round and delicate. An extremely small and waspish-looking waist can never be considered handsome. It is exceedingly hurtful to those who attain it by tight-lacing, and doubly ungraceful, since it prevents all graceful movements.

7. SHORT CLOAKS. Short cloaks are very unbecoming to short and clumsily built persons, but to a tall figure the reverse.

HOW TO DRESS THE HAIR.

1. DRESSING THE HAIR. Light hair is generally most becoming when curled. For an oval face, long and thick ringlets are suitable; but if the face is thin and sharp, the ringlets should be light, and not too long. Open braids are

very beautiful when made of dark hair. A simple and graceful mode of arranging the hair, is to fold the front locks behind the ears, permitting the ends to fall in a couple of ringlets on either side behind. Great care should be taken to part the hair directly in the centre of the forehead. Persons with very long, narrow heads, may wear the hair knotted very low at the back of the neck. If the head is long, but not very narrow, the back hair may be drawn to one side, braided in a thick braid, and wound around the head. When the head is round, the hair should be formed in a braid in the middle of the back of the head If the braid is made to resemble a basket, and a few curls permitted to fall from within it, the shape of the head is much improved.

2. CAPS. Caps are becoming to most ladies, but they should be trimmed with as few bows and as little lace as possible. Upon a long head they look well with a narrow border of lace lying close to the face and forehead.

THE MOUTH.

1. PURITY OF BREATH. Purity of breath is an advantage that cannot be too highly prized, as the want of it is the most unfortunate circumstance that can befall beauty, and is alone sufficient to annihilate in an instant the most perfect and otherwise inviting charms.

2. A fetid breath may be the consequence of various causes. When it proceeds from a diseased state of the lungs, riding on horseback, fresh air, and the use of gargles of myrrh, or the infusion of oak bark, with proper attention to the state of the bowels, may palliate the affection, and ultimately remove it, if not too deeply seated.

3. If it arise from causes which derange the digestive organs, the causes must be removed by proper medicines before the effect can cease; but cleanliness, and attention to the state of the mouth and teeth, morning and night, will assist to remove the inconvenience.

HINTS TO YOUNG MEN.

CHOICE OF A WIFE.

1. YOUNG gentlemen, a word of advice to you in the choice of a wife. Don't allow yourself to be deceived and fascinated by a gay, dashing young lady, fond of company, extravagant, vain, artistical and showy in dress. It is not a doll or a coquette you want for a partner. Choose rather one of those retiring, modest, sensible, neat young ladies who have learned to deny themselves, and possess a decided mind, and have acquainted themselves with the domestic cares of a family.

2. HOW TO TREAT A WIFE. You may have great trials and perplexities in your business with the world ; but do not therefore carry to your home a clouded or contracted brow. Your wife may have had trials which, though of less magnitude, may have been as hard to bear. A kind, consoling, and tender look, will do wonders in chasing from her brow all clouds of gloom.

3. Notice kindly her little attentions and efforts to promote your comfort. *Do not take them all as a matter of course*, and pass them by ; at the same time being very sure to notice any *omission* of what you may consider her duty to you. Do not treat her with indifference, if you would not sear and palsy her heart, which, watered by kindness, would, to the latest day of your existence, throb with sincere and constant affection.

4. *Sometimes* yield your wishes to hers. She has preferences as strong as you, and perhaps just as trying to her to

yield her choice as to you. Do you find it hard to yield it *sometimes ?* Think you it is not hard for her to give it up *always ?*

5. Again, show yourself manly, so that your wife can look up to you, and feel that you will act nobly, and that she can confide in your judgment.

STYLE AND DRESS OF GENTLEMEN.

I. The importance of dressing properly can scarcely be overrated. It not only influences the opinions of others in regard to us, but governs our own self-respect. A shabbily dressed man is likely to feel shabbily, and to commit shabby actions. A man with his coat out at the elbows, a shocking bad hat, and boots run down at the heel, will do things of which, in his dressed moments, he would be heartily ashamed.

2. A dandy farmer, an over-dressed mechanic, and a finical tradesman, are ridiculous ; but there is no reason why people of all employments should not wear clean linen and dress with perfect neatness.

3. A plain, simple style, is most proper for people of every class—the richest as well as the poorest. Flashy dresses, fancy colors, and excess of ornament, are the distinguishing marks of blacklegs and prostitutes.

Full dress for gentlemen, admits of but two colors, black and white. Undress allows of grays, browns, olives, indigoes, and other quiet colors.

"Neat but not gaudy," is the best possible maxim for both sexes and all conditions, though the ladies are allowed a greater variety and a more fanciful display.

Perhaps the best way is to have a sensible tailor, and leave the whole matter to his discretion ; that is, if you can rely upon his disinterestedness.

The best rule for both sexes, is to dress so that no one can remember what you wore, or anything about it, except the generally pleasing effect.

CHAIRMAN'S GUIDE ;

Or, Rules for the Orderly Conduct of Public Debate and Public Meetings.

ELECTION OF CHAIRMAN.

1. THE chairman selected should be a man held in respect.

2. He should be a man of maturity and commanding personal appearance.

3. He should possess a fitness for the office. This includes standing in society, intelligence, business tact, self-possession, etc.

4. The chairman should be chosen, in small meetings, by nomination ; and each person named, the motion being seconded, should be voted for until a choice is made.

5. The chairman chosen should always be properly conducted to the chair, and he may be introduced to the meeting in a brief speech.

6. On taking the chair a few words of remark on the part of the chair is in order, and generally expected.

THE POWER AND DUTIES OF THE CHAIRMAN.

7. In a public meeting the chairman should be elevated above the assembly.

8. It is improper for a chairman to hold conversation with any person while the floor is occupied by a speaker.

9. No person should accept the office of chairman unless he is prepared to resign all thoughts of promoting any private views of his own.

10. When a motion is presented to the meeting, it should be read by the chairman, and objections called for ; there being none, the motion should be put to the meeting, and decided by a majority of votes.

11. Persons wishing to advocate the motion should be allowed to do so.

12. If there be an objection, it must take one of the following shapes: it must be an *amendment*, or *negative*, or to *postpone*, or for the *previous question*, or to *adjourn the meeting*.

13. The right of reply, as it is termed, exists in the mover of the original proposition ; but belongs not to the mover of an amendment.

14. The rule of speaking is one speech for each person on each motion.

15. If a vote be doubted, it will be the duty of the chairman to " divide the *house*," and decide the question by count.

16. If there be amendments to an original motion, the amendments must be acted upon first.

17. At an adjourned meeting, the chairman should cause the minutes of the last meeting to be read.

18. If it is desirable to get rid of a chairman, it may be done, 1st, by refusing to do any business; or 2d, by an adjournment of the meeting, *sine die*.

19. No speaker should be interrupted while speaking, unless called to a point of order by the chairman.

20. When a point of order is raised, the person speaking should cease, and await the decision of the chairman.

21. When several persons rise to speak at the same time, the preference should be given to the one whose eye was first caught by the chairman.

A MANUAL FOR FARMERS AND THEIR WIVES.

FOR FARMER.

1. APPLES. Winter apples are better for remaining on the tree till well grown and ripened; it improves their flavor.

2. BEES. How to catch the moth or miller. Dr. Waterman says; I took two white dishes (I think white attracts their attention in the night), or deep plates, and placed them on the top of the hives, and filled them about half full of sweetened vinegar. The next morning I had about fifty millers caught; the second night I caught fifty more; the third night being cold, I did not get any; the fourth night being very warm, I caught about four hundred; the fifth night I got two hundred.

BEES—to prevent them from fighting. To stop bees from fighting and robbing one another, break the comb of the robbers so that the honey will run down among them, and they will go to work at home.

BUGS—to preserve vines from bugs. The best remedy we have tried, is to plant onion seeds with the cucumber, and after the plants are up to sprinkle ashes on every hill just before a fall of rain, which makes a *ley*, and kills the bugs, etc., almost instantaneously; the smell of the onions when up will keep the flies off. We have adopted this method for a number of years, not only on our vines, but on vegetables, such as beets, parsnips, etc. It promotes their growth and loosens the earth around the roots. Ashes sprinkled on young cabbages will also destroy worms and increase their growth.

5. ANOTHER. Lay two shingles flat on each hill among the plants ; early in the morning, and just before night, visit them and you will find plenty of bugs sticking to the shingles on the other side—clap them together, and the slaughter is sudden and immense.

6. CHEAP PAINT FOR A BARN. An excellent and cheap paint for rough wood work is made of six pounds of melted pitch, one pint of linseed oil, and one pound of brick-dust or yellow ochre.

7. CORN. Soak your seed corn in saltpetre. It destroys the worm, is not relished by crows or by squirrels, and yields much more abundantly than when it is planted without.

8. ANOTHER. Soak a few quarts of corn in whisky, and scatter it over the fields for the crows, who after partaking one such meal, and getting pretty thoroughly *corned*, will never return to it again.

9. CORN SOAKED FOR SWINE. Soak corn till fermentation is produced, and it will make excellent food for hogs.

10. CALVES—keeping calves with sheep. We have often recommended the keeping of calves with sheep, as we have found it an excellent plan, and highly approved of by others who have tried it. In this way there is less trouble, and the calves keep in fine condition upon the coarse part of the fodder which the sheep leave. In such cases, calves are never afflicted with vermin, and if any are on them before, they will soon disappear after the calves are among sheep.

11. Corn Rule for measuring corn in the ear in a crib.— Multiply the length, width, and depth of the bin together, and their product by $4\frac{1}{2}$. Cut off the right hand figure, and the remaining figures will be the number of bushels of shelled corn, and the figure at the right the decimal of a bushel.

12. COLTS—to prevent them chewing their halter. Take the scab from the wart or issue on the inside of the leg, rub the halter thoroughly with that, and they will not be caught chewing their halter very soon. I have tried pepper, tobacco, etc,, but nothing to so good purpose as their own or kindred musk.

13. CATTLE—feeding, etc. If all the grain fed out to stock were chopped, a saving of at least 25 per cent. in the quantity consumed might be made. The cattle would thrive better, as the food would be converted into nutriment without making so violent a demand upon the digestive organs.

14.—FOWLS—to fatten. Confine your fowls in a large and airy enclosure, and feed them on broken Indian corn, Indian meal, or mush, with raw potatoes cut into small pieces, not larger than a filbert, placing within their reach a quantity of charcoal broken into small pieces. Boiled rice is also good.

15. ANOTHER. It is astonishing with what rapidity fowls increase when well fed, kept in confined cribs, and in a darkened room. Fed on a mixture of 4 lbs. of oatmeal, 1 of suet, and half a pound of sugar, with milk for drink, five or six times a day, in summer, a dorking will add to its weight 2 lbs. in a week, sometimes $1\frac{1}{2}$ in four days. A young turkey will lay on 3 lbs. a week under the same treatment.

16. GEESE—feeding Geese, etc. An experiment has lately been tried of feeding geese with turnips, cut up fine, and put into a trough with water. The effect was that six geese, weighing only nine pounds each, after three weeks' feeding with this food alone, weighed fifteen pounds each.

17. GRAFTING—time of grafting. The most favorable time for grafting, is from the time the buds are bursting till the tree is in full foliage. Scions take well at this season, and being set soon after vegetation commences, they will attain a good growth; but though this may be the most favorable time, yet the work may be attended to for a longer period, as circumstances require. It may be commenced the first of March, and continued till the first of August. When the scions are set quite early, as the weather is cold and vegetation dormant, more care is necessary to ensure success. When scions are set late, they of course get a smaller growth and are more liable to get winter-killed.

18. GRAFTING—composition for. Take one part of tallow, two parts of beeswax and four parts of rosin. Melt the

whole together ; turn the mixture into water, and work in the hands as the shoemaker does his wax, to incorporate the parts. The warmth of the hand will soon bring it to a proper consistency when wanted for use, and a little grease will prevent its adhering to the fingers. A small piece is broken off, flattened in the hand, and covered over the cleft or wound. If of the thickness of a shilling it will neither melt, crack, or peel off.

19. HORSES—-salting horses, etc. A good lump should be kept in a box by the side of every animal, without fear that it will ever be taken in excess.

20. HORSES—feeding with Oats, etc. We were lately told by the proprietor of an extensive livery stable, that he had experience of several years in feeding the yellow carrots to his horses, and that he considers them the most valuable articles for winter food that he ever used. He considers a peck of carrots and a peck of oats worth more for a horse than half a bushel of oats.

21. HORSES—Marks of, etc.

> One white foot, buy him ;
> Two white feet, try him ;
> Three white feet, deny him ;
> Four white feet and a white nose,
> Take off his hide and throw him to the crows.

22. HENS—feed with oats, etc. Hens will, it is said, be sure to furnish an extra quantity of eggs, if you deal to each about a gill of oats per day.

23. HENS—How to protect from vermin. A gentleman from Hanover requests us to state the fact, that pennyroyal woven in their nests, will perfectly and certainly protect hens from vermin. He generally makes the nest entirely of this strong-scented herb.

24. HAWKS—to prevent their depredations. One or more Guinea hens in a flock of flowls it is said will effectually prevent molestation from hawks.

25. INSECTS IN ORCHARDS. Worms and insects in orchards may be destroyed by allowing swine to run beneath

the trees. As fast as the wormy and immature fruit falls, they will eat them, worms and all.

26. MANURE FOR MELONS. The best is pigeon dung, and from the use of this it is said the Persian fruit derives its superiority. Hen dung is probably next in value, and after this guano, which is the manure of sea fowls.

27. MILK SPREADING. This may be remedied by pressing the teat full of milk against a stone and rubbing it smartly.

28. HOW TO SAVE IN FEEDING HORSES. Bruise or crush your oats in a mill, or otherwise, as convenient, and your horse will become fatter on half its usual allowance than on double the quantity unprepared. If you cannot bruise the oats, pour hot water on them and let them soak for a few hours.

29. TO RENDER OLD AND BARREN ORCHARDS THRIFTY AND PRODUCTIVE. Early in the spring plough the entire orchard and enrich with a compost of manure, swamp-muck, lime and ship manure. Scrape off all the old bark with a deck-scraper, or a hoe, ground sharp. Apply half a bushel of slacked lime, and the same of charcoal, round each tree. Apply then soft soap or strong soap suds on the trunks and limbs as high as a man can reach. While the trees are in full bloom, throw over them a quantity of fine slacked lime.

30. OINTMENT—for cattle. Excellent ointment for cattle can be made by taking equal parts Venice turpentine and hogs' lard well beaten together.

31. POISON—cure for poison. It is said that a gill of melted lard poured down the throat of a sheep poisoned by eating laurel, a shrub that retains its foliage in winter, and grows abundantly on the margin of some of our streams, and in mountainous districts, is a certain cure.

Cattle are sometimes poisoned by eating the same shrub —would not the same remedy, in larger portions, be equally efficient?

It is also stated that poison on the hands or other parts, occasioned by the running ivy, or poison vine, may be cured by rubbing the part affected a few times with hogs' lard.

32. SCIONS. Every fruit-grower should get his scions ready in due season. Wrap them in a moistened mat, or cloth, put them in a close box, and keep them in a cool cellar. Keep the mat moist. If the scions mould it will do no harm

33. SALT FOR STOCK. When animals are first turned to grass they need more salt than at other seasons ; at least we infer this, as they eat it more freely.

34. SILKWORMS—noise disturbs them. A friend of ours, who has had much experience in managing silkworms, says that noise disturbs them, especially at the time of moulding. The sound of a hammer, a burst of laughter, or loud talking disturbs them. Their food should be gently laid down by them, not thrown on them. He uses as much caution in entering the rooms as approaching the cradle of a sick infant.

35. SHEEP—how to give them an appetite. Give to your sheep pine boughs once or twice a week; they will create appetite, prevent disease, and increase their health.

36. SEEDS—How to preserve, etc., for planting. Mix the seeds with clean sand which shall be occasionally slightly moistened, to prevent the seeds from drying, and put in a cool place. The seeds of stone fruit should not become much dried internally. Expose them sufficiently to evaporate the external atmosphere, and pack as above.

37. SWINE—substitute for ringing. A Mr. Tub, an English breeder of stock, recommends a mode of dealing with these mischievous animals, which it is said may supersede the necessity of putting rings in their nose. It consists simply of shaving off with a razor or sharp knife, the gristle on the top of the noses of the young ; this place soon heals over, and the pigs are thus rendered incapable of rooting.

38. SUNFLOWER. It is said of this unornamental but intrinsic flower, that it is destined to become one of our most

valuable agricultural products. One hundred pounds of the seed afford forty pounds of oil. The refuse of the seeds after expression, furnishes an excellent food for cattle. From the leaves of the plant segars are manufactured of singular qualities ; the stock affords a superior alkali, and the comb of the seeds is a choice dainty for swine.

39. TREES—setting trees. In setting trees, do not place them deep, and let the earth around them remain concave, that it may catch the water.

40. TREES—to prevent young trees from becoming hide-bound. An excellent mode for preventing young fruit-trees from becoming hide-bound and mossy, and for promoting their health and growth, is to take a bucket of soft soap, and apply it with a brush or old cloth to the trunks from top to bottom ; this cleanses the bark, destroys the worms, or the eggs of insects, and the soap becoming dissolved by rains, descends to the roots, and causes the tree to grow vigorously.

41. TREES—transplanting, etc. The trees to be removed are selected, the situations chosen, and the holes dug, while the ground is yet open, in autumn. Then, just before the ground is frozen, dig a trench at some distance around the tree to be removed, gradually undermining it, and leaving all the mass of roots embedded in the ball of the earth ; the whole ball is then left to freeze pretty thoroughly (generally till snow covers the ground), when the ball of earth containing the tree is rolled upon a sled and transplanted to the hole previously prepared, where it is placed in its proper position ; and as soon as the weather becomes mild, the earth is filled in around the ball. On return of growth, the trees scarcely show any effects from being removed.

42. TREES—budding, etc. If stocks are young and very thrifty it will be in season to commence budding the first of August, for if they are set earlier they will be likely to start the present season, and then liable to be winter-kiled. In this way some have suffered great loss for want of experi-

ence. If trees be rather old and of slow growth, they should be budded the latter part of July ; but the better way is to put all stocks in a very thrifty condition before budding or grafting.

43. TREES—to form new bark on old trees. ".Scrape the loose bark, and apply a mixture of cow-dung and urine, made into the consistency of paint. Apply the mixture with a paint brush. This softens the old scaly bark, which peels off the following spring, and is succeeded by fine, new, smooth bark."

44. PLANTING FOREST TREES. The best time for planting acorns, walnuts, as well as peaches, cherries, and other stone fruits, is in the fall of the year, as soon as they are ripe. If they are kept long after becoming thoroughly ripe, they are apt to lose their vegetative principle.

45. TREES—to keep away the Borer. Coal-pit dust has proved beneficial to fruit-trees, by placing a few shovelfuls about the roots of each tree ; it keeps away the grass, prevents the borer from entering the bark, and withal, makes an excellent manure.

46. WHEAT—rust in wheat. This seems to take place when it is nearly ripe, after a heavy shower of rain, succeeded by an intensely warm sun. The straw then bursts, and the sap exudes. This is the cause of rust. Steeping the seed in strong brine twelve hours, and then sifting lime over it, is the best preventive.

47. WORMS AND GRUBS. A mixture of salt and saltpetre (nitre), in proportion of eight parts of the former to one of the latter, applied about the roots, will, it is said, destroy the worms, and greatly promote the health and thrift of the tree.

FOR FARMERS' WIVES.

48. DAIRY SECRET. Have ready two pans in boiling water ; and on the new milk coming to the dairy, take the hot pans out of the water, put the milk into one of them, and cover it with the other. This will occasion great augmentation in the thickness and quality of the cream.

49. EGGS—preserving eggs. A Mr. Jayne, of Yorkshire, England, obtained a patent for the following receipt, for preserving eggs, which we think worthy of trial :

One bushel of quick lime, 32 ounces of salt, 8 ounces of cream of tartar.

Mix the same together with as much water as will reduce the composition to consistency that an egg when put into it will swim. It is said eggs have been kept, in this way, sound, for two years.

50. ANOTHER. Put a layer of salt in the bottom of a jar, and stick the eggs, point downwards, into the salt, and so on layer after layer.

51. CHEESE—to prevent its cracking. The best method to prevent the cracking of cheese, is to salt them in the milk, or after the cheese is formed which may be done with much more certainty than in the curd, which is a bad method.

52. TO PRESERVE APPLES AND PEARS. Wipe the fruit dry, then take a varnished crock or wide-mouthed jar, at the bottom of which is to be a layer of fine and very dry sand : on this place a layer of fruit, and so alternately fruit and sand until the jar or crock is full. Put a thick coat of sand on the top, and place it in a dry place. Apples or pears thus treated will keep good all winter.

53. CANDLES—how to make. Prepare your wicks about half the usual size, wet with spirits of turpentine : put them into the sun until dry ; then mould or dip your candles.

Candles thus made last longer, and give much clearer light. In fact they are nearly or quite equal to sperm, in clearness of light.

54. BACON—How to preserve. Make a lye of wood-ashes.

and boil it till it is strong. Dip each piece of the meat in it, let it dry and hang it in a smoke-house; and no insect will injure it, and the taste of the lye will not be perceived, even on the outside.

55. HAMS—how to preserve. Mr. Robert Wilson, of Fairfield, Conn., says he preserves his hams from flies, etc., by packing them in oats. In the fall he mixes his oats with corn, and grinds them to make more ham.

56. INSECTS—to destroy insects on plants. Tie up some flour of sulphur in a piece of muslin or fine linen, and with this the leaves of young shoots of plants should be dusted ; or it may be thrown on them by means of a common swans' down puff, or even by a dredging-box.

57. TO DRIVE ANTS AWAY. To prevent this little intruder from committing depredations on your dairy, safes, etc., smoke the bottom of your dishes, or other vessels, over a fire of oak chips or limbs; smoke empty vessels, and set your full ones in them. You must repeat the process every day or two, which will probably cause them to change their haunts. A small quantity of green sage, placed in the closet, will cause ants to disappear.

58. CASKS—foul casks made clean. Tainted wooden casks of every description may be rendered perfectly sweet and wholesome by washing them with diluted sulphuric acid [oil of vitriol] and water, and afterwards with lime-water, and then pure water.

59. BEEF AND PORK—a pickle for. The following recipe is strongly recommended ; Six gallons water, 9 lbs. salt, coarse and fine mixed; 3 lbs. sugar; 3 ounces saltpetre ; 1 ounce pearlash ; 1 gallon of molasses to every 6 gallons of water. In making a larger or smaller quantity of pickle, the above proportions are to be observed. Boil and skim the ingredients well.

DIET AND REGIMEN.

THE natural and uppermost question a patient puts to his medical man, after having received his instructions about medicine, is, " Well, doctor, how am I to live ?" The reply is usually, "Oh! sparingly—temperately; be careful. You must avoid spirits—take your medicine—and let me see you again."—" May I eat meat ?"—"Y-e-e-s, only moderately." " May I take exercise?"—" Y-e-e-s, yes,"—May I—I had something else to say, but I have forgotten it. Good day." And thus ends the colloquy; and how little wiser is the patient for his instructions. The medicine may be admirably prescribed, and excellently adapted for the case.

If there be any virtue in physicing by measure, there surely must be in dieting by the same principle. A pill, or draught, or powder, or dose of some sort or other, is advised to be taken every three, four, or six hours; and should not food and drink be taken with similar regularity? The only interpretation I can put upon the seeming fact is that it would appear, if a man fall ill, he has only to take some nauseous stuff, and he will or will not, as it may turn out, get well. The study of diet is left to the public to learn, as they would astronomy and chemistry, if they would desire to be more learned than their neighbors. We are all fashioned so differently, that there are extremes of every kind; some people can digest any thing, while others are compelled to hesitate before they take a mouthful. The multitude, however, are influenced by common laws. In a general way, certain articles of diet are generally indigestible, and overfeeding produces corresponding results to the strong and the weak, in proportion to the excess. These facts are ascertained only by experience. Youth lifts us over many difficulties. The appetite is the only guide, and the stamina of a growing boy helps him over the abuse which an elder person dare not commit. Many youthful habits are continued some time with impunity, that would be followed by serious inconveniences ten years afterward. It is very common to observe young persons drink off a tumbler of water or beer before commencing their dinner, which, although it may gratify a little morbid thirst, necessarily interferes with the digestion of the forthcoming meal ; it distends the stomach, dilutes the gastric juice, and is a shock to the nervous tone of the stomach. Many elder persons commit the same error; but it is difficult to persuade them that it is an error, and that the flatulence and weight after the subsequent meal is the result of the water or drink taken beforehand. Abertheny forbade his patients to drink at all at dinner-time ; and it will presently be seen that drink, at that period, is not only unnecessary, but also, as has been shown above, very prejudicial, and, if obstinately persisted in, ultimately productive of disease.

Consequently, as I observed before, unless there be specific instructions how to live given with the physic that is ordered to be taken, the treatment is sadly imperfect ; and it is too much to expect the patient to know by inspiration how he should diet himself to get well when probably it was only his careless living, of which he was ignorantly guilty, that caused his illness. Even the reform from intemperate habits, the relinquishment of spirituous drinks—in a word, teetotalism, unquestionably the greatest step ever made in a nation toward the improvement of health and security of universal happiness—how was it achieved (say to the wonderful extent it has already been)? Not by the preaching of the parsons, or by the advice and writings of the doctors, whose almost exclusive province it was, but by philanthropic individuals, by men chiefly from the hnmbler classes, who made the discovery themselves, and became the leaders of others.

If any man, living or dead, deserves the benediction of his fellow-creatures, Father Mathew is that man. It was not his position as a priest which gave him power; it was his homely, his common-sense understandable exposition of the injurious consequences of drink, to both the mind and body, to the home, to the family, and to the self of the drunkard, that enabled him to lead the thousands to the shrine he himself worshiped, namely, Temperance.

But while giving him credit for the change that he has effected, for the moral triumph he has gained, and the misery he has averted, his scheme is not wholly unattended with certain inconsistencies. Father Mathew, I presume, was not a physiologist, nor is teetotalism founded upon physiological principles; else wine, spirits, and beer, would not be entirely excluded from the table of man. Teetotallers admit that they may be taken medicinally; but medicine is usually administered to persons only when ill. Now, stimulatives are allowedly useful, not only in illnesss, but to prevent illness. There are some individuals who cannot subsist without stimulatives; they are not unwell, but they would be liable to become so, if denied *in toto*, the prohibited *stimuli*. It is difficult, I admit, to keep people within bounds; and perhaps the best way to avoid mischief on a large scale is to disallow spirits, etc., altogether, merely permitting the exceptions to infringe the rule. But of this as we go on; the advantages as well as disadvantages should be equally exhibited, and then those who infringe the laws of nature as well as of man, knowing beforehand the punishment in store, have only themselves to thank for their pains, and they deserve no commiseration.

SUMMARY OF DIET AND REGIMEN, WITH REMARKS.

In summer, rise at six, or earlier; in winter, not later than seven. If your pursuit confine you within doors all day, take an hour's exercise the first thing in the morning. If it prove wearisome to walk before breakfast, provide yourself with a biscuit or crust, or if you can get it, and need it, a cup of coffee. If you reside in the country, pursue the same plan. A light breakfast afterward will refresh you, and remove all fatigue. If you once commence the habit, you will find it more difficult to leave off than you found it to begin. A cold shower-bath, health permitting it, in the morning, is most salutary. It is no use, however, in taking it only occasionally ; it should be used daily, in all weathers, and all the year round. Where that is not practicable, cold ablution, or sponging the body and chest, particularly, with cold water, or deluging the head in a " bucket from the well," is sure to do good. These are such agreeable processes, that one day's omission will occasion such a want of comfort that the habit of persistence will become a delight to you.

I have offered a few comments on the beauties of bathing, generally, elsewhere, but no person should pass his or her life, without taking, for purposes of cleanliness and health, where it be practicable, a *warm bath* at least once a fortnight—certainly one a month ; but it would not be unwise nor dangerous, as by many it is foolishly feared, once a week.

If the weather be unfavorable, and you cannot go out, there are various means of taking exercise within doors : pacing a passage or room, with windows open ; some light game, skipping, battledore and shuttlecock, dumb-bells, fencing. A man in search of health must not mind being laughed at for seeming puerility. Even singing or reading aloud, or the practice of declamation, are severally serviceable. The most salutary of all early movements is a ride on horseback. A city business man may easily ride ten miles before breakfast. The immense benefits of sleeping out of town I have already expatiated upon ; and the morning ride in the fresh air furnishes you with health and strength that will carry you through the day. We now come to the eating part.

Breakfast is usually the first meal. Some people, from habit—from suppers, perhaps—although early risers, do not breakfast until eleven o'clock, when they will have a chop and a mug of ale. It is impossible to furnish such rules as shall be universally applicable. Dr. Combe rididicules the idea of fixed dietaries, or, indeed, prohibitions or allowances of any kind, inasmuch as men differ so in their capacities and appetites that scarcely two individuals will be found whom the same regimen will suit. And where, therefore, man is master of himself, and his means can command any thing he requires out of the common routine, he can the better study his feelings, which he is perfectly justified in doing.

However, this principle is good, that as we require both solids and fluids, it is better to adapt our resources to our wants; the first meal required is necessarily a fluid one, from the exhaustion we sustain during the night by perspiration, and the escape of other secretions. Like the earth, we need moisture; and instinct dictates that the commencement and close of the day are the best periods for partaking of it, and that those times render the enjoyment most congenial to our feelings, and productive to our personal comfort.

The materials of the tea-table are very simple in this country, hut epicures convert it into a *dejeune a la four-chette*. The ordinary breakfast consists of tea or coffee, with bread and butter, or toast, to which is occasionally added eggs, fried ham or bacon, cold meat, chicken, etc.; but usually the appendages are taken but sparingly of; indeed, except one has to wait till a five o'clock dinner, or to undergo much exercise or fatigue, the quieter the breakfast the better. A very hearty breakfast is difficult to dispose of; it is productive, especially if three or four cups of liquid be swallowed, of much flatulence and eructations, with a degree of puffiness that continues disagreeable for the next two or three hours. Exercise should not be taken immediately after a good breakfast. It is advisable also to drink slowly, as well as to eat slowly. The stomach becomes more reconciled to a fluid meal when introduced gradually, than when poured in all of a heap ; the thirst is better allayed, and the palate better satisfied. In selecting what we should drink for breakfast, we must be governed by our individual experience. Many people cannot take either tea or coffee, in which case, cocoa, or chocolate, or broma, or milk and water, or boiled milk with bread, or farinaceous food, or oatmeal porridge, or whatever else the ingenuity of the housewife or nurse may suggest, or the palate of the individual may fancy. From half to three-quarters of a pint is sufficient, with a round or a round and a half of toast, buttered when cold, the allowance to be increased according to appetite and circumstances; a reasonable time for breakfasting is between eight and nine o'clock.

The next function of life which is most universally exercised immediately after breakfast, is the evacuation of the bowels. This affair is one of very great importance, and which no morbid delicacy should suffer to be disregarded. It is an ordination of nature, and a sure sign of something wrong when not obeyed. Constipation is a very marked symptom of indigestion, and may be looked upon as an indication that the diet is of too dry a nature, too astringent, or that the bowels are irritable, that the stomachic and intestinal secretions are at fault. So formidable an interruption to health, and so productive is constipation of general uneasiness, that various methods, dietetical, medical, and mechanical, are from time to time suggested for its relief ; but the very remedies only keep up the disease, and when once resorted to, cannot be dispensed with. Many people never obtain an evacuation of the bowels without medicine. or the use of the lavement, whereas the only two certainties to procure efficient relief are watchful living and exercise, both of which are miserably neglected. When possible, an evacuation should be secured ; the daily habit of visiting the closet at the same hour is a method very likely to insure success, and the practice cannot be too much insisted upon with regularity in early life : among the dietetic provocatives, apart from the simplicity of feeding, is the brown bread instead of white, and the unfermented (where it can be obtained or made) in preference to that prepared with yeast.

Constipation is indeed a great nuisance, but it is always confirmed by medicine-taking rather than cured by it. When once the bowels become regular, be wise, and never take another purgative pill or dose but upon stern necessity. Constipation is mere irritation, inducing deficient secretion, and morbid apathy or positive constriction of the rectum and bowels generally.

The next consideration is how the time between breakfast and dinner should be filled up. If this be read by the man of business, he can better answer the question than I can ; if by one, happily, controller of his own time, and one in search of health, I need scarcely say, that from ten to two is the best and most agreeable time for taking pedestrian or equestrian exercise. The ride by steamboat, railroad, or omnibus, or even foot journey, to the city or house of business, is of incalculable advantage, but how much more so is the liberty the uncontrolled man possesses of rambling out either in the green fields, on the cheerful river, or in the highways and byways of this beautiful world. From two to three hours thus spent daily, makes our stay here an elysium. It furnishes the meal for the soul, if I may be allowed such an expression, and which I employ without prejudice ; the mind is gladdened—the perceptions brightened—and contentment reigns throughout. It completes the process of the transmutation of the food we consume into the blood that animates the mortal man—it is the last handiwork of nature in digestion. How blest, indeed, is he, and also ought he to feel, who possesses the inestimable privilege of having all things made to his desires—of being born to live, not to struggle—and of serving others rather than needing service himself. This is not the language of discontent, it is from one who believes *whatever is, is right ;* and one who, from the naturally restricted privileges of a working bee, the more duly appreciates the freedom of a day's holiday—the ramble abroad, where the only buffets he encounters are those of the friendly breeze, and the only homage he is called upon to pay, the cheerful thanksgiving to the only Master he serves.

Exercise, in whatever shape availed of, in the bustle of trade, or the sports of the field, or in any of the other duties or pleasures of life, is indispensable to secure health.

The question of " Have you been out to-day ?" pre-supposes generally that the morning was the time selected ; it certainly has its advantages ; but where it cannot be obtained in the forenoon, the remaining half of the day is amply sufficient to make man content. The afternoon jaunt and evening stroll have severally admirers, and it is well we cannot all select the same time, else we should jostle each other. The weather and seasons forbid and invite alternately, and circumstances must guide us in our selection.

The dinner should be the substantial, the nourishing meal of the day. One strong reason why it should be taken early in the day, in preference to late in the evening, is, that as the food has to be digested as well as swallowed, and which former requires some energy for its purpose, the meal ought to be taken before man is exhausted by the fatigues of the day, besides to allow time for the necessary exercise which should accompany the completing process of digestion.

Digestion usually takes from four to five hours before it is completed ; the time is not invariably the same with everybody. With some the process is much more rapid ; with others double the time is occupied. The stomach all this time is absolutely at work. Happily, except in disease, we are ignorant of what is going forward, scarcely cognizant we have a stomach ; and there is certainly in health no feeling to tell us exactly whereabout it is situated. It is, however, as well to know so much of anatomy, that if we should experience a twinge we might form some idea which part of our digestive machinery was attacked. I have hitherto presumed it to be of less importance that a reader should be rendered anatomically learned, than that he knew simply what the office of the stomach was, and also have some idea of its powers.

Now it follows, and the policy is borne out in the universal maxim, that it is better to finish one thing first before we commence another, and so it is with digestion. Digestion is a specific process that involves certain duties, that cannot well be performed is subject to interruptions or additional imposts. The stomach, on receipt of the food supplies promptly, that is to say, it secretes or pours forth from its surface a certain and limited amount of a powerful solvent fluid, called gastric juice ; this mingles with the food, and rapidly dissolves the portion it comes in contact with. To render the contact more general, the stomach is furnished with a power of contracting upon itself and squeezing as it were the food from one part to another. When the food is sufficiently pulpy or dissolved, it passes onward to the intestines, where the nutritious portion which is to form the blood of the body is taken up, and the extraneous carried forward and given off in the usual manner.

Now it is well known that every act and movement of the body, or even exercise of the senses, is followed more or less with fatigue, and there is no reason why the stomach should not have a little breathing time, after having completed its work, as well as the legs and arms. Such a respite is necessary ; and hence the prudence of allowing a little time to elapse beyond when the digestion is to be completed before fresh work is imposed, A quiet breakfast, being a fluid meal, is disposed of in perhaps three hours ; therefore, if taken at eight or nine o'clock, dinner may follow at one or two. If protracted beyond that time, to five or six ; or later, some little refreshment is advisable, proportioned, of course to the exercise and bustle going on. Lunches, else, are tantalizing interruptions, and except necessary to prevent faintness or exhaustion, had better be dispensed with. Besides, the materials of the lunch are usually some sweet or spongy substance—a bun, tartlet, or biscuit, with a glass of wine. It must be told that there is as much ceremony in digesting a mouthful as in a meal ; and the digestive process being set in motion too quickly, enervates its powers, and disturbs the sympathies of appetite and relish that are usually in attendance when in a healthy condition.

Frequently and little, or much and seldom, must be adopted according to each man's capacity, of which, as I have observed before, every person should judge for himself. It is so easy to find out which best agrees ; but if the order be reversed, overfeeding or underfeeding are the consequences ; there is less fear from the latter than the former. Now, with regard to the dinner, *it should be eaten slowly, and masticated thoroughly*, and the grand rule regulating the whole should be, *that we do not eat too much*.

Persons in feeble health must vary their table fare according to the instructions already given. The propriety of drinks at dinner is a matter of opinion. Unquestionably, dinner being a solid meal, requires only so much fluid as shall help to relieve the *dryness* of the repast, or to aid its miscibility; but then there is almost sufficient moisture in the meat and vegetables for that purpose, and in the salivary and other secretions. If the said dryness prevail, and man's aptitude requires it, there is no reason why drink should altogether be excluded ; and I should say, there can be no great harm in half a pint of mild table ale, if experience bespeak the necessity. When the digestion is feeble, and persons seem to need it, from one to three glasses of wine may be taken if preferred. These dietetic instructions to one in health may well be laughed at ; to the sick man, the case is different ; and as to him they are chiefly addressed, allowances must be made for this wearisome minuteness. With regard to taking stimulants in the shape of wine and beer at dinner, or at any time, by the healthy or by the sick, a main consideration is, *do they excite?* or, on the other hand, do they *produce lethargic feelings?* The mere exhilaration of spirits, the cheerfulness which follows, or the general comfortable sensations which prevail after wine, beer, or spirits, do not determine that mischief is going on, nor should a man be always feeling his pulse to know whether his life is running too fast; but there are other indications which cannot be mistaken—the sensible increased beating of the heart, the throbbing in the forehead, the evidence of powerful mental excitement, the flurry following a quickened step, the confusion of thought, the puffiness and general distension— all of these, and many more, known by experience to the free liver, determine the mischievous tendency of stimulants, and prove, by the absence of these feelings, when not partaken of, that they had better be avoided.

Dining is a much more important affair than many people suppose. It is true a hungry stomach is a most unruly fellow, and a man is up in arms if compelled to go without his dinner: but it is often looked upon as the mere link between body and life, and it is considered sufficient so long as we can fill our stomachs. Now, there are certain conditions, if we desire really to benefit by the meal, that should be observed, independently of regularity and a wholesome supply of the daily fare. Nothing is so injurious as hurried eating, or proceeding to dine when overheated or fatigued. There are many persons in cities, who allow themselves not more than half an hour to *run* to their dinner, consume it, and *run* back again. Many there are also, who defer it till hunger pinches their stomachs; and on the strength of a good appetite exhaust themselves by a five or six mile ride, or corresponding walk home to join the dinner-table, and by the time the repast is over, they are absolutely fitter to go to bed than remain up for several hours, in which lethargy the stomach joins, and digestion is more or less suspended. Dinner being a cheerful meal, and also of its not being taken immediately after exertion ; at least a quarter of an hour's respite is advisable. It is equally imprudent to return to active duty without a corresponding pause after, as well as before.

Supposing little drink be taken at dinner, and allowing from three to four hours for its digestion, a fluid meal comes in very *apropos* at this time ; and by its miscibility, completes the solution of the food, and facilitates its transmission into the bowels. Tea, therefore, may be taken about this time. The comfortable and refreshing feelings which ensue test the propriety of the repast.

As we are not merely sent here to feed and repose, but to fulfil various other duties, among which recreation as well as toil has its demands, custom has assigned the evening for general pastime and association among each other ; and, accordingly, the body being hereby invigorated, the mind is fitter for its lighter occupation. The pursuits of the evening are multifarious ; to dictate which amusement should be followed would be trespassing upon other people's taste, which is beyond the privilege of a writer on dietetics ; certain it is, that exercise should form a part. The walk out and home and family dance are alike serviceable ; and where the one be impracticable, the other should not be dispensed with.

An early dinner admits of a light supper, but it should be taken by weight and measure. The tempting things put upon table often induce one to eat more than is wholesome ; and it is indeed a wretched recompense for the short-lived gratification of pleasing the palate by an extra plate or a glassful, of having to pass a night of nightmare and hideous dreams ; besides, the punishment is extended over the next day, by the feelings of lassitude consequent upon loss or rest.

I need not say a word about the unwholsomeness of hot meat suppers to a person in uncertain health ; they are proverbially mischievous, and a man of any experience is rarely found to be a guest thereat. Of late hours I have already spoken at length. With regard to sleep, it should be remembered that ventilation of a sleeping apartment is of as much importance as that of the day-room, and hence it is well to choose large and lofty bed-rooms; if the sleeper be not very suscepible of taking cold, I would advise the windows—or at least one of them, if there be more—to be kept half down during the night. Slumber should be sought for not later than ten or eleven o'clock, by the valetudinarian, and he thereby may secure from eight to nine hours' rest, which is sufficient, and not too much, for the invalid, or for the preservation of health.

A happy and even temper, is an invulnerable shield against the misfortunes—worldly, bodily, and mental—of human life; and as I am convinced it can be acquired where not already possessed, it is a study I would urge every one in need of to carry out to the letter.

Thus may the twenty-four hours be passed; remembering, meantime, the hints furnished regarding the control of the passions, that no matter whatever the exercise of the mind or body may be, nature has its limits, and the transgression invariably draws down its punishment. The last words of Dr. Spurzheim were, that "man never will be happy till he learns God's laws, and has wisdom to obey them." If this aphorism be fairly carried out, and the trouble be taken to make the same our especial study, we shall assuredly escape the prickly thorns of a corrupt body or a distempered mind.

SULLIVAN'S CAMPAIGN.

A Full and Truthful Account of the Expedition of Gen. John Sullivan and an American Army through the

CHEMUNG VALLEY IN 1779

To Destroy the Power of the Six Nations of Indians.

Compiled from the Historical Address of the *Rev. DAVID CRAFT,*

FOR SUBSCRIBERS OF THE WEEKLY GAZETTE.

SULLIVAN'S EXPEDITION.

The expedition of Gen. John Sullivan through the Valley of the Chemung in the summer and early fall of 1779 to break the power of the Iroquois Indians was one of the most interesting incidents of the Revolutionary War. The following account of it, drawn from the historical address of the Rev. David Craft, published by the state, may be relied upon as substantially correct.

When the Revolutionary War broke out there were living through the central part of New York the confederate Five Nations of Indians called the Iroquois. They were the Mohawks, the Oneidas, the Onondagas, the Cayugas and the Senecas. All together they had about 2,000 warriors. Before the union of these tribes they had suffered greatly from wars with the western and southern tribes, and the union was made for mutual protection and safety. They prospered under it and showed many signs of civilization. Their confederation was an anticipation of our own Republic. They lived in log huts covered with bark and having glazed windows and chimneys, instead of the lodges of poles set up and covered with skins, which is the shelter of the savage. They raised abundant crops of corn, potatoes, beans, squashes, pumpkins, melons and cucumbers, cultivated fruit orchards raised and cared for cattle, horses, swine and fowls, and were in short farmers on a rude but quite large scale. We believe, however, that the squaws did all the farm work, the bucks spending their time between hunting, fighting and loafing.

The Iroquois were, however, friends of the British. They had been their allies in the war against the French, and the British had so treated the Indians as to retain their friendship afterward. Sir William Johnson, the popular Indian agent, died in 1774, and his son in-law, Col. Guy Johnson, succeeded to the agency. His son John succeeded to his title and estate. Col. John Butler, a speculator in Indian lands, was their neighbor. They were all British loyalists and had great influence with the Indians in turning them against the Americans. Joseph Brant, a Mohawk chief, whose sister Mollie was mistress of Sir William Johnson, was taken to England, educated, shown much attention, and became a warm adherent of the British. In 1775 Sir John Johnson and Colonel John Butler called a secret council of Indians at Oswego. It was attended chiefly by the Senecas and Cayugas, who were henceforth British allies and prominent enemies of the Americans. Early in 1776, Sir John Johnson went to Canada, was commissioned a Colonel in the British service, and raised two battalions of troops, called the "Royal Greens". They were joined by some British sympathizers from America, and in co-operation with the Iroquois were a dangerous force to be in rear of the patriot army.

The Americans had feared the hostility of the Iroquois and at the very beginning of the struggle for independence had sent a delegation to the great council of the Iroquois to inform them of the situation and ask them to be neutral. The request was well received and agreed to ; but the agreement was not kept. In 1777 the forces of Indians and whites under Col. Butler and Joseph Brant were with the British in the Burgoyne campaign, in the siege of Fort Schuyler and in the battle of Oriskany. The Americans made another attempt for peace with them. Congress sent a deputation to meet them at Johnstown. There were some 700 Indians present and three of the tribes showed a disposition to make peace. But the Senecas and Cayugas, who had attended the council with the British in Oswego, only sent a defiant message and showed that they were for war.

HOSTILITIES IN 1778.

The year 1778 was marked by a series of attacks on the most important frontier towns in New York and Pennsylvania. In January, predatory excursions were begun against the settlers on the Susquehanna, and before the close of spring, of more than a hundred families scattered along the river, above the Lackawanna, not one remained. Then came the destruction of Wyoming, and the piteous tale of sorrow and distress and death had hardly been told when there followed in swift succession the destruction of Andrustown, of the German Flats and Cherry Valley. As the terror-stricken fugitives fled to the adjoining settlements, they told with every conceivable exaggeration, the story of their sufferings, and the hideous cruelty and savageness of both Tory and Indian. Every messenger from the frontiers brought a new tale of butchery, of prisoners tortured, of scenes where every refinement of cruelty was in sharp competition with the most shocking barbarism.

During the winter of 1778-79, bands of savages or disguised Tories were incessantly prowling around the border settlements, keeping the people in constant alarm and terror. Military men began to discuss the feasibility of what had for a year been advocated by Washington—carrying the war into the enemy's country. It was argued that the surest and easiest way to protect the border settlements was to weaken the power of the adversary. It was known that in the fertile valleys of the Genesee and along the lakes of Central New York, large crops of corn and other vegetables were raised, not for the support of the Indians alone, but as supplies for the British army. It was thought that if these crops should be destroyed, and the Indians driven back upon the British garrisons which were maintained at Niagara and Oswego, it would largely increase the expense of the British government in carrying on the war, embarrass their operations through the failure of their expected supplies, place a greater distance between the Indians and the frontiers, and teach them wholesome lessons of the power of the colonies to visit upon them the vengeance which their cruelties deserved. The territory it was proposed to lay waste was that occupied by the Senecas and Cayugas, the two most powerful nations of the Iroquois, and the most haughty and implacable in their enmity to the people of the States.

In the autumn of 1778, the New York authorities had determined to send a strong force into the very heart of the Iroquois country, to punish severely the Mohawks and Onondagas for their breach of faith, and their cruelties upon the patriot frontiersmen, but it was abandoned on account of the lateness of the season. In September, however, Colonel Thomas Hartley of the eleventh Pennsylvania Regiment, with about two hundred men, penetrated the Indian country by way of the West Branch, the Lycoming and Towanda creeks as far as Tioga, intending to form a junction with a detachment from General Clinton's Brigade. But finding the enemy in force at Chemung, and not meeting the expected reinforcements, after recovering some property stolen by the savages, he retired to Wyoming, reaching that place October 1, in safety. The subject was formally brought to the attention of Congress, and that body, February 27, 1779, passed a resolution authorizing General Washington to take the most effectual measures for protecting the inhabitants of the States and chastising the Indians. The Commander-in-Chief determined to carry out this resolution with vigor. General Hand, Colonel Zebulon Butler, Captain John Franklin and Captain Simon Spalding, of Wyoming, each of whom had extensive knowledge of the Indian country, were consulted. Lieutenant (after Colonel) John Jenkins, by profession a surveyor, who had recently been a captive among the Indians, and had traveled over the very country into which it was proposed to send the army, was able to give information of great value, and was retained as chief guide to the expedition. General Phillip Schuyler, at his headquarters on the Hudson, was also gathering and transmitting most important information from those conversant with the movements of the enemy.

The plan of a vigorous campaign contemplated the entire destruction of everything upon which the Indians depended for food or shelter. The invading army was to enter the Indian country in three divisions ; one from the south up the Susquehanna ; another from the east down that river, the third from the west by the way of the Allegany. These were to form a junction at some convenient point, advance against the strongholds of the enemy in such force as could not possibly be resisted, and then overrun the whole Iroquois country, west of the Oneida villages.

THE PERSONNEL OF THE EXPEDITION.

Washington's first task was to select a commander for the expedition. April 14, 1779, he wrote to Congress that he considered " this command of the second, if not of the first, importance of the campaign." He offered it to General Gates, but Gates declined it because it required youthful strength. Then he offered it to General John Sullivan, who was 39 years old.

General Sullivan accepted the command and immediately began preparing the details for the expedition. It was determined that the center or main division of the army should rendezvous at Wyoming, whence baggage and supplies could be transported to Tioga and beyond, by water. This division was to be made up of three brigades—the New Jersey, commanded by Brigadier-General William Maxwell, composed by First Regiment, under Colonel Matthias Ogden ; the Second, under Colonel Israel Shreve ; the Third, commanded by Colonel Elias Dayton, and the Independent or Fifth, better known from the name of its commander, as Colonel Oliver Spencer's Regiment ; also David Forman's Regiment, and Colonel Elisha Sheldon's Connecticut Riflemen, both subsequently merged into Spencer's Regiment. The Second, was the New Hampshire Brigade, commanded by Brigadier General Enoch Poor, comprising from that State, the First Regiment, under Colonel Joseph Cilley ; the Second, commanded by Lieutenant-Colonel George Reid, the Third, or Scammel's Regiment, under command of Lieutenant-Colonel Henry Dearborn, and the Second New York commanded by Colonel Philip VanCortlandt. The Third, was a Brigade of Light Troops, under Brigadier-General Edward Hand, composed of the Eleventh Pennsylvania Regiment, commanded by Lieutenant-Colonel Adam Hubley; the German Regiment, or what there was left of it, commanded by Major Daniel Burchardt; Captain Simon Spalding's Independent Wyoming Company; the Wyoming militia, under Captain (afterward Colonel), John Franklin, and Schott's Rifle Corps, with Captain Selin in command. It was expected that the Pennsylvania and some other companies would be filled up by enlistment, when the whole number would be about 3,500 men. There was also a section of Artillery under command of Colonel Thomas Proctor of Philadelphia.

The right division of the army was the New York Brigade, commanded by Brigadier-General James Clinton, consisting of the Third Regiment, under Colonel Peter Gansevoort, who in 1777 gained great renown for his heroic defense of Fort Schuyler against St. Leger; the Fourth, or Livingston's Regiment, under Lieutenant-Colonel Frederick Weissenfels, the Fifth, or Independent Regiment, commanded by Colonel Louis Dubois; the Sixth Massachusetts, or Alden's Regiment, commanded by Major Whiting—Colonel Ichabod Alden having been killed the autumn previous, at Cherry Valley, and Lieutenant-Colonel Stacia being a prisoner with the enemy; the Fourth Pennsylvania Regiment, under Lieutenant-Colonel William Butler; companies of Morgan's Riflemen, with Major James Parr the senior officer, and a small command under Colonel John Harper. The nominal strength of the Brigade was about 1,600 men.

The left division was to consist of troops at Pittsburg, numbering about 600 or 800 men, under command of Colonel Broadhead. As this force never became connected with the main army, and never received orders from General Sullivan, nothing further need be said of it.

DIFFICULTIES OF THE START.

Gen. Sullivan reached Easton, Pa., May 7, 1779, and wrote to General Washington that he should do everything in his power to set the wheels in motion for the expedition. There were many difficulties. The Indians knew of his movements, and there were spies in camp. Some of the Jersey troops were in a state of mutiny because they were paid in Continental currency, which had very little value. Many people of Pennsylvania opposed the expedition, especially the Quakers, who said the Indians deserved more pity than blame. The " Wyoming controversy" over the title to lands on which Connecticut people had settled, was also raging, and the Wyoming claimants desired to have the Indians keep the whites off until the war was over; they therefore opposed the expedition. The route was also mountainous and difficult.

Gen. Sullivan succeeded in overcoming all these obstacles so as to start from Easton on June 18th, at 3 o'clock in the morning. He was accompanied by three New Jersey and two New Hampshire regiments and Proctor's artillery. They marched days and camped nights through the Blue Ridge mountains, and reached Wyoming June 23d. Here there were more difficulties. The expected supplies were not on hand. The salted meat was not fit to eat The cattle were too poor to walk. The whole commissary was in a sad condition. The Pennsylvania authorities had shamefully failed in their duty.

The army lay at Wyoming five weeks, with few incidents. Mutiny and desertion had to be punished and the army disciplined. The British and Indians in the meantime were active in making raids, but Gen. Sullivan paid them little attention, and hastened his preparations for a move forward.

On the last day of July, everything being in readiness so far as circumstances would permit, about one o'clock in the afternoon the army broke camp at Wyoming and began its forward march. Two captains, six subalterns and one hundred men were left as the garrison for Wyoming, under command of Colonel Zebulon Butler, who was charged with forwarding such supplies as might be collected. The artillery consisted of eight brass pieces, viz : two six-pounders, four three-pounders, two howitzers, carrying five and a half inch shells, together with a light piece for carrying either shot or shell, called a cohorn. The artillery, ammunition, the salted provisions, flour, liquors and heavy baggage, were loaded on two hundred and fourteen boats, manned by four hundred and fifty enlisted boatmen, Colonel Proctor's regiment, and two hundred and fifty soldiers, all under the command of Colonel Proctor. To General Hand and his light troops was assigned the post of honor, the front of the column, which was directed to march in three columns, and keep about a mile in advance of the main body. Hubley's regiment and Captain Spalding's Independent company formed the centre column and proceeded on the main road; the German regiment and Captain Schott's Independent corps formed the right column, the left being a detatchment from the centre. Colonel Armand had on the

30th of June been ordered with his troops to join the army of Washington. Advanced and flanking parties were kept out to guard against surprise from the enemy, and the brigade was so arranged as to be instantly effective in case of sudden attack. Then Maxwell's brigade, advancing by its left in files, sections or platoons, according to the nature of the country; then Poor's brigade, advancing by the right in the same manner. Then followed the pack-horses, about twelve hundred in number, and seven hundred beef cattle. A regiment, taken alternately from Maxwell's and Poor's brigades, was detailed as rear guard. Sixty men, under Captain Gifford, of the Third Jersey regiment, were directed to go up on the west side of the river to prevent any surprise or interruption from that quarter, and four light boats, well manned, were ordered to keep abreast of them and bring them over to the main body, in case of an attack by a superior force.

The firing of a gun from the "Adventure," Colonel Proctor's flag boat, at one o'clock, P. M., was the signal for the fleet to weigh anchor. In a few moments the whole army was in motion, with flags flying, drums beating, fifes screaming, and Colonel Proctor's regimental band playing a lively air. Passing the fort, a salute of thirteen guns was fired, which was answered by a like number from the fleet. When the whole line got in motion the distance from front to rear was about two miles, and sometimes farther, while the fleet was spread out at least an equal distance.

ON TO TIOGA.

The army encamped the first night at Coxton, the next night about seven miles from Lackawanna, and then pushed on to Wyalusing. August 11th it reached Tioga, the site of an Indian town on the peninsula between the Susquehanna and Tioga or Chemung rivers. In its last day's march the army had passed over the ruins of Queen Esther's town, burned by Col. Thos. Hartley the year before, as punishment for the Queen's barbarous conduct at Wyoming.

On the first flat above the present village of Chemung stood the Indian town Chemung in 1779. The old town, abandoned several years previous, was nearly three miles below and near the present village. Gen. Sullivan determined to destroy the Indian town, and sent a reconnoitering party to discover the situation. The party found the Indians expecting an attack, and returned to camp. Without delay the greater part of the army marched on the village, but when it was reached, with much difficulty, the Indians had fled. Gen. Hand, with Hubley's regiment and the Wyoming troops, pursued, and about a mile above Chemung, on the broken ground called the "Hog Back," came upon them suddenly. The Indians, from ambush, fired on the party and killed six men, all of the 11th Pennsylvania. The troops returned the fire, and, pushing on, the Indians fled, losing certainly three of their number. Gen. Hand was recalled by Gen. Sullivan. About 100 acres of corn, just in the milk, were near this town, and all but forty acres (which were left for the future use of the army), were destroyed. While entering a field, the troops were fired on by Indians and one man killed and five wounded. The army returned to Tioga Aug. 13th, carrying their seven dead and fourteen wounded. The dead were buried, and the location of their graves is now unknown. The wounded recovered.

For the protection of the stores and boats to be left at Tioga during the absence of the army, a fort was erected and named Fort Sullivan. The site selected was near the centre of the present village of Athens, where two rivers approach near each other.

THE NEW YORK EXPEDITION.

The New York government had determined, prior to the Sullivan expedition, to send a strong force against the Iroquois by way of Mohawk, and Gen. Clinton was preparing for it. Then it was thought best to punish the Onondagas for their treachery and General Clinton, by direction of General Schuyler, sent a force to break up their haunts. The work was done by the First New York regiment, 558 strong, under Col. Van Schaick. Twelve Indians were killed and 33 taken prisoners; three villages, with a quantity of corn, beans, etc., were destroyed, the council house disabled and their council fire extinguished.

Gen. Clinton then marched to Lake Otsego, the head of the Susquehanna river, and encamped July 3d, 1779. His force consisted of the 3d, 4th and 5th New York regiments, the 6th Massachusetts, the 4th Pennsylvania and four companies of Morgan's Rifles, altogether 1,600 men and two pieces of artillery.

This army lay in camp until Aug. 9th, when, by order received from Gen. Sullivan, it started down the Susquehanna. Gen. Sullivan sent a force to meet them. The meeting occurred near the present village of Owego, and the Indian village of that name was burned as a bonfire in honor of the meeting. The united force then proceeded to Tioga and joined Gen. Sullivan August 22d. They were welcomed with cannon, cheers and music.

PUSHING THE EXPEDITION.

In the meantime Gen. Sullivan was preparing for his advance. The army was now reorganized All cumbrous and unnecessary baggage was stored at Tioga, where a garrison of 250 men was to remain. Gen. Hand's brigade now took the advance, Gen. Poor's the right, Gen. Maxwell's the left and Gen. Clinton's the rear. The artillery, preceded by the pioneers and followed by the pack horses and beef-cattle, was in the centre.

August 26th this army took up its line of march into the unknown country, into the very heart of the enemy's country. It was an expedition more daring than Sherman's march to the sea in 1864.

The army reached the site of Old Chemung the evening of the 27th. A scout came in with news that the enemy were at work on a fortification a few miles above. On the 29th the army moved, but with great circumspection. Before going two miles small bodies of Indians were seen. Two miles further and the fortifications were in sight.

ABOUT ELMIRA.

Consulting the map of the State of New York it will be seen that nearly opposite the present village of Wellsburg, the Chemung (old Tioga) river runs first in a southerly direction, then sweeping around to the northeast, it forms nearly a semi-circle, of which the road leading to Elmira is the diameter. The road to Wellsburg divides this space into two nearly equal areas or quadrants. Coming down between the hills from the north is Baldwin's creek, which, a little south of the main road, turns sharply to the east, and reaches the river some distance below. Beginning near the river, and nearly opposite to what was formerly the lower point of Baldwin's island now, owing to a change in the main current of the stream, near the middle of it, begins a ridge of land, running in a southeasterly direction for about three thousand five hundred feet, and crossing the Wellsburg road, when it turns nearly at right angles, and extends in almost a direct northerly course about one thousand two hundred feet further, until it reaches the creek. The side of this ridge toward the streams was steeper and higher than it now is, it having been measurably levelled down by ninety years of cultivation. Between this ridge and the hill on the north on which the monument stands, now called Sullivan hill, is a hollow, along which the Elmira road is laid, and which a mile to the west of the creek expands into a wider flat. where was an Indian town of twenty-five or thirty houses, called Newtown, which gave the name to the battle-field. At present only two or three old apple trees indicate its site.

A mile or more to the north of the main road, Baldwin's creek runs between two high ridges parallel with the stream, the slope of the western one, which is Sullivan hill, coming sheer down to the water's edge. Where Jacob Lowman's sawmill now stands, in the woods, on both sides of the creek, were about twenty or thirty houses, which had never been inhabited, and were supposed to have been built for storing the crops growing in the vicinity. A few houses near the bend of the creek were torn down by the enemy, and the logs used in their fortification One hundred and fifty to two hundred acres of magnificent corn just ripening for the sickle, were on the flats near the river. The Indian path from Chemung, probably, was nearer the creek than the present road ; after the creek was crossed, the path turned to the right, until it reached the Elmira road, when it took about the direction of the highway to Newtown. The slope of Sullivan hill was covered with pine and dense growth of shrub oaks.

Along the crest of the ridge, or "Hogback," from the river to the creek, the enemy had erected a fortification in most places breast high or more, in others lower, but pits or holes were dug in which the defenders could be protected The work was very artfully masked by the slope of the ridge being thickly set with the shrub oaks cut the night before from the hillside. A little in front of the line of fortifications were one or two log houses which served as bastions for the work.

The enemy had concentrated their main force at the angle in the fortified line. From this point a thin line was continued on one side to the river, and on the other to the creek. On the crest of the ridge, just above the sawmill before spoken of, a considerable force was stationed to repel any flank movement which might be attempted and was connected with the main force by a scattering line. On the very summit of the hill, where the monument stands, was placed a corps for observation, as also one on the opposite hill, on the east side of the creek.

The plan of the enemy seemed to have been this :—Presuming their fortifications to be perfectly concealed, and that the army would follow the Indian trail, as it turned to the right after crossing the creek, a sudden and severe fire opened on its exposed flank would create confusion in the ranks, and in the surprise of the unexpected attack, the party on the eastern hill, and that over the river having fallen back and crossed over, would fall on the rear of the army, increase the consternation, stampede the cattle and packhorses, and, if they did not destroy it, would so cripple its resources, as to prevent its further progress. For the purpose of the enemy the place was admirably adapted. In addition to occupying a position naturally strong, they had the inside line, and could concentrate their forces in much shorter space than their opponents.

The troops behind the ramparts consisted of a few regular British soldiers, the two battalions of Royal Greens, Tories and Indians. The whites were commanded by Colonel John Butler, with his son, Captain Walter N. Butler, and Captain MacDonald, and the Indians by the great Mohawk warrior, Joseph Brant. Other celebrated Indian Chiefs, but of less note, were also present.

The advanced guard having discovered the enemy's position about eleven o'clock, A. M., General Hand ordered the riflemen to form at about three hundred yards from the enemy, and hold their position until the remaining part of the brigade should come up or until further orders. This was scarcely done, when about four hundred of the enemy made a sortie, delivered their fire, and quickly retreated to their works. This was a number of times repeated, with the manifest intention of drawing our men into their lines. The scheme which had too often been successful in alluring the militia into ambush, failed with the disciplined troops of this army, and, at length, the enemy sullenly retired behind his entrenchments to await the issue of the attack.

In the meanwhile, General Hand advanced his brigade in line of battle to support the riflemen, and informed General Sullivan of his discovery and the disposition he had made of his brigade.

Ths commander at once summoned a council of his general officers, who, after thoroughly reconnoitering the ground, agreed upon the plan of attack.

It was three hours from the time the enemy was discovered, before the ground was reconnoitered, the plan of attack matured, and the troops came up. It was determined that the artillery should be stationed on a slight rise of ground about three hundred yards from the angle of the enemy's fortified position in such a way as to enfilade his lines and command the space behind them ; General Hand to advance a portion of his light troops near the breastwork, and divert the enemy's attention from the movements on the flank, and the rest to support the artillery ; the left flanking division to push up the river as far as prudent, in order to gain the enemy's flank, cut off his retreat in that direction, and join in the pursuit when he left the works ; General Poor with his brigade, the riflemen, and the right flanking division, supported by Clinton's brigade, to march by a circuitous route, and gain the mountain (Sullivan hill) on the enemy's left ; Maxwell's brigade to remain a *corps de reserve*, to act as occasion might demand.

THE BATTLE OF NEWTOWN.

It was about three o'clock P. M,, when a point a little more than a mile to the eastward of where the path crossed Baldwin's creek, "marching by columns from the right of regiments by files," followed by Clinton, who was ordered to march to the rear and the right of him, Poor struck off to the right from the path, his movement being concealed from the enemy by a considerable hill, which also hid a swamp that was directly in his path. He had not proceeded far before he found himself floundering in this morass, which was so thickly grown up with alders and bushes that his men could only with great difficulty make their way through them. An hour had been allowed as sufficient time for Poor's troops to be in position to turn the enemy's left, at which time the attack should be made in force on the front, the artillery fire being the signal for a simultaneous attack on both front and flank. The advance of Poor's brigade, had, however, just reached the creek where the group of houses stood near the sawmill, when General Sullivan, ignorant of Poor's delay, ordered the artillery to open fire, and the light infantry to advance. They pushed forward and formed in line under the bank of the creek, which afforded a sure protection within one hundred and twenty yards of the enemy's line. Proctor, whose battery, consisted now of six three-pounders, the light cohorn, and two howitzers, carrying 5¼ inch shells, opened with a sharp, severe fire of shell and solid shot. Such a scene this valley never before witnessed, and to such music never before did these hills send back their answering echoes.

To endure a protracted cannonade is one of the severest tests of the discipline and fortitude of experienced troops, while to the Indian the roar of cannon is as terrifying as though it were the harbinger of the day of doom ; yet such was the commanding presence of the great Indian captain and such the degree of confidence he inspired, that his undisciplined warriors stood their ground like veterans for more than half an hour, as the shot went crashing through the tree-tops or plowing up the earth under their feet, and shells went schreeching over their heads, or bursting in their ranks, while high above the roar of the artillery and the rattle of small arms, could be heard the voice of Brant, encouraging his men for the conflict, and over the heads of all, his crested plume could be seen waving where the contest was likely to be most sharp. At length, from the party on the mountain top, whose keen eyes had discovered the advance of Poor's brigade by the gleaming of their arms in the sunlight, word came of the threatened attack on the flank. With a chosen band of his warriors, Brant hastened to repel this new danger, leaving a few of his Indians, with troops under Butler, to hold the ground in front.

Emerging from the swamp, Poor bore off considerably to the left ; General Clinton following, with his left exactly in the rear of Poor's right, and his right as he turned toward the creek, sweeping over the lower part of the hill on the east side of the creek, uncovered the party of the enemy stationed there and compelled their precipitate retreat.

On reaching Baldwin's creek, Poor drew up his brigade in line of battle— Lieutenant-Colonel Reid's 2nd New Hampshire regiment on the left, Lieutenant-Colonel Dearborn's 3rd New Hampshire next, then Alden's, the 6th Massachusetts, and Colonel Cilley's, the 1st New Hampshire, on the right ; and on the right flank of the brigade, the two hundred and fifty picked men under Colonel Dubois, while the riflemen were deployed in front of the line as skirmishers.

By this time the advance of General Clinton, who was to support Poor, began to arrive, and his brigade was placed in order of battle with Gansevoort's regiment, the 3rd New York on the left, then Livingston's, which was the 4th New York and VanCortlandts', the 2nd New York, on the right.

Having formed the line of battle, Poor advanced his brigade with as much rapidity as the nature of the ground and the heat of the day would admit. No sooner had he crossed the creek than he was met by a sharp but somewhat random fire from the enemy stationed along the slope toward the creek, and protected by the trees which thickly studded the hillside. The riflemen returned the fire, but the brigade pressed rapidly forward, without firing a shot, and with fixed bayonets, steadily driving the enemy before them, who as our men advanced, retreated, darting for cover from tree to tree with the agility of panthers.

When about two-thirds the distance up the hill, the left part of the brigade was met by the party of the enemy from the breastwork, led by Brant in person. They, falling like a thunderbolt upon Colonel Reid's regiment, which was the left wing of the brigade and nearest the foe, checked his advance, and before he had time to recover from the shock, his men being out of breath from their run up the hill, he found himself in the midst of an Indian force outnumbering his own, three to one, who were swarming in a semi circle about his regiment, threatening to cut it off from the support of the rest of the brigade from which he was already separated by nearly a gun-shot, and leaving him the alternative either to fall back on Clinton for support or force his way through at the point of the bayonet. General Poor being with the right wing of the brigade, urging forward his men that he might cut off the retreat of the Indians toward Newtown, was not aware of the serious danger which threatened Reid, but Colonel Dearborn, whose regiment was on Reid's right, immediately and on his own responsibility ordered his regiment to change or reverse front, by a right about face, and just as Reid had given orders to charge, Dearborn's regiment poured in a volley upon Brant's force which first staggered them, and then a second volley, when they beat a hasty retreat.

About the same time Clinton perceiving the critical condition of Reid pushed forward Gansevoort's and Dubois' regiments for his support, who reached him just in time to hasten the flight of the enemy. Brant observing the movement toward his rear and understanding its meaning, sounded the retreat, and the enemy fled from all parts of the field towards Newtown and the ford of the Chemung, pursued by Hand and the riflemen. The two regiments on the right of Poor's brigade and the flanking division of Dubois, reached the river above Newtown, at a point where the old Fountain Inn, now owned by Willard Harrington, stands ; but this force was not sufficient successfully to resist the demolished mass of the enemy, whose only means of escape led in this direction ; and which being thus intercepted, they broke through Poor's line with such impetuosity, as for a time, to endanger his flank. Some shots were exchanged, without serious casuality to our troops, although General Sullivan and others say the enemy did not so escape. At the same time Colonel John Butler himself came very near being taken prisoner.

General Clinton with his two remaining regiments followed in the track of Poor, burning the houses which lay in his path, and joined the other troops near Newtown. It was now about six o'clock in the afternoon, and seven hours since the first gun was fired, when three rousing cheers announced that the battle was ended, and General Sullivan's gallant army was in possession of the contested battle-field. Our men fought with great valor and determination. The horrors of Wyoming, of Cherry Valley, of the

West Branch, of Minnisink and German Flats, were fresh in their recollections, and many of the soldiers had lost some of their nearest relatives in these strifes, where savage hordes and Tory outlaws held high carnival. There is a tradition, that as Poor's men began the charge up the hill, some one cried : " Remember Wyoming," which was taken up along the line as the watch word and battle cry of the hour; but there is not a lisp in confirmation of this in any of the numerous journals which have been preserved.

The exact numbers engaged on either side cannot be ascertained. General Sullivan and his officers, after going over the whole field, examining the line occupied by the enemy, and comparing the accounts and estimates of those in best position to know, put their strength at one thousand five hundred men, while the two men who were captured on the evening of the battle gave the number as low as seven or eight hundred. Somewhere between these extremes is doubtless the truth.

The loss in General Sullivan's army was three killed on the field, viz : Corporal Hunter and two privates; the wounded were Benjamin Titcomb of Dover, Major of the 2d New Hampshire, through the abdomen and arms ; Elijah Clayes, Captain of the 7th company of the 2d New Hampshire, through the body ; Nathaniel McCauley of Litchfield, First Lieutenant of the 4th company of the 1st New Hampshire; Sergeant Lane, wounded in two places; Sergeant Oliver Thurston, and thirty-one rank and file, all but four of whom were of Poor's brigade, and nearly all from Reid's regiment. Lieutenant McCauley had his knee shattered, making amputation necessary, and died before morning, and Abner Dearborn died a few days after he was removed to Tioga. Sergeant Demeret Joshua Mitchell and Sylvester Wilkins died previous to September 19th, making a total of eight.

Those who died upon the field were buried separately, near where they fell, and fires were built upon their graves to conceal them from the enemy, lest after the departure of the army their bodies should be desecrated ; a practice shamefully prevalent on both sides in Indian warfare. It seems strange that in a contest waged between such numbers and for so long a time, the casualties should have been so few. But our men were well protected by the bank of the creek in front, and the Indians probably shot over the heads of those coming up the hill.

Twelve of the enemy were found slain on the ground, and two prisoners were taken, one a negro, the other "one Houghtailer from the Helder Barrack." A British account says : " In this action Colonel Butler and all his people were surrounded, and very near being taken prisoners. The Colonel lost four rangers killed, two taken prisoners and seven wounded." Butler also lost his commission and private baggage, besides jewels and hard money. The Indian account, found four days afterward, near Catherine's town is as follows : "Sept. 2d, this day found a tree marked 1779, Theandagava, the English of which is Brant; twelve men marked on it with arrows pierced through them, signifying the number they had lost in the action of the 29th ultimo. A small tree was twisted round like a rope and bent down, which signified that if we drove and distressed them, yet we would not conquer them."

Disheartened, terror-stricken, and hopeless of further resistance, the enemy fled with all possible speed, not daring even to look behind them; and such was the moral effect of the victory, that without thought for else but their lives, they abandoned their villages to the torch and their cornfields to the destruction of the victorious foe.

The day after the battle was spent in destroying the crops in the neighborhood, sending the wounded, four heavy guns, ammunition wagon, etc., back to Tioga; and while here, owing to the prospective scarcity of beef and flour, snd the abundance of corn, beans, potatoes, squashes, etc., the army agreed, without a dissent, to subsist on half rations of the former articles.

PUSHING ON.

On the 31st of August the army again started westward, to complete the work for which the expedition had been organized.

About two miles above Newtown a little village of eight good houses was found, which was burned, and the army passed to Kanawaholla, a pleasant town situated on the point, at the junction of present Newtown creek with the Chemung, near the city of Elmira, and four and a half miles above the battle-ground. Here, as at Chemung and Newtown, the cornfields bore marks of having been planted under the supervision of white people, whom it is well known were directed by the British government to aid the Indians in raising supplies for the British army and garrisons.

From this point, Colonel Dayton, with the Third New Jersey regiment and a detachment of riflemen, was sent up the river in pursuit of some of the enemy whom the advanced guard saw escaping in their canoes. He chased them for eight miles up the river, but their speed was too great, and the nimble-footed savages escaped At this point, Colonel Dayton found an Indian village which was near present Big Flats, where he encamped for the night. The next morning he burned the village, destroyed about thirty acres of corn and a quantity of hay, and rejoined the main army just as it was leaving its encampment.

From Kanawaholla the path turned northward; the army marched about five miles farther and encamped for the night near the present village of Horseheads. The next morning, tents were struck at eight o'clock, and for three miles the path lay through an open plain, then they entered the low ground which forms the divide of the waters flowing into the Susquehanna and the St. Lawrence, at that time a deep, miry swamp, covered with water from the recent rains, dark with closely shadowing hemlocks, the path studded with rocks and thickly interwoven with sloughs; it was the most horrible spot they had met with. It was past seven o'clock, just in the dusk of the evening, when the advanced guard emerged from the gloomy shadows of the morass and formed themselves in line on the outskirts of the village Sheaquaga, or French Catherine's town

It was pitch dark before Hand's brigade got out of the wilderness. To the rest of the army it was a night of horrors. It was so dark the men could not see the path, and could keep it only by grasping the frocks of their file leaders. Poor's and Maxwell's brigades did not reach the town until ten o'clock. Many of the soldiers, utterly worn out with heat and fatigue, fell by the wayside, and did not join the army until the next day. Clinton's brigade spent the night in the swamp without supper or shelter. Two of the pack horses fell and broke their necks, others became exhausted and died in the path, while the stores of food and ammunition were sadly depleted. The town was built on both sides of the inlet to Seneca Lake, and about three miles from the lake, on the site of present Havana. It consisted of between thirty and forty good houses, some fine cornfields and orchards. The soldiers found a number of horses, cows, calves and hogs, which they appropriated.

TO SENECA LAKE.

The next day (Thursday, Sept. 2d), the army rested. An old squaw was found who gave a little information, and said the Indians were discouraged by the result of the battle of Newtown. Friday the army marched twelve miles and encamped at what has since been called the Peach Orchard. There were a few Indian houses and plenty of corn; Indians were roasting corn there, but fled as the army came up. Saturday the army proceeded to what is now North Hector The Indian town there was called Con-daw-haw. The single log house and corn crops were destroyed. Sunday the army marched to Kendaia, or Appletown. There, pleasantly situated, half a mile from the lake, stood twenty or more houses of hewn logs, roofed with bark, and some of them well painted. There were apple orchards, one having sixty trees, beside others, peach orchards and other fruits. The houses were burned, the trees cut down or girdled and the crops destroyed. About this town also were shown the tombs of chiefs, made of hewn planks. On Monday and Tuesday the army tramped along Seneca Lake, and Tuesday night reached Kanadesaga, an important Seneca village of fifty houses, surrounded by orchards and cornfields, and about two miles northwesterly from the foot of the lake. The army had passed through or near what is now Geneva. It rested Wednesday at Kanadesaga, and then detatchments were sent out to explore the country. One detachment of Jerseymen, under Col. John Harper, found a village (Skoi-yase) where Waterloo now is. It was surrounded by orchards and cornfields, all richly laden, and there were some artificial fish-ponds—the only instance known among the Indians. It was the capital of the Cayugas. Everything was destroyed and the detachment returned to Kanadesaga. Another detachment under Major Poor went seven miles up the west side of the lake and destroyed the town of Shenouwaga. There also were cornfields, peach and apple orchards, stacks of hay, hogs, fowls, and all the evidences of agricultural prosperity. The houses were well-built and the fields fenced. The work of destruction occupied so much time that reinforcements of 400 men were sent for.

TO CANANDAIGUA LAKE.

Kanadesaga was a large and important town, consisting of fifty houses, with thirty more in the immediate vicinity, and being the capital of the nation was frequently called the Seneca Castle. Its site was on the present Castle road, a mile and a half west from Geneva. The town was divided by Kanadesaga or Castle creek. It was regularly laid out, enclosing a large green plot, on which, during the "Old French War" in 1756, Sir William Johnson had erected a stockade fort, the remains of which were plainly visible to our army, and spoken of in a number of the journals. Orchards of apple, pear and mulberry trees surrounded the town. Fine gardens, with onions, peas, beans, squashes, potatoes, turnips, cabbages, cucumbers, watermelons, carrots and parsnips, abounded ; and large cornfields were to the north and northeast of the town. All were destroyed on the 8th of September. Here was found a little white boy, about three years of age, who had been stolen by the Indians from the frontiers. The little fellow was nearly starved when our men found him. No clue to his parentage was ever obtained. The officers of the expedition were greatly interested in the little waif and tenderly cared for him. Captain Machin adopted him and christened him Thomas. He died in Kingston, N. Y., some two years after, of small-pox.

On the 9th the army resumed its journey toward the Genesee, and after an uneventful march of eight miles, encamped in the woods near a stream of water now called Flint creek.

Starting the next morning at eight o'clock, after marching eleven miles, the army came to "Kanandaigua lake," and fording its outlet marched a mile farther, when they found the town of "Kanandaigua," consisting of twenty three elegant houses, some of them framed, others log, but large and new, pleasantly situated about a mile from the west shore of the lake, partly on the site of the present Canandaigua At this place the rear guard of the enemy remained so long that their fires were found burning. The torch was soon applied to the buildings, and the army advanced a mile farther where the cornfields were, and encamped, when fatigue parties were detailed for the destruction of the crops, which was pretty thoroughly accomplished before dark.

Before daylight on the morning of Saturday, September 11th, the troops were again in motion. A march of fourteen miles brought them to the Indian town of Han-ne-ya-ye, which contained about twenty houses, and was near the site of present Honeoye, at the foot of Honeoye lake, on the east side of its outlet.

The General now estimated his distance from the principal Genesee town at about twenty-five miles, and that he might not be burdened with unnecessary baggage and stores, all except about four days' half rations, the baggage, cattle and horses, except a few of the strongest, were left here in charge of Captain Cummings and fifty men, together with the "sick, the lame and the lazy," which amounted to three hundred men all told. The Captain took possession of the strongest block-house, cut port-holes through the sides, protected it with abatis made from the limbs of apple trees, placed the two three-pounders left with him in proper position, strengthened the walls with kegs and bags of flour, so that altogether it was capable of offering a formidable defense against any force that could be brought against it. Thus lightened, the army proceeded with its work with increased celerity.

Sunday, Sept. 12th, the army started again, and Monday reached Kanaghsaws, also called Adjuton, a place of eighteen houses on the east of the inlet to Conesus lake. It was the home of the Seneca chief Big Tree, who had been very friendly to the Americans, but afterward turned against them.

FIGHTING AGAIN.

Immediately after the battle of Newtown, the forces of Butler and Brant had retired to Canawaugus, near the site of present Avon, in Livingston county, but having received considerable reinforcements, they determined to make another attempt to arrest the further progress of the army.

At the head of Conesus lake was a soft, miry bottom, along the south side of which ran the Indian path to the Genesee towns, nearly on the site of the present highway, crossing the sluggish inlet by a bridge, which Butler had destroyed on his retreat, probably a few feet south of the present one. On the west of the lake and running parallel with it, is a steep bluff of considerable height, which reaches nearly to the water's edge, at that time covered with trees, and then, as now, deeply gashed with several ravines which came straight down its face. The path led up to the crest of the hill between two of these ravines, but with a southerly trend, following nearly or exactly the line of the present road. This was the place selected by the enemy to surprise the army, and, if possible, to destroy it.

Learning from his scouts that General Sullivan was approaching this difficult place, early on the morning of the 12th Butler left Canawaugus, and in the afternoon had his forces posted on the crest of the ridge and in the ravines, overlooking the south end of the lake and flanking the path to the Genesee towns. Here, though himself perfectly concealed, he was in full view of General Sullivan's army and within musket shot of the inlet crossing.

As late as 1770, the principal Genesee town, called Chenussio, was located near the confluence of the Canaseraga creek with the Genesee river, and here it was marked on the most recent maps to which General Sullivan had access. He was not aware that its location had been changed to the west side of the river, and seems to have known nothing of another town two miles farther up the Canaseraga.

When, therefore, General Sullivan reached his encampment on the evening of the 12th, he supposed he was near the great Genesee castle of which he had heard so much, and which was the objective point of his expedition. In order to secure more accurate information, he ordered Lieutenant Thomas Boyd of the riflemen to take five or six men with him, make a rapid reconnoissance, and report at headquarters as early as sunrise the next morning. He took, however, twelve riflemen, six musketmen of the Fourth Pennsylvania regiment, and eight volunteers, making, with himself and Hannyerry, an Oneida Indian guide, and Captain Jehoiakim, a Stockbridge Indian, twenty-nine men in all. The party left camp north of Kanaghsaws at eleven o'clock in the evening and set out on the trail leading to the Great Town. Owing to his misinformation, General Sullivan's directions had been confusing and misleading. It was found that the principally traveled trail took a direction different from what was expected. Boyd did not lose his way, but instead of taking the unused path that led to the abandoned Chenussio, he took the one which brought him to an important town two miles farther up the Canaseraga, the only one between the army and the Genesee. In the darkness, he had passed Butler's right flank, without either party having discovered the other. Boyd reached the town which the enemy had abandoned, early in the morning, without having encountered any difficulty. Halting his force at the outskirts of the village, with one of his men he carefully reconnoitered the place, then joining the rest of the party, they concealed themselves in the woods near the town. He sent back four of his men to report the discoveries he had made, and awaited the light of day, which was just breaking. Soon four Indians on horseback were seen entering the town, and Boyd sent a party to take or kill them. One Indian was killed and another wounded. The wounded man and the other two escaped. Boyd then set out for camp. Having gone four or five miles, and thinking the army must be on its march toward him, he sat down to rest. After a short halt he dispatched two of his men to inform the General where he was, and of his intention to await the coming of the army. In a short time these men returned, with the information that they had discovered five Indians on the path.

Boyd again resumed his march and had gone but a short distance, when he discovered the same party and fired on them. They ran, and Boyd, against the advice of Hannyerry pursued them. The chase was kept up for some distance, the Indians succeeding in alluring the scouting party near the enemy's lines. They then allowed the party to approach sufficiently near to draw their fire, but kept out of danger. Butler, hearing the firing on his right, as his force was arranged facing Conesus, and fearing that he had been discovered, and that an attempt was being made to surprise his camp, hastened to the spot, where he found Boyd's party still following the Indians. Without being aware of their presence, Boyd was already within the fatal embrace of the enemy, and before he was aware of it, Butler had given such orders as to completely surround him. Once and again he attempted to break their line, but without success; he then sought to retreat, but he was encompassed on all sides. The odds were fearful, eight hundred of the Indians and Tories to twenty-five Americans, but the scouts determined to sell their lives as dearly as possible; and relief from our army, which was only about a mile distant, was expected every moment. Covered by a clump of trees, our men poured a murderous fire upon the enemy as they were closing around them, numbers of whom were seen to fall. In all, fifteen of Boyd's party, including Hannyerry probably, were slain, eight escaped, Boyd and his sergeant, Michael Parker, were captured, and four had been sent early in the morning to report to General Sullivan. The bodies of the slain were found on the 16th by Captain William Henderson, of the Fourth Pennsylvania regiment, who with sixty men had been detailed to search for them, and buried with military honors, that of Hannyerry with the others, although literally hacked to pieces. Of those who escaped, one was the noted Timothy Murphy, from Northumberland, Pa., of Boyd's company, an account of whose hair-breadth escapes and deeds of reckless daring would fill a volume. Boyd and Parker were hastened to Little Beard's town, where they were put to death with cruel tortures.

It has been currently reported that after his capture, Boyd approached Brant under the sign of a Free Mason, of which ancient fraternity both were members, that the chieftain recognized the bond of brotherhood and promised him protection, but having been unexpectedly called away the captives were placed in charge of Butler (probably Walter N.) who, becoming exasperated with Boyd's persistent refusal to disclose any information in regard to the army handed them over to the Indians to be put to death. The whole story, however, is extremely doubtful, and it is now difficult to ascertain how much of it, if any, should be received as true. The most, that can be said with certainty is, that the next day the bodies of the unfortunate men were found by our troops, horribly mangled, and bearing marks of having suffered unspeakable torture.

MORE DESTRUCTION.

Having destroyed Kanaghsaws General Sullivan pushed on seven miles to Gathtsegwarohare, an Indian town of twenty-five houses on the east side of Canaseraga creek, two miles from its confluence with the Genesee. These grounds are now known as the Hermitage. As the troops neared the town (Sept. 13) they met a considerable force of Indians and rangers drawn up in battle array ; but they fled without firing a gun. The army encamped on the ground. It took 2,000 men six hours the next day to destroy the extensive cornfields. Then the army marched on to the great Genesee town. The valley was found to be wonderfully rich and fertile. The Seneca Castle was found on the west side of the Genesee river, near Cuylersville on the opposite side of the valley from Geneseo. It consisted of 128 houses, mostly large and elegant, surrounded by 200 acres of cornfields and gardens filled with vegetables. It was the western door to the Long House to which the Iroquois were accustomed to liken their confederacy.

On the morning of September 15th the whole army turned out to destroy the crops, orchards, houses and gardens. Everything that could be was burned. It was the largest corn the men had ever seen.

THE RETURN.

On the afternoon of the same day (Sept. 15) having destroyed, it was supposed, all the villages of the Senecas, the army started on its return tramp, and on the evening of the 19th reached Kanadesaga. There General Sullivan was met by a delegation from the Oneidas who came to excuse themselves for not joining the expedition, and to intercede for the Cayugas east of the lake, who were said to be friendly. General Sullivan said the Cayugas had shown too much duplicity, treachery and hostility and must be chastised. On the 20th he sent Colonel Smith up the west side of Seneca lake to destroy Kershong and its cornfields. He also despatched Colonel Peter Gansevoort with 100 men to go to Albany and bring forward baggage stored there. Colonel William Butler with 600 men was also sent to destroy the towns on the east side of Cayuga lake. This party reached Cayuga Castle the 22d, containing fifteen large square log houses. Two other towns nearly as large, Upper Cayuga and East Cayuga, were near by. There were in the vicinity 110 acres of corn, besides apples, peaches, potatoes, turnips, onions, pumpkins, squashes, etc All were destroyed. Then the force marched four miles and a half to Chonadate, where there were some 1,500 peach trees, besides apple trees, corn, etc. The town included fourteen houses. The force encamped there and next morning destroyed everything with fire and ax. The 2ith the party reached the southern end of Cayuga lake.

Meantime the main body under General Sullivan had not been idle. Colonel Dearborn was sent to the west side of Cayuga lake and destroyed houses and crops. Six towns were found and destroyed one of them, Canoga, the birthplace of Red Jacket, the great Iroquois orator. Colonel Dearborn rejoined the main army the 26th.

HORSEHEADS.

In the meantime General Sullivan with the main army had been marching on homeward. On the morning of the 21st he left the south side of Seneca river and in two days reached Catherine's town. On the 24th he started early but some of his horses were worn out and could go no further. A halt was made and a number of the poor animals killed. This was apparently the site of the present village of Horseheads. The Indians afterward found the bones and taking the skulls arranged them in a line by the side of the trail.

TO THE END.

One day later General Sullivan reached the junction of Newtown and Tioga creek where Captain Reid returning with the sick and wounded, had erected a palisade. The army was received with a salute. Remaining until the 29th General Sullivan again broke camp and camped that night two miles below Chemung. The next day Fort Sullivan at Tioga was reached. There were great rejoicings. The army remained until October 3d, then destroyed the fort and set out for Wyoming, which was reached on the 7th.

The expedition accomplished its whole purpose. On October 14th Congress voted thanks to General Sullivan. Forty villages, 200,000 bushels of corn, and thousands of fruit trees, etc., had been destroyed. The Indians returned to their blackened homes and wasted cornfields, and looked with despair upon the waste and ruin before them. They now began to feel the iron they had so ruthlessly thrust into the bosom of others. Mary Jemison says, there was nothing left, not enough to keep a child. Again they wended their way to Niagara where huts were built for them around the fort. The winter following was the coldest ever known, and prevented the Indians going on their winter hunt. Cooped up in their little huts and obliged to subsist on salted provisions, the scurvy broke out amongst them, and hundreds of them died. Those the sword had spared, the pestilence destroyed.

The power of the Iroquois was broken. That great confederation, whose influence had once been so potent, crumbled under the iron heel of the invader, and the nation which had made so many tremble, itself quailed before the white man's steel.

THE END.

Send The Gazette Company, Elmira, N. Y., One Dollar and Six Cents, and secure the Weekly Gazette for one year and this book FREE.

Belle Anderson's Pies—Kittie's Popcorn Balls, and Mrs. Northop's Recipes.

BELLE ANDERSON'S PIES.

HAPPY HOUSEHOLD: Please find recipes for excellent lemon pies with two crusts:

Cream Lemon Pie.—One lemon, one cup o white sugar, and one cup of sweet cream. Prepare the juice of the lemon, grated rind, an sugar first, then add the sweet cream. Sometimes we add the white of an egg w ll be Bake with two crusts, and serve cold.

Lemon and Raisin Pie.—The juice and rind of one lemon, three-quarters of a cup of seeded raisins, one cup of sugar. Bake with upper crust. The cream, lemon, and sugar, with a spoonful of corn-starch added, is an excellent filling for layer cake.

Belle C. Anderson, Beaulah, Okla Ter.

POPCORN BALLS.

HAPPY HOUSEHOLD: Emma J. Hand requests a recipe for popcorn balls. Please find a good one:

To a six-quart pan of popcorn allow a teacup and a half of good molasses. Put on the stove and let boil until it ropes from the spoon. Have the corn ready, grease the pan with butter, so it will not stick, then turn the molasses on the corn slowly, and stir as you turn it on, until it is thoroughly mixed. Grease the hands, and form into balls.

Mrs. E. A. Northrop, Newark, N. Y.

KITTIE'S POPCORN.

HAPPY HOUSEHOLD: I am a daughter of G. F. Hummell, Co. I, 17th Ohio, and an interested reader of THE NATIONAL TRIBUNE. Hair and eyes, brown; weight, 130 pounds; hight, five feet three inches; age, 19.

In response to Emma J. Hand, I send my recipe for popcorn balls:

Have the corn popped nicely, and take out all hard or burnt grain. Allow nearly one pint of white sugar for a gallon of corn. Put it into a stewpan with enough water to cover and boil until it will harden in cold water. Pour this over the corn, mix thoroughly, and mold into balls quickly.

Kittie H rell, Sugar Grove, O.

RHEUMATISM AND WOUNDS.—One of the very best liniments for rheumatism is made as follows: One pint spirits turpentine, two ounces of camphor, two ounces of spirits of ammonia, and one ounce oil of sassafras. One of the best liniments for wounds is made by melting pine tar, adding one quart linseed oil, and half a pint spirits turpentine; it is just the thing for any wounds on man or beast, and it is one of the best remedies to apply to brittle feet.

BEET PICKLES.

if you want them fresh, sweet and tende for use next winter. Cook them in salted water until tender, taking care when cleaning not to cut them or they will bleed badly. When done throw them in cold water and let them stand a few moments, then the outer skin will slip off easily. Slice them and place carefully in cans and pour boiling vinegar, with a half a cup of sugar allowed to each two-quart can of pickles, over them and seal immediately. The color will be better preserved if kept in the dark. Now I come to the last and what we all consider best pickles of the list and these are

PEARS

are very nice made the same way, with the exception of soaking in brine. Now is the time to make your

MIXED MUSTARD PICKLES.

One quart of cucumbers cut in small pieces, one quart of small cucumbers, all placed in salt and water over night; two quarts small onions, two quarts of green tomatoes cut in pieces or sliced, three large green peppers sliced, two heads of cauliflower cut in pieces half a finger long. Scald all except the cucumber in hot salt and water, i. e., put them in cold weak brine and allow them to come to a boil. Drain the brine off and place all the ingredients in a crock and pour boiling vinegar over them and let stand 3 days. Take one half pound of Coleman's English mustard (this is the only kind I can recommend, as common mustard will make them bitter), 3 cups of light brown sugar, 1 cup of flour mixed with a little cold vinegar. Pour 3 quarts of boiling vinegar over the mustard, sugar and flour and stir well together. After the pickles have been well drained from the vinegar, pour the above mustard preparation over them and they will keep a year—if you can keep the big boys awa from them—and when you eat and call them delicious thank THE STOCKMAN.

BECKY SHARP.

Homemade Soap.

First try out and strain the grease. This done, more than half the work is done. The directions for making the soap are on every can of potash. You can make hard soap very nice, white and hard. Here is the recipe: Hard soap—empty the contents of the can of potash into a kettle with a quart of cold water. Stir it with a spoon or stick. The lye will dissolve immediately and become quite hot. Allow it to cool. Now take 6 pounds of clean grease, tallow or lard. Melt it until lukewarm; then commence pouring the cold lye into the melted grease gradually in a small stream until it is thoroughly mixed and drops from the stirrer the thickness of honey. To be properly done the stirring should continue for 10 minutes. It is then ready to pour into any mold.

If you will follow this recipe closely, you cannot fail in getting nice soap. There is also a recipe for soft soap on each can of potash.

A Cheap Sponge Cake.

Three eggs, 2 tablespoonfuls of water and a teacupful of sugar, mix together. One and a half cups of flour, 2 teaspoonfuls baking powder and a pinch of salt, stirred in quickly. Season with a teaspoonful of vanilla or juice of half a lemon. Bake in three jelly pans in a quick oven. For the filling grate 2 good sized apples, add the grated peel and juice of a lemon, a well beaten egg and sugar to taste. Boil five minutes and spread between the layers. This is very good if eaten fresh.

Cooking Recipes.

CABBAGE SALAD.—Cut the cabbage very fine, and put into a dish in layers, with salt and pepper between. Then take two teaspoonfuls of butter, two of sugar, two of flour, two of mustard, one cup of vinegar and one egg. Stir all together, and let it come to a boil on the stove. Pour it hot over, and mix well with the cabbage ; cover up.

—A down-east druggist claims that the following will cure an incipient cold in five minutes: Take about half a teaspoonful of laudanum and dilute it with an equal amount of water. Then thoroughly saturate a piece of absorbent cotton with this mixture, and holding the cotton to the nostrils draw in a deep breath. The liquid will pass through the nostrils, down into the throat, and hen be discharged.

Simple Breakfast for Commuters.

Farming.

Make cornmeal mush this way: Put two quarts of water to boil, add to it a teaspoonful of salt. Meanwhile mix yellow cornmeal to a good smooth paste in cold water; then put this into the boiling water and it won't get into lumps. Stir it now until the whole becomes thick enough to hold the spoon upright. While doing this let the fire be only sufficient to let it bubble gently. It ought to cook an hour. Turn it out into square bread pans three or four inches deep, and in the morning, if to be fried for breakfast cut in slices an inch thick, dip into flour to bind it, then fry in lard and butter mixed, turning until a golden color.

HOT WATER SPONGE CAKE.

One cup sugar, one cup flour, two eggs, one teaspoonful baking-powder, one small teaspoonful vanilla and one-third of a cup of boiling water. Beat the eggs very light, whites and yolks separately. Add the sugar, then the flour and baking-powder sifted together. Beat well, then add the boiling water, and lastly the flavoring. Bake in a moderate oven.—Ellen J. Huntley, Great Barrington, Mass.

HAPPY HOUSEHOLD.

Star Prairie Cake, and Mrs. Ewing's Nice Chicken Croquets.

C. C. BRIDE'S CAKE.

FRIENDS OF THE C. C.; Cream together one scant cup of butter and three cups of sugar; add one cup of milk, then the beaten whites of 12 eggs. Sift three tablespoonfuls of baking powder into one cup of cornstarch mixed with three cups of sifted flour, and beat in gradually with the rest; flavor to taste. Beat all thoroughly, then put into a tin lined with letter-paper well buttered; bake slowly in a moderate oven. Ice the top. Double the recipe if more is required.

LEMON LAYER CAKE.

Two cups of sugar, one and a half cup of butter, one cup of sweet milk, three eggs, three cups of flour, and two teaspoonfuls of baking powder; bake in layers.

Jelly for cake.—One cup of sugar, one egg, one tablespoonful of butter, the rind and juice of one lemon; boil all together until thick.

HAPPY HOUSEHOLD.

Valuable Recipes for Those Who Love to Cook.

RASPBERRY VINEGAR.

To four quarts of raspberries add one quart of good vinegar. Let it stand 24 hours, then strain, and to one pint of juice add one pound of sugar. Boil 15 minutes, bottle hot, and seal the corks.

RIPE CUCUMBER PICKLES.

HAPPY HOUSEHOLD. Peel your pickles and soak 24 hours in salt water; then take them out and scald in clear water enough to cook them, not too soft, but just enough. Skim them out, and put into the jars you are going to leave them in, and sprinkle sugar over them; then heat enough vinegar, with spices of all kinds, to cover them; pour over the pickles scalding hot, then cover and set in a cool place. This is my recipe for tomato sweet pickles also. I hope you will all try it.
M. A. Seward, San Diego, Cal.

CHICKEN CREAM SOUP.

Boil a chicken with five or six onions in five quarts of cold water until it has boiled down to two-and-a-half quarts. Take chicken out of the pot and let it cool; cut off the breast and chip quite fine; mix the cut meat with mashed yolks of two hard-boiled eggs and rub fine. Cool, skim and strain the soup into a saucepan, season to taste, then add the chicken and egg mixture. Let it cook over a slow fire for 15 minutes; add one pint of boiling milk; pour into a tureen and serve hot. It is delicious, and very nourishing.
Mary A. Morrison.

HAPPY HOUSEHOLD,

Recipes Tried and True from Loyal Home Workers.

CHOCOLATE CREAM PIE.

One cup of sugar; butter size of egg; two eggs; one-half cup of milk, and one-half teaspoonful of cream tartar; one-fourth of a teaspoonful of soda, and one and one-half cups of flour. Bake in three layers.

Filling: Two squares of chocolate, one-half cup of milk; five tablespoonfuls of sugar. Cook until thick and spread while hot.
Carrie A. Briggs.

LIGHT ROLLS.

Take one quart of warm water, one cake of yeast (I prefer the "Magic"), dissolve in warm water, and add flour to make a stiff sponge. Let it raise over night, and in the morning, when light, add one quart of warm water, two tablespoonfuls of salt, and flour enough to make a stiff dough. When light, make two loaves of bread, which can be sliced in thin slices and buttered and served. Take the remaining portion of the dough, and pinch off bits large enough for your rolls; work in a little lard in each. One teaspoonful of lard will be enough for four or five rolls of medium size. This recipe never fails. After adding the flour knead for 20 or 30 minutes, but do not knead the second time.
Rhoda I. Woodruff.

MOCK BISQUE SOUP AND SALTED ALMONDS.

—The time is fast approaching when the housewife will begin her fight with the carpet bugs. E. C. Waldson, of the Oswego woolen mills, a practical chemist, claims that he has discovered a compound that causes the death or departure of carpet bugs in short order after its application. Your druggist can compound it for you if you ask for it: One ounce of alum, one ounce of chloride of zinc, three ounces of salt. You should mix with two quarts of water and let it stand over night in a covered vessel. Then, in the morning, pour it carefully into another vessel without sediment. Dilute with two quarts of water and apply by sprinkling edges of the carpet for a distance of a foot from the wall. This is all that is necessary. They will leave boxes, beds or any other resort they may have chosen, on the shortest possible notice, and the carpets will not be injured in texture or color.

New York History Review Press explores and publishes all aspects of New York State's rich and diverse local history.

Other New York History Review Press publications

Victorian Pride - Forgotten Songs of Central New York 1841-1885
Victorian Pride - Forgotten Songs of Central New York Music CD
Victorian Pride - Forgotten Songs of Upstate New York 1850-1884
Victorian Pride - Forgotten Songs of Upstate New York Music CD
Victorian Pride - Forgotten Songs of Pennsylvania
Victorian Pride - Forgotten Songs of America
The Great Inter-State Fair, Elmira, New York 1890
Carl Albert Janowski Goes to War and Back
Janowski Gardens Cookbook